D1627094

WITHDRAWN
UTSA LIBRARIES

HISTORY, LITERATURE, CRITICAL THEORY

DOMINICK LACAPRA

CORNELL UNIVERSITY PRESS
Ithaca and London

Copyright © 2013 by Cornell University

All rights reserved. Except for brief quotations in a review,
this book, or parts thereof, must not be reproduced in
any form without permission in writing from the pub-
lisher. For information, address Cornell University Press,
Sage House, 512 East State Street, Ithaca, New York 14850.

First published 2013 by Cornell University Press
First printing, Cornell Paperbacks, 2013

Printed in the United States of America

Library of Congress Cataloging-in-Publication Data
LaCapra, Dominick, 1939– author.
    History, literature, critical theory / Dominick LaCapra.
       pages cm
    Includes bibliographical references and index.
    ISBN 978-0-8014-5197-3 (cloth : alk. paper) —
    ISBN 978-0-8014-7865-9 (pbk. : alk. paper)
    1. Literature and history.   2. Literature, Modern—
History and criticism—Theory, etc.   3. Fiction—
History and criticism—Theory, etc.   4. Violence
in literature.   5. Holocaust, Jewish (1939–1945),
in literature.   6. Holocaust, Jewish (1939–1945)—
Historiography.   I. Title.
    PN50.L33 2013
    809—dc23   2012047659

A version of chapter 4 appeared in *History and Theory* 50
(February, 2011): 71–97.
A version of the Epilogue appeared in *Variations* 18
(2010): 9–28.

Cornell University Press strives to use environmentally
responsible suppliers and materials to the fullest extent
possible in the publishing of its books. Such materials
include vegetable-based, low-VOC inks and acid-free
papers that are recycled, totally chlorine-free, or partly
composed of nonwood fibers. For further information,
visit our website at www.cornellpress.cornell.edu.

Cloth printing   10 9 8 7 6 5 4 3 2 1
Paperback printing   10 9 8 7 6 5 4 3 2 1

Library
University of Texas
at San Antonio

For Jane, Molly, and Véronique

The ghost of Roger Casement is beating at the door.
—William Butler Yeats

❦ Contents

HISTORY, LITERATURE, CRITICAL THEORY

Introduction

This book begins with a frame essay on the general problem of relating history, literature (specifically the novel), and critical theory. This topic is vast, and my approach is selective. But the manner in which problems are addressed has more general implications for relating history and literature as well as historical and literary analysis. At issue is how best to elaborate a form of inquiry where history and literature are brought into mutually provocative contact—where historical understanding is challenged by critical (including literary) theories, and literary criticism is not only informed but insistently interrogated by historical questions.

My focus in the discussion of history is on violence, with particular attention to the Nazi genocide or "final solution." More generally, I am interested in the nexus linking the sublime, the sacred, the "postsecular," and a variable quest for a redemptive absolute, as well as possible implications of such a quest for violent and at times sacrificial or quasi-sacrificial practices involving radical transgression, scapegoating, and victimization.[1] As the dubious dimensions of these initiatives become more evident in the wake of catastrophic events, the quest may be emptied of content, purely formal,

I thank Katy Meigs for her copyediting and Franz Hofer for his assistance in preparing the index. I also thank Jane Pedersen and two anonymous readers for Cornell University Press for their helpful critical readings of this text.

or perplexingly opaque, a quest for a quest that nonetheless may be presented in extreme terms, prompting a leap into the unknown or an empty utopianism, at times attended by violence as a valorized practice or rite of passage.[2] In certain theoretical discourses, the very term "violent" becomes like a perfunctory seasoning that peppers any and every allusion—to language, to affect, to change, to relationships, and to putative origins.

One objective of this book is to foster thinking about the increasingly prevalent but ill-defined notion of the postsecular, a term that may perhaps be best "defined" by its various settings and contextual uses and abuses.[3] This multidimensional, contested notion arises in the wake of debates about secularization, which often stressed either the continuity of the religious and the secular or the radical break between them, as many defenses of the Enlightenment tend to do,[4] notably in attempting to establish the "legitimacy of the modern age."[5] The most thought-provoking approaches to problems bearing on the postsecular are, I think, those that point to an intricate understanding of displacement, involving both repetition and change, at times traumatic change (at least for those undergoing a crisis or even a loss of faith, epitomized in the "death of God" or in the way religious language, such as prayer, becomes incoherent or unavailable).[6] To the extent that a notion of the "postsecular" is at play in the work of figures such as J. M. Coetzee and W. G. Sebald (as well as Jacques Derrida), it is in this complicated sense. (To the best of my knowledge, none of them uses the term.) It is also interesting to note that Hans Blumenberg, despite his emphasis on the discontinuity between the premodern and the modern, directed against a "secularization thesis" stressing continuity, develops a concept of "reoccupation" whereby sites and even conceptual or imaginary spaces that were formerly invested by religion (a chapel or church, for example) may come to acquire "secular" functions that nonetheless remain imbued with sacral dimensions. And running counter to his insistence elsewhere on epistemological breaks between historical periods, Michel Foucault as well, in his 1961 *Folie et déraison: Histoire de la folie à l'âge classique*, employs at crucial junctures a model of repetition with change, referring, for example, to the relation between premodern unreason and modern madness in terms of "torsions in the same anxiety" and indicating, for example, the manner in which leprosariums when converted into insane asylums nonetheless produced intense concern as loci of contamination and possible contagion.[7] Moreover, one may mention the way the French Revolution gave rise to feast days, a new calendar, and a quasi-sacred liturgy of celebrations as well as quasi-sacrificial violence during the Reign of Terror.[8] Indeed, once the notion of the postsecular arises, one is inclined belatedly to see earlier phenomena and texts in its light (for example, the works of certain Romantics, such as Wordsworth, Friedrich Schlegel, or Novalis, which might not be explicitly "religious" in any conventional sense. A touchstone would be Wordsworth's "Ode. Intimations of Immortality from Recollections of Early Childhood.")[9]

I think that, in the course of this book, my own subject-position with respect to the "postsecular" may be characterized as open-minded, or at least nondismissive, yet at times questioning. (A mode of the postsecular of which I remain critical is that which appeals to a variant of the sacrificial and its supposed regenerative or redemptive powers, involving some form of victimization or scapegoating.) One of the most difficult, fraught terms and problems in this respect is of course the "Holocaust" itself, which often moves in the space between the postsecular and the more manifestly religious (evoking sacral or even sacrificial connotations, for example, as a *tremendum* whose victims were martyrs). Certain discussions of the Holocaust may insist on its uniqueness even while acknowledging the extremity of other events or processes. Because of its possibly sacrificial connotations and its etymology as a burnt offering, the term Holocaust may be avoided, as it is emphatically by Giorgio Agamben and in a more subdued manner by figures such as W. G. Sebald and Saul Friedländer.[10]

I hesitantly use the term "Holocaust" and address issues related to it, especially toward the end of this book, with the stipulation that the term is problematic, that it should not be fixated on but used along with other terms (such as Shoah, Nazi genocide, and "final solution"), that most people in the recent past probably use it not because of sacral or sacrificial connotations but because it is the term current in their culture, and that this very usage may help wear away any residual sacral or sacrificial dimensions that are questionable. Even the appeal to uniqueness may be defensible not in any universal or absolute sense but contextually and with qualifications in situations where it may counter tendencies toward denial or nomalization, as was the case during the 1986 *Historikerstreit*, an important reference point for the thought of Friedländer and to some extent of Sebald. Moreover, a special, non-numerical sense of "unique" might be to refer, however tentatively, to that which is so extreme and unsettling that it somehow stands out however many times it may or may not occur.[11] But my more basic point is that, with respect to the Nazi genocide and to other genocides as well, one is on contested ground, and there are no innocent or unproblematic terms, certainly not "final solution," which is always to be used or at least understood in scare quotes as a Nazi, neutralizing, bureaucratic term that one invokes only faute de mieux. There may also be an important sense in which "uniqueness" is not a significant issue and may even have become diversionary in that the more important concern is to investigate the course of the Nazi genocide and to analyze it in noninvidious terms with respect to other genocides or forms of extreme violence and victimization, raising the question of how to account for various subject-positions and possibilities of transformation with respect to understanding, responding to, and attempting to address certain extreme phenomena that may raise intractable problems. Indeed the "Holocaust" and its various uses and abuses should be something that makes one especially wary (although not dismissive) about appeals to the postsecular and what they may entail or, however unintentionally, validate.

A key problem in relation to literature is how to account in a nonreductive manner for its relation to history, a relation that may be best formulated in terms of a process of mutual interrogation, pressure, and provocation. The following chapters explore this relation, including discussions of Joseph Conrad, Gustave Flaubert, J. M. Coetzee, W. G. Sebald, Jonathan Littell, Saul Friedländer, and Jacques Derrida. I take the discussion of Derrida into an analysis of fascism and especially Nazism, a topic that preoccupied Derrida himself toward the end of his life but that he did not explicitly relate to his reflections on religion and the sacred. Friedländer, a historian, has often been praised on stylistic grounds and even hailed as developing a new "literary" approach to the problem of "representing" the voices of victims of the "final solution." Derrida is, of course, often seen as a "literary" philosopher, one who both stresses the importance of literature for the investigation of philosophical problems and who writes in an unorthodox style that has a seemingly literary quality or impetus. For many he transgresses or blurs the boundary between the literary and the philosophical as well as other "fields," including the historical. He has been criticized if not execrated by philosophers, for example, Jürgen Habermas, who in this respect joins many in the analytic tradition such as Ruth Barcan Marcus.[12] By contrast, Derrida is praised or emulated by many in literary and continental philosophical circles, including probably his two primary disciples or interlocutors, Jean-Luc Nancy and Philippe Lacoue-Labarthe.[13] Derrida's appearance in the last chapter of this book, which has a more historical and decidedly critical-theoretical emphasis than the other chapters, should not be surprising.

Violence and fascism, more specifically Nazism, are also topics related to the work of W. G. Sebald, who lived in the melancholic aftermath of the Nazi genocide. This genocide and its aftermath are a concern of J. M. Coetzee, but in his work apartheid arguably has an analogous place as a historical phenomenon that exerted pressure on his writing and exists as an oppressive force field even in texts where he does not explicitly address it (as he does to some extent in *Disgrace*). Of course, disastrous events and melancholic aftermaths have proliferated in the recent past to such an extent that the contexts pertinent to the work of any given writer are blatantly overdetermined. Although Flaubert and Conrad wrote well before the catastrophic events of the more recent past, the excessive and even genocidal dimension of colonialism is evoked in *Heart of Darkness,* explicitly in Kurtz's infamous words: "Exterminate all the brutes." And the narrator in Flaubert's works, including *Madame Bovary,* seems to have genocidal or at least nihilistic tendencies in his desire to negate and transcend an ugly, mediocre, unlivable bourgeois reality. Such, at least, was Sartre's contention in his monumental *L'idiot de la famille* (*The Family Idiot*).[14]

The mutual relation between history and literature tends to be disavowed or misconstrued in various approaches that I investigate in the first chapter: a contextual reductionism in which literature becomes a function explained by one or another set of contextual forces (such as capitalism, colonialism, or the autonomization of spheres in modernity); an ultraformalistic conception of the literary for which history is ultimately irrelevant or becomes at best mere raw material, background, or ballast; and "high theory" (or "theoreticism") that goes beyond necessary speculation and uses both literature and history simply as illustrations or more or less fleeting touchdown points for its transhistorical, if not quasi-transcendental, claims.[15] Such a transhistorical perspective arises not only in the work of figures such as Giorgio Agamben and Slavoj Žižek but even at times in the self-understanding and novelistic practice of certain writers such as Jonathan Littell and, arguably, at points W. G. Sebald, where a transhistorical fatalism may seem pronounced or even, as in Littell, assume a mythological or metahistorical cast.[16] Yet how to trace the intricate, variable, at times bewildering relations between history and literature, while being attentive to contextual pressures as well as to the role of literary form and deformation, is an admittedly difficult undertaking where the promise of success cannot be the primary motivation for making the attempt.[17]

One motif in this book is the importance of transgressive excess and its relation to a quest that in the modern period tends to become empty and may veer in the direction of a participatory fascination with, if not celebratory apology for, violence, itself at times seen as a regenerative, transfiguring, or redemptive force in history. I have intimated that, especially insofar as any specific objective or revolutionary subject seems increasingly unavailable, the quest itself may turn into a metaquest or quest for a quest, perhaps eventuating in a blank utopianism that provokes a desire for radical transcendence or transformation in a willing suspension of disbelief concerning where it may lead.

This quest may take on postsecular or quasi-religious overtones and resonate with negative theology or with something that seems imperceptibly close to it. Such a quest took a specific, violent, genocidal form in Nazism, which may at times have uncanny echoes or resonances in other quests that should not be identified with it and, however contestably or ineffectively, may even resist or criticize it.

What may perhaps be termed a postsecular, if not a more explicitly religious or theological, orientation has at times been seen in the work (notably the later work) of Jacques Derrida, who himself attempted to engage in a critique of fascism, and especially Nazism.[18] One of the more intriguing general phenomena of recent literary criticism and critical theory is the way Derridean discourse has captured the imagination and inflected the style of a significant sector of the academic and literary community (including a writer such as J. M Coetzee, at least on a certain level). The turn to (as well as the almost visceral turn away from) Derrida has involved not only strategies of textual reading and the role of complex (non)concepts such as *différance* or the trace, along with a propensity for enigmatic, paradoxical, at times mind-boggling formulations. It has also engendered an intensely mimetic relation to Derrida's own idiosyncratic style, which might even be seen, in a non-disparaging sense, as a kind of linguistic analog of a computer virus. Or, to change the metaphor, Derrida's style gets under your skin in both the positive and negative senses of that colloquial expression. Moreover, those looking to Derrida may track and follow his interest in various topics, texts, and orientations, resulting in a situation in which a move by Derrida generated—and even after his death may still generate—a cottage industry around one of his concerns (the origin of language, supplementarity, the aporia, the uncanny, the "critique of violence," generosity, the totally other, the autoimmune, the literary, and so forth).

The foregoing series signals that Derrida's role has indeed been pronounced in literary studies, which may even have its problems or lines of analysis directed by questions he enunciates or explores.[19] More generally, the lines between literature and philosophy have become indeterminate if not blurred, and even those who insist on the specificity or even sui generis status of the literary "as such" (such as Derek Attridge, for example, in his important study of Coetzee) tend paradoxically to see the literary in terms largely shaped by a certain approach to philosophy (in Attridge's case, Derrida's).[20] As I have intimated, these terms have themselves recently become increasingly postsecular with a problematic relation to religion, thus repeating on a spectral or phantomlike level the traditional relation between philosophy and theology, with this relation becoming more explicit in the recent past. A text in which the postsecular turn in Derrida seems especially pronounced is his "Faith and Knowledge: Two Sources of 'Religion' at the Limits of Reason Alone."[21] I begin chapter 5 with a brief, highly selective discussion of this text and then go in directions not pursued by Derrida (although he does pursue them elsewhere in his own way)—directions that take me back to issues circulating around the problem of fascism and Nazism.

Another phenomenon in the recent past, accentuated by the death of Derrida and other major figures, is the rise to prominence in theoretical circles of Giorgio Agamben, Alain Badiou, and Slavoj Žižek, who have almost become the "ABZs" of contemporary critical theory. Žižek arguably has achieved pride of place in this threesome, at least in terms of the frequency of references to him and his publications, which have taken on a very significant role in the work of literary critics with an avowed interest in politics. Despite his encompassing interests, Žižek's primary focus has been on film and modes of popular culture, along with at times arresting forays into history and politics. Yet his prominence as a theorist has inspired others, including those who do focus on literature. In the first chapter, I briefly discuss Paul Eisenstein's noteworthy "Žižekian" study, *Traumatic Encounters: Holocaust Representation and the Hegelian Subject.*[22] And, as an epilog, I include a discussion of Žižek, focusing on his influential treatment of violence that combines political advocacy, literary flair, and rhetorical flamboyance. For many, Žižek is a very "exciting" writer (and speaker), if not what the French would term an "*exalté.*"

Among my concerns are the ways literature inscribes, at times by resisting, contextual forces and historical constraints; indeed in certain respects it may actively disorient reference or attempt to transcend contexts. This sometimes unsettling initiative (as in Derrida or, in a different register, Flaubert or, say, Samuel Beckett) may involve a practice of insistent decontextualization that seems to place the bewildered reader on a barren lunar landscape or in a desert where s/he is invited to wander blindly, devoid of a sense of direction or a goal. In seemingly less uncanny or disorienting forms, this relation of text and context may enact reversals and run from quotidian happenings in the French provinces (experienced by Emma Bovary, and perhaps rendered by the Flaubert-narrator, as ultimately deadly) to the unfolding and aftermath of genocide. It is, for example, noteworthy that a telling reversal in *Madame Bovary* is the manner in which the fictitious towns of Tostes and Yonville l'Abbaye are extensively described in "realistic" terms, while the real city of Rouen is barely sketched and Paris, the center of Emma's dreams and hopes, remains a vague, suicidally inflected ideal—an analog of her elusive ideal lover. One may also find in certain tendencies, including what has been seen as a form of "modernism," a preference for suggestive allusiveness or perplexing vagueness that may situate context or setting in a twilight zone, if not a "heart of darkness," and render uncertain any ascription of a referential context or decided point of view (such as racism or misogyny). More generally, underspecification may be an explicit strategy of representation, and it has many possible functions from evasiveness and equivocation to the provocative implication of the reader in the problems being explored. Another way the reader's expectations may be upset, at least with respect to understanding and meaning, is through a surfeit of context or historical and pseudohistorical detail, a practice (or at least an effect) of certain of Flaubert's novels (notably *Salammbô*) and in evidence in Littell's monstrously, and at times repulsively detailed, seemingly historical novel, *Les Bienveillantes* (*The Kindly Ones*).[23]

The uses of language or, more generally, signifying practices should be taken as an important historical problem as well as an object of literary and rhetorical study. Despite the much heralded, more rarely practiced, and often reductively construed "linguistic turn," historiography may still not give sufficient attention to the problem of language-in-use as a prominent object of inquiry, and this is one reason why much history does not include sustained, careful attention either to the historian's own use of language or to literature, philosophy, and the arts as important sociocultural practices, supplemented but not altogether displaced in the recent past by media, film, and other forms of popular culture. Perhaps even less attention is devoted to the problem of how to read texts and signifying practices with an attentiveness to the way they involve complex uses of language, having variable relations to language use and associated signifying practices in different social groups or categories that are more familiar to historians. Yet at present the influential opposition between *langue* and *parole*, derived from Ferdinand de Saussure, as well as the postulates of difference and the arbitrariness of the signifier, may fruitfully · be displaced in the direction of the complex relation between (abstract) system (or certain forms of theory) and signifying practice (including but not restricted to language) in historical use. In historical processes (including literary practices) language is always caught up in a variable interplay between demotivation (or, at the limit, radical decontextualization, dissemination, and arbitrariness) and (re)motivation, notably through changing uses effected by various agencies with different degrees of power and authority, from the state through social groups to the individual writer engaging various traditions, genres, and other writers as well as the discourses of social and political life. This, in any case, was the valuable view of Mikhail Bakhtin and at times of Derrida—a view of greatest pertinence to those with a marked interest in the relation between history and critical theory.

The question of the history of language use indicates the importance of such issues as narrative structure, voice, perspective, and subject-position—issues that arise not only in the novel but also in the writing of history and that provide a basis for nonreductive comparisons and contrasts between literature—including fiction—and historiography. An important novel, such as *Madame Bovary* or any of the other novels discussed in this book, should be seen as a significant event in history—a significance to which the trial of Flaubert itself bore witness. This variant of the linguistic turn does not isolate or reify language. Nor does it give language a causal or formatively sovereign, radically constructivist power. On the contrary, how language is used and how that use varies over time and place—at times in the same text or discourse—is a problem bound up with many other crucial problems and processes, and for that very reason it deserves a prominent place in a critical and self-critical historiography.

The specific figures I discuss provide the occasion to inquire into more general issues in a manner that allows for comparative study and requires close reading sensitive to problems of language as well as translation. The groundbreaking work of Flaubert is a key reference point for other novelists I discuss. His relation to French was both intimate and alienated. At times it seemed to him to be a foreign language or at least a language on which he had to engage in now legendary labor in quest of a distinctive style, sometimes described in terms of a prose that would attain the rigor of poetry. The *"affres du style"* attested to an asceticism or *askesis* that brought both suffering and "joy"—a kind of sadomasochistic practice reminiscent of the self-flagellating spiritual exercises of saints and martyrs. This style was far from the fluency of ordinary language or the ease of a linguistic habitus that bespoke the immediacy of a second nature, even when the results of such a style in Flaubert seem to parallel or mimic the most everyday if not banal speech; and the radical transitions (for example, in the opening sections of *Madame Bovary* in which the narrative voice and perspective move from the first-person plural to a third-person form of narration) seem so smooth and seamlessly made as to screen the disruptive nature of the movement. This style is related to the "rigor" (or "exigency") that later writers saw as a requirement of their craft. It is evoked in the self-commentaries of the Polish novelist (writing in English) Joseph Conrad, the ill-at-ease South African (who grew up speaking Afrikaans and late in life moved to Australia) J. M. Coetzee, and the German (living in East Anglia and uncomfortably writing in German) W. G. Sebald, as well as the recent phenomenon Jonathan Littell (an American writing in French and a long-time resident of Paris) whose massive prize-winning novel, a first-person account by an SS officer of experiences and events during the Nazi genocide, I discuss together with Saul Friedländer's two-volume prize-winning history, *Nazi Germany and the Jews*, whose goal is to recapture—and punctuate his own narrative with—the unsettling "voices" of victims.

By the time one gets to Littell and Friedländer a belated recognition arises that may apply retrospectively to other writers, beginning at least with Flaubert: the very notion of a "mother" tongue may be illusory once one's relation to language becomes problematic and is continually placed in question. This assertion could not apply to anyone more than Jacques Derrida, whose Algerian past became an insistent concern and whose writing is markedly diasporic and orphaned. My epilog addresses one crucial dimension of the thought of Slavoj Žižek, whose relation to language also warrants more attention than I give it in my focus on violence. Yet there is a sense in which Žižek (a Slovenian) has a relation to language that is not simply problematic, most obviously in his heavily inflected, insistently dramatic use of English, but overpowering, as he forcefully translates popular culture into a Lacanian dialect and turns English itself into a recognizably "Žižekian" idiom that rivals the idiosyncratic, yet almost contagiously imitable, usage of other major figures, including the more gentle inflections, melodic sweeps, and chiasmic complexities of Derrida. I argue that Žižek's provocative, indeed hyperbolic thinking contains certain questionable elements that at times echo, uncannily, earlier reflections on, or apologies for, political and seemingly regenerative, even sacralized (or "divine"), violence. My discussion touches on the most disturbing and politically dubious dimension of a thinker who never fails to unsettle.

With respect to the intricate issue of the postsecular and its increasingly prevalent role in recent thought, I do not claim to occupy an uninvolved or detached position that puts me above the fray or "*hors jeu*."[24] I make no effort to rehabilitate either religion in general or any specific religious tradition, such as one or another form of Christianity or Judaism. Instead, my objective is to inquire critically into the role of sacred and sacralizing forces in history, including in philosophy and literature as well as critical theory. A goal of critique is to disentangle the sacred from sacrifice, indeed critically to construe sacrifice that requires victimization and violence (whether with respect to humans or to other animals) not as the epitome or even the origin of the sacred but rather as its distortion or disastrous abuse, often if not typically its anthropocentric appropriation oriented toward generating a sense of purification, regeneration, and redemption, at least for its human officiators or agents (should one say perpetrators?). In other words, I see the value of understanding religion (with Émile Durkheim) in terms of the sacred (rather than, say, with reference to a god or godlike analog, however hidden, radically transcendent, or "totally other"). I would, however, argue against construing sacrifice as the crux of the sacred (as did Georges Bataille),[25] or taking a given religion as exceptional in transcending sacrifice or at least providing the sacrifice that presumably ends (but has clearly failed to end) all sacrifice (as did René Girard with respect to Christianity).[26] The effort to disambiguate sacrifice and the sacred is an ongoing process, as is the attempt to delineate what in the sacred (or in a certain construction of religion or the postsecular) may be worthy of affirmation, for example, the role of nondiscriminatory rituals in articulating transitional points in life—rituals that situate humans in a broadly relational network in which neither scapegoated humans nor other animals are victimized in either quasi-sacrificial or seemingly secular, even antiseptic ways.[27] In any event, a recurrent motif of this book is the role of the sacred, its problematic status in sacrifice, its virulent manifestation in social and political violence (as in the Nazi genocide), and its multivalent expressions in postsecular hopes, anxieties, and quests.

✎ CHAPTER 1

The Mutual Interrogation of History and Literature

There has been a recent tendency in the historical profession that calls for a turn, perhaps a turn back, to a close relation with the social sciences and social history. This tendency is in evidence in William H. Sewell's widely acclaimed *Logics of History: Social Theory and Social Transformation*,[1] as well as in the collection *Practicing History: New Directions in Historical Writing after the Linguistic Turn*, edited by Gabrielle Spiegel.[2] Also evident in these books, notably in Spiegel's introduction to the volume she edits, is a certain resistance to the so-called linguistic and cultural turns that stressed history's relation to the humanities, including literature and critical theory. In my judgment, it would be self-defeating to decide between the social sciences and the humanities in the definition of historiography. The historian's own version of a double consciousness is both valuable and in need of continual rethinking.

I would like to focus on one dimension of that process of rethinking with respect to the relation between history and literature. I think the most cogent and thought-provoking way to envision that relation, including what might be called the pressure exerted by the historical on the literary, is in terms of intricate and variable forms of interaction, especially modes of mutual interrogation. In other words, history and literature may be seen as posing questions to one another, the answers to which are not foregone conclusions. One crucial question is precisely how literary texts inscribe or process historical contexts, both in symptomatic, perhaps unconscious ways and through formal procedures that may be quite explicit and well crafted. A related question concerns the relation between historical and trans-historical forces that are intertwined and impinge on texts in different ways, with the epitome of the transhistorical perhaps exemplified at present by the Lacanian "real"—the traumatic void or break that resists or even annihilates symbolization yet may provoke it as well. Another issue, which at least warrants mention, is the way texts are read differently over time in relation to changes both in the literary field and in the larger sociocultural and political context. (I note at the outset that, for the most part, I shall refer to literature, but the question I would leave open is the extent to which points I touch on might apply to other forms of art as well.)

The two polar, more or less extreme and rather confining responses to the problem of relating history and literature may well disavow or diminish mutual interrogation, but each has had noteworthy proponents. One might be seen as an "immanent" quest for thoroughly grounded knowledge in relation to which literature or "the literary" may be an object to be assimilated, perhaps even taken to be an irritant. The other is at times a variant of the quest for transcendence, with the literary given a transcendental or quasi-transcendental status that may be construed in postsecular or displaced religious terms.

Perhaps the primary modality of the immanent quest is contextual reductionism in which a literary text is a mirror image or at least a symptom of some sociohistorical or perhaps transhistorical process or structure such as capitalism, colonialism, the rise of the individual, the emergence of a distinctive if not unique form of experience or subjectivity, even castration anxiety or the "real." The text thus becomes a document of the times or perhaps of transhistorical forces. A distinctive variant of this approach, more sensitive to literary developments themselves, at least on a societal or general cultural level, traces the development of the so-called institution of literature, especially as a differentiated system or field of modern culture. The literary in this sense comes to form its own context, which is more or less open to other contextual pressures and similar in its dynamic to other differentiated systems or fields in modern society and culture (for example, science, business, or the professions).

The other response is a vision of the literary text as detached or disimplicated from, or in some basic sense transcending, historical contexts. The text may, however, be situated within the differentiated field or institution of literature in a more or less unself-questioning way or, on the contrary, in a radically contestatory, even self-deconstructing manner. Literature may be understood not only as engaging at times in modes of decontextualization but postulated as essentially in excess of or radically beyond its contexts, negating and/or transcending them, perhaps toward absence, impossibility, perplexity, ironic indirection (or "permanent parabasis"), and unreadability, if not "madness."[3] Literature may appear to be a displacement of religion, and literary criticism may seem to be related to negative theology.[4] The object of study may be taken as tantamount to a sacred or perhaps a postsecular text whose exegesis suffices to reveal truth and whose close reading approximates a pious practice or in itself embodies an ethic. In a more domesticated vein, the literary text, or the text read in its "literariness," may be subject only to formal analysis in terms of its self-referential way of bending back on itself or being "about" the play of language. As Leo Bersani put it with reference to Flaubert, in terms which now seem more familiar than uncanny: "Flaubert's novels are most interestingly about . . . the arbitrary, insignificant, inexpressive nature of language. . . . Fundamentally, language refers to nothing beyond its own impersonal (and discouraging) virtuosity."[5] On this reading, Flaubert marks the linguistic turn inward of literary language. And language itself is to be construed as a formal system similar to the manner in which music, mathematics, or abstract art is often seen.

By contrast, in contextual reductionism, literature becomes a document with referential functions, perhaps a symptom of history's hidden or secret dimensions. Historians, sociologists, Marxists, and, in a somewhat different sense, Freudians and Lacanians have often taken this approach to literature and art in general.[6] For example, from a sociohistorical point of view, one reads Stendhal's *The Red and the Black* for what it discloses about the play of factions in early nineteenth-century France or perhaps about the suicidal fate of the alienated individual whose subjective values can find no home in existing society. Or one reads Balzac for his insight into the development of capitalistic forces, themselves the deregulated but systemic generators of excess and madness. And one reads Flaubert for his enactment of the autonomization of art as a differentiated sphere of activity that parallels the development of other autonomy-seeking professions. Two especially important theorists, separated by a generation, who propose variants of this approach are Georg Lukács and Pierre Bourdieu.

In his influential *Theory of the Novel* of 1920, the young Lukács elaborated a contrast between the epic, as a form in which there were answers without questions, and the novel, as a form in which there were questions without answers. Typical of the novel was the role of abstract idealism and romantic disillusionment in which the alienated hero could not realize values in the existing world and so generally had a tragic fate. In his own preface of

1962 Lukács situated *The Theory of the Novel* as an overly abstract work whose interest was at best symptomatic of its context. The later Lukács turned from his early Hegelianism to a Hegelian Marxism in which the texts of so-called critical realists such as Balzac and Thomas Mann are valued, while the works of others, who are often seen as among the more experimental writers, esteemed by the young Lukács himself—for example, Flaubert—are understood as escapist or formalistic symptoms of bourgeois decadence.[7]

The later Lukács stresses the way critical realists provide perspective on social and historical developments—perspective that may even contradict their explicit ideology, for example, royalism in the case of Balzac. For Lukács, Balzac was more insightful about the forces of modern history than was the affirmed leftist Zola, who produced what Lukács presents as a merely photographic, uncritical realism close to positivism in the sciences. Hence, whatever their explicit ideologies, figures such as Balzac and Mann may be recuperated and used by Marxists in sociopolitically progressive, even revolutionary ways. One might say that the impossible quest of the early Lukács to find in art the presumably lost, integrated world of totality in which one could be at home was itself displaced onto social and political action, and Marxism became the way to realize in historical reality the values that art could enact only in the mode of the impossible dream, the unattainable utopia, or the tragic quest. Still, even in the later Lukács, the critical dimension of art—often in ways unbeknownst to the writer or artist—was itself reflective of social forces, specifically the rise of the proletariat as the revolutionary subject of history.

In his 2005 impressive yet controversial analysis and critique of colonial violence, which he sees as the origin of later genocides including the Holocaust, Olivier Le Cour Grandmaison is on one level close to Lukács when he reads Conrad's *Heart of Darkness* as an instance of critical realism in its analysis and indictment of colonial practices.[8] Unlike more simplistic advocates of contextual reading, Grandmaison does not present Conrad himself as an exponent of colonialism, racism, and imperialism.[9] Rather, following the lead of Sven Lindqvist in *"Exterminate All the Brutes,"*[10] he understands *Heart of Darkness* as drawing from documentary sources and Conrad's own experience to render a literary account of colonial activity typical not only of the Congo but of colonialism in Africa more generally, especially with respect to peoples, such as the "Arabs," who (at times analogized to American Indians) were seen as untamable, wild or savage beasts such as jackals—prey whose tracking was "certified" by taking a head as a trophy (157). More docile sub-Saharan blacks (at times analogized to American slaves) were perceived as *bêtes de somme* (beasts of burden), who could be a reliable labor force and even used for domestic service, although they too might go bad and become unmanageable like Arabs, as was the case with the Herero in 1904 (82). For Grandmaison, Conrad's novel is a more reliable history of these empirical processes than were actual histories of the time and even subsequently, histories that were misleading vehicles of ideologies of progress, imperial glory, and the "civilizing mission." He concludes that "the literature of Conrad, at least that which has held our attention, is a literature of radical and brutal disenchantment. That's why it was rebellious at its time; it remains so today, for it allows one to take the just measure of what was the conquest and colonization of Africa for the populations that were subjected to it" (167; my translation). Despite his trenchant formulations and incisive analyses, Grandmaison, while not reducing texts to symptoms of contexts and instead recognizing, perhaps even exaggerating, their critical power of provocation, does not inquire into their internal tensions or self-contestations, for example, that between Tocqueville's violent, at times exterminatory response to North African peoples (or to the working class in France after 1848) and his democratic liberalism, reserved for "civilized" peoples. He also does not look into the different if not divergent movements in *Heart of Darkness* itself. In Conrad's text (discussed in the following chapter) there is both a radical condemnation of, and a fascination with, the violent excesses personified in Kurtz, a fascination that affects Marlow, the unnamed narrator, and arguably even the implied author and perhaps the reader as well, who is drawn in by the way a quest narrative almost inevitably endows its object (be it the "heart of darkness") with an ambivalent allure.

Pierre Bourdieu, in his *Rules of Art*, does not share Lukács's Marxist assumptions and is situated in a different sociological tradition, stemming from Durkheim.[11] Bourdieu may, like Grandmaison, often subsume specific texts in a sweeping argument but at times without the sensitivity to the critical power of certain texts at their own time and over time. Bourdieu reads literature, specifically Flaubert's *Sentimental Education*, rather one-dimensionally as symptomatic of social forces. The forces in question for Bourdieu are those bound up with the division of labor and more particularly with the functional differentiation and autonomization of spheres or fields in modern life. (His approach is a distinctive variant of a more widespread mode of analysis, probably most rigorously developed in systems theory, notably in the work of Niklas Luhmann.)

Bourdieu argues, plausibly enough, that one should not take art for art's sake and formalistic analysis at face value. One should situate them in the larger context of the division and autonomization of spheres as well as the spread of professionalization in modernity. However, for Bourdieu, art simply falls in line with the tendential regularities of modernity in general, and sociology is able to explain and provide the proper demystifying perspective on art for art's sake, an ideology that artists or literary critics often inhabit from the inside. Aesthetes may believe art is an end in itself or a transcendent value, just as an academic may assert a fully disimplicated, objectifying "outsider" position on topics of inquiry or a CEO may believe that business is business or transfigure the market into a supernal blue flower or inviolable divinity.

Contextualizing theorists have the virtue of attempting to see and interpret literature and art in larger sociohistorical and cultural contexts, at times with an eye to political practice. It is, for example, informative to see Flaubert in the context of the emerging literary field of his time and to trace his relations, including his resistances, to figures and processes typifying that field, prominently including the commodification of literature. One of Flaubert's motivations was to resist being like crowd-pleasing commercialized writers such as Paul de Kock or Alphonse Karr. (He was more inclined to identify with ascetic saints and monks, for example, Saint Anthony subject to maddeningly bewildering temptations.) But the difficulties with contextualism when it becomes reductive should be evident. A reductive contextualism does not sufficiently account for the work and play of the text or of art in general, including its formal devices and the variably divided ways it may have a critical and possibly transformative relation to contexts and not simply be symptomatic of them. Thus Flaubert's *Sentimental Education*, the very novel on which Bourdieu grounds his symptomatic sociological analysis, may be seen to a significant extent as questioning and destabilizing the autonomization of spheres in modernity and not straightforwardly illustrating or enacting it, for example, in the manner in which the novel itself may be construed as a historically and critically pointed reading of the times or the way in which, in the novel itself, religion, art, economics, and intimate relations, as well as private and public "spheres" in general, intersect or implode to the point of confusion.[12]

The view of literature and art as always in excess, negating and transcending sociohistorical contexts or forces, takes what contextualism underplays or denies and gives it an accentuated, at times an exorbitant, role. In its most challenging form, this approach stresses the role of the imagination, improvisation, and the nonrepresentational performative dimensions of literature and art, even the ways in which the latter place themselves—and oneself—in radical question. Literature may then become the site of a sustained self-interrogation bearing on its conditions of possibility or impossibility. Literature in this sense may even be situated in the wake of religion, in the dual sense of being both in its turbulent passage and in a relation of impossible mourning with respect to it. Insofar as religion is unavailable but still beckons, literature explores the space religion has vacated yet may still haunt. It approaches what may be an absence, or at least a darkening, of the sacred and engages in an attentive waiting, at times with no expectation of salvation—what Derrida terms *une attente sans attente* (translatable as a waiting without expectation, say, for a redeeming moment, total insight, or recovery of a putatively lost totality). It may also raise the specter of utopian hope and longing but may leave it totally blank or at least not invest it with politically specific objectives or self-transformative rhetorical power. And literature may, like the funereal wake, merge mourning with gallows humor, at times exploring the often violent nature and effects of a deficit of effective ritual in modern society and the way even intended festivals or carnivalesque scenes may backfire and become undone. (Nothing may be more frequent in modern literature, especially literature involving gallows humor, than the spectacle of carnival gone awry.) Literature is of course also open to at times daring and risky experimentalism and improvisation, more or less constrained by deficits in cultural forms that might provide sustaining points of reference. Experimentation may include the writer's transferential involvement (or self-implication) in the text and the issues it explores, an involvement mediated and at times dislocated by formal procedures that may, at the limit, attempt to "erase" the traces of the writer and his or her "experience."[13]

The literary "field," viewed from this perspective, makes Bourdieu's concept of field seem too much like a well-tended victory garden. Literature may even be construed as postsecular as well as postapocalyptic, oriented toward some form of transcendence or perhaps a disastrous yet sublime vortex-like black hole—an all-consuming "heart of darkness" that threatens to turn us all into the living dead. Here literature moves vertiginously in an area in which religious concern and intensity occur in opaque, displaced, disguised, distorted, even disavowed ways that make the very distinction between the secular and the religious seem to dissolve, perhaps giving rise to some emergent, ill-defined postsecularism—at times a kind of religious atheism, or what Derrida terms a messianicity without messianism.[14] And the postapocalyptic sense of surviving in the wake of a catastrophe or extreme event may either leave that event unnamed or name it in ways that are more or less explicitly seen as problematic. Such problematic namings include the "death of God," "Auschwitz," "Hiroshima," and the "postcolonial" as well as the "postmodern." (Uncertainty about conceptualization and naming, a "no longer not yet" sense of belatedness and a reaching for some indeterminate future or "beyond" are at play in the frequent appeal to the prefix "post.") At least until recently, the Holocaust or Auschwitz has

been a privileged name for the unnamable, but one may also relate traumatizing events to, or even questionably subsume them under, a transhistorical
source of disruption or disorientation, such as original sin, the passage from
nature to culture, the separation from the mother, the entry into language or
symbolism, the abject that precedes and unsettles subject and object, or the
encounter with the traumatic "real."

This second mode of construing literature is more provocative, uncanny,
and captivating than *terre-à-terre* contextual reductionism. And in more or
less distinctive ways it informs the work of some of the most important and
demanding thinkers and writers of the last century, figures such as Mallarmé,
Kierkegaard, Beckett, Heidegger, Blanchot, Kristeva, de Man, and Derrida.
Stéphane Mallarmé's famous statement about poetry, "rien n'aura lieu que
le lieu," epitomizes the challenge and the enigmatic uncanniness of this approach. "Nothing will take place but the place" places or displaces poetry,
perhaps all that is literary (assuming one may approximate poetry and the
literary), into a no-place in which nothing and everything seem to happen.
This place is not about other places but insistently carves out or performs
its placements and displacements, at times seeming to be improvising (or
skywriting) in the void. How it relates to other historical places, processes,
and displacements becomes problematic and at times inscrutable. In one
sense there seems to be an active decontextualization of the literary text that
becomes intransitive and nonrepresentational. In another sense the literary
text loses any putative autonomy and becomes radically open in unpredictable ways.[15] Somehow (as for Derrida) the text that has no outside gestures
toward the totally other. In any case, history may be problematized and temporality reconfigured, often in varying modalities of repetition with change,
at times traumatic change (for example, as in Virginia Woolf, William Gad-
dis, or Thomas Mann).[16] Especially in certain theorists, perhaps more so than
in the literary texts they treat, history may also be transfigured into a literary
trope or liberated signifier construed in purely literary or theoretical terms,
for example, as excess, trauma, violence, or the sublime.[17] And disconcerting
reversals or warps may arise in the relation of life and art. As Kierkegaard
once put it, his texts might blush at certain aspects of his life. Or, as he wrote
with respect to his use of pseudonyms (in a sense, a series of fictional doubles
as narrators or commentators related to the role of indirect communication),
pseudonymity "has not had an accidental basis in my *person* . . . but an *essential* basis in the *production* itself, which, for the sake of the lines, of the
psychologically varied differences of the individualities, poetically required a
disregard for good and evil, contrition and exuberance, despair and arrogance,
suffering and rhapsody, etc., which are limited only ideally by psychological

consistency, which no actual or factual person dares allow himself or wishes to allow himself in the moral limitations of actuality."[18] Here, experience with respect to literature seems to become literary experience or the writing and reading of the literary text itself.

Kierkegaard's comment clearly contests certain kinds of realism, but it also indicates that a rather different relation to ordinary reality (or actuality) and its possibilities nonetheless informs apparently nonrealistic aesthetics and their import for various contexts. For Kierkegaard seems to be saying that what is possible or even demanded in literary production may not be desirable in life. Here two points made by Kierkegaard are pertinent to my analysis. The first applies to the role of a corrective that becomes misleading or confusing when it is simply taken as the norm or as a hegemonic form. Kierkegaard applied this to Lutheranism and, I think, to himself as polemicist and gadfly. One might perhaps apply it to recent theories when they are learned as a first language or an exclusive mode of analysis. Kierkegaard writes: "Lutheranism is a corrective—but a corrective made into the norm, the whole, is *eo ipso* confusing in the next generation (when that which it was meant to correct no longer exists)."[19] (As someone who once gave a course whose unofficial title was "Deconstruction as a Second Language," I take this injunction to heart.)

The second point bears on the relation between the indirect (or maieutic) and direct communication or style in an approach to problems, a point Kierkegaard makes with respect to religion but that might also be made pari passu with respect to the literary, especially when the latter seems to serve as a displacement of the religious in terms of radical alterity or (transgressive-transcendent) excess.

> The communication of Christianity must ultimately end in "bearing witness," the maieutic form can never be final. . . . In Christendom the maieutic form can certainly be used, simply because the majority in fact live under the impression that they are Christians. But since Christianity is Christianity the maieuticer must become the witness. In the end the maieuticer will not be able to bear the responsibility because the indirect method is ultimately rooted in human intelligence, however much it may be sanctified and consecrated by fear and trembling. God becomes too powerful for the maieuticer and so he is the witness though different from the direct witness in that he has been through the process of becoming one. (146; the quote dates from 1848)

Kierkegaard insisted on the differences between the religious and the aesthetic and saw allusion, indirection, irony, parody, parable, and so forth, as particularly suited to the aesthetic, prominently including the literary. But "maieutic" indirection, related to midwifery rather than to more participatory involvement in gestation and birth, was not self-sufficient and had to be supplemented by directness, even though there was no simple transcendence of formal devices and no possibility of unmediated or transparent (immediate and nontransferential) directness. Moreover, the extreme of unrelieved indirection (perhaps including abyssal Romantic or post-Romantic irony, approximated if not epitomized in figures such as Friedrich Schlegel and Paul de Man), like the opposite extreme of direct witnessing as well as asymmetrical grace, creation ex nihilo, and full "presence" (or "absence" and total otherness), was a divine prerogative. In any event, a life of indirect communication (including parable and paradox) was available only to the God-man.

> It is not true that direct communication is superior to indirect communication. No, no. But the fact is that no man has ever been born who could use the indirect method even fairly well, to say nothing of using it all his life. For we human beings need each other, and in that there is already directness.
>
> Only the God-man is in every respect indirect communication from first to last. He did not need men, but they infinitely needed him; he loves men, but according to his conception of what love is; therefore he does not change in the slightest toward their conception, does not speak directly in such a way that he also surrenders the possibility of offense—which his existence (*Existents*) in the guise of servant is.[20]

A problem arises with respect to what is arguably the displaced religious or theological construction of literature itself as radical alterity, abyssal excess, endless negativity, asymmetrical nondialogism, or a quasi-transcendental "beyond," when, unlike Kierkegaard, one absolutizes this view and makes it into an all-or-nothing consuming object of concern (perhaps a "postsecular" fixation). When the latter occurs, literature and history do not have a mutually interrogatory relation because one is either alienated from or consumed by the other, hence arriving at a situation not altogether unlike that reached by contextual reductionism. One obvious question is the extent to which one can recognize and even participate in the uncanny, at times compelling movements of a self-questioning notion of literature and still pose the problem of historical context, which requires a certain mediated directness in modes of address that are nonetheless nonreductive and thought provoking. Posing the problem of context in this sense would be neither a reductive "explanatory" move nor an inert, unreflective association, conjunction, or montage of formal experiment (if not phantasmatic projection) and documentary information. (One may take this as a key problem in the writing of literature and in both cultural studies, including postcolonial studies, and the historical approach to literature and art.)[21]

A further question is how a self-questioning, insistent, extremely discomfiting approach to literature may give rise to a formalistic methodology or to a more or less compulsive return to certain discursive strategies that resort exclusively to allusiveness, indirection, paradox, aporia, and the *mise en abyme*, with openings to history or to ethics and politics either being foreclosed or formulated in ways that remain enigmatic or circular (for example, with history construed as a trope or a literary fiction). When an approach becomes a methodology or the premise for a repetition compulsion, certain distinctions may be not only problematized (as well they should) but obliterated, including the distinction between literature and sociopolitical life or between everyday ethics and what sublimely exceeds and questions it.[22] And, in a more technical vein, a formalistic methodology may take the place of an insistent mode of inquiry that cannot be codified or contained in a methodology. It would be misguided to conflate self-referential formalism with a defensible concern, in literature and in other genres as well, for the significance of form (along with the attempt to explore the intractable). A crucial dimension of form is to resist immediate identification, say with characters or even with a narrator or a style, and to serve as the type of mediation that allows for some degree of critical distance and self-questioning. Such mediation need not be seen in stereotypical "dialectical" ways that are indentured to closure, totalization, or a progressive, all-encompassing movement of integration or *Aufhebung.*

Aufhebung is a key concept in Hegelian dialectics. It is generally understood as comprising three different and perhaps dissonant meanings: to negate, to affirm, and to lift to a higher level. It may be countered (as in Kierkegaard), deconstructed (as in Derrida), or even understood (as in Žižek) in terms of displacement involving a repetition or variation that may possibly involve traumatic, disorienting, unpredictable, or aleatory change. The relation of theory to its object may be construed either as "traditional" *Aufhebung* (as at times in Lukács or even Bourdieu) or as a mode of more or less radical displacement. Indeed, however much a theoretical construction or analysis tries to be "faithful" to its object, it arguably entails some mode of alteration and displacement, although the latter may be more or less cogent and convincing.

On the back cover of Paul Eisenstein's *Traumatic Encounters: Holocaust Representation and the Hegelian Subject* Žižek hails the work in the following terms: "The book [is] a must: a forceful redemption of the power of theory." Žižek sees the "traumatic encounter" of the book's title not as "that of Holocaust, but the one between two seemingly incompatible events: the Holocaust and Hegelian dialectics. The result is simply shattering: both terms undergo a profound transformation." This transformation is for Žižek the basis of the book's "redemption of the power of theory." One may well think that the attempt to approach the Holocaust in terms of a revised understanding of Hegelian dialectics—in Eisenstein (as in Žižek) approximated to Lacanian psychoanalysis (an approximation that is itself a dazzling if not mind-boggling feat)—is a significant theoretical project, if not quite "simply shattering" or the "redemption of the power of theory." Of principal significance would be not the "traumatic encounter" of a theory and a genocide but the extent to which a theory assists in, and is tested by, the analysis of a genocide and of texts or signifying practices that themselves address it.

One may recognize the value in the Žižekian approach validated by Eisenstein in its repeated encounter with the Lacanian real (or structural trauma) if one sees that approach as a kind of high-level transhistorical "fort-da" game that may serve to engage and perhaps mitigate existential anxiety, while almost compulsively addressing it time and again. But its pertinence for an understanding of the actual and possible relations of history, theory, and literature may be restricted. Here a critical observation by Sebald is to the point, and his comment about the reading of *Doctor Faustus* may not be restricted to its "originally intended" readers, although the reasons for a certain reading may shift in valence from idealistic reaffirmation to a carte-blanche indictment of what exists combined with a seemingly "radical" desire for a thoroughgoing, even violent breakthrough to something completely different: "In *Doctor Faustus*, Thomas Mann wrote a comprehensive historical criticism of an art that was increasingly inclined to take an apocalyptic view of the world, at the same time confessing his own involvement. It is likely that few of the readers for whom this novel was originally intended understood him; the lava barely cold under their feet they were too preoccupied with the reaffirmation of their higher ideals, too anxious to free themselves of any taint. They did not go deeply into the complex question of the relationship between ethics and aesthetics that tormented Thomas Mann."[23]

I think that what tormented Thomas Mann was not so much the transhistorical role of structural trauma or how it might explain Nazi behavior but what specifically the Third Reich did to Jews and other victims, what those actions meant for the understanding of Germany, its history, and its postwar possibilities, and how a literary work, while remaining literary, might address such momentous problems. In *Doctor Faustus*, the importance of the specifically historical is insistent, even if there may be problematic aspects of the novel in this respect (notably the invocation of the Devil, although one may take this reference as a metaphoric appeal to the traditional exemplar of radical evil, with the Devil being in one important sense a projective embodiment of Adrian Leverkühn's own "internally dialogized" self-questioning and self-doubts, notably in the central chapter treating the encounter of the musical genius and the shape-shifting wily one where the latter at times quotes Leverkühn to himself).

Eisenstein does not account for the way the intricate formal relations in the novel (notably between implied author, interposed narrator [Zeitblom], "mad" musical genius [Leverkühn], various characters, Germany, and the reader) function to resist any unmediated identification on the part of the reader and instead critically open various possibilities in reading. In *Traumatic Encounters* Leverkühn's quest for the aesthetic breakthrough, enabled by a pact with the Devil, is itself an object of Eisenstein's own, and by implication the reader's, unmediated identification or at least uncritical affirmation, and it is linked to an interpretation of Leverkühn's varied and different compositions as "fundamentally a music of witnessing . . . to that structural [that is, transhistorical or even universal] trauma for which [the Nazi] regime promised redress" (120–21). Eisenstein even presents *Doctor Faustus* as "provid[ing] us with a manifesto or blueprint for how to proceed" in and through the character and approach to music of Adrian Leverkühn. Not only is the Nazi regime construed abstractly as somehow responding immediately to structural trauma, but Leverkühn is seen as a Žižekian tragic or post-tragic hero who, in his musical "breakthrough" (associated in the novel with his mental breakdown), takes problems to an implosive limit and thereby does not give up on his desire, traversing the fantasy into a consuming suicidal abyss—a kind of existential *mise en abyme* (a "*fort*" or "away" movement that seems to obviate any resisting or impeding "*da*" or "there"). Indeed, the crux of the novel is taken to be Leverkühn's act of exemplary witnessing to the "holocaustal" process.

By contrast, one might argue that Leverkühn is not figured in the novel univocally as a model witness to a holocaustal process or as the ethical or political answer to Nazism, its rise, and the dangers arising in its aftermath. Instead, he has a complex relation to these forces, which has both its sublimely elevating and its extremely dubious sides. Except for the intricate central chapter, we see Leverkühn largely through an indirect lighting provided by his devoted, even adoring, yet disconcerted and increasingly agitated friend, Serenus Zeitblom, a Catholic and a humanistic child of the Enlightenment who does not fully understand Leverkühn and is presented as untimely and ineffective yet not simply to be dismissed. One thing that causes Zeitblom (and, in a different key, the implied author) such concern is the relation between Leverkühn, his music, and the preconditions for the Nazi regime.

Indeed, there are many indications in the text that Leverkühn's desperate, ultimately apocalyptic music may be implicated in the currents leading up to Nazism that are explored in the novel. But it is significant that three years elapse between Leverkühn's Nietzsche-like subsidence into a coma, with an uncanny return to his mother's womb-like protection, and the Nazi accession to power in 1933, perhaps indicating not only the absence of a direct relation of Leverkühn to the Nazis but that even into the 1930s there were still other possibilities in German history. One might also suggest that Leverkühn in some sense fictively undertakes on the level of personal tragedy and self-sacrifice what the Nazi regime, by scapegoating others and construing them as causes of pollution and dislocation in the phantasmatic *Volksgemeinschaft*, came to enact historically through collective atrocity and murderous excess. Hence, one may agree with Eisenstein that Leverkühn is misread simply as an avatar of the Nazis. In an important sense he represents one alternative to them on a personal but not, I think, on a general or collective level. In any case, it is dubious in the extreme, on the basis of a reductive reading that is insufficiently alert to questions of both form and historical implication, to identify with and propose Leverkühn as a man for all seasons—the hero of his time and a model for ours.

In the novel, Leverkühn is figured as a highly equivocal being who embodies the best and the most questionable, if not the worst, in Germany, perhaps in modernity more generally. His transgression of limits is bound up with a self-destructive repetition compulsion and does not lend itself either to generalization (whereby Leverkühn becomes a potential everyman) or to a rather one-dimensional, symptomatic reading.[24] Eisenstein argues for the acknowledgment of, or what he sees as the unmediated encounter with, structural trauma (the Lacanian real)—a notion reminiscent of an important Christian version of the authentic relation of the believer to the Hidden God. Eisenstein even maintains (like Žižek at times) that this encounter with structural trauma (or the real) serves, and apparently suffices, ethically and politically as a counterforce to fascism and a holocaustal process. In this unqualified form, the idea may well be a theoreticist fantasy out of touch with historical and political problems. It not only skirts specific historical issues in the rise and functioning of Nazism, prominently including the nature and course of the Nazi genocide, but ignores the possibility that some fascists and Nazis may not have sought "redress" but, in their own way, were fascinated by, played out, or demonstrated "fidelity" to the structural dimension of trauma related to excess, transgression, risk, and sublimity, which for Nazis were bound up with repeated scenes of victimization and violence. There are elements of the latter orientation in Himmler's Posen speech (which I discuss in chapters 4 and 5) as well as in the behavior of notorious Nazis such as Kurt Franz, Hans Kaltenbrunner, Christian Wirth, and others. (There are also indications of this orientation in Max Aue, the SS protagonist and narrator in Jonathan Littell's *Les Bienveillantes,* which I also discuss in chapter 4.)

One may, however, possibly argue that one dimension of the Nazi phenomenon was a refusal to recognize sources of anxiety and vulnerability in oneself (which might conceivably be related to a disavowal of the "real" or of structural trauma in its bearing on oneself), along with a concomitant projection of all sources of anxiety onto a group of vulnerable scapegoated others. Here the results of such disavowal, eliminating the possibility of resistance to enacting excessive traumatizing violence that one acknowledges as a threat to one's vulnerable self, would be similar to the acting or playing out of what is, on the contrary, affirmed [as in Himmler's Posen speech]— the need to ruthlessly eliminate others perceived as contaminating presences, however difficult such action might be for those who perpetrate, witness, and bear up under it. But, to be pertinent to an analysis of the Nazis and their actions, any such appeal to structural trauma (or the real) would have to be qualified and articulated with a specific analysis of historical processes, including the construction of Jews in Nazi Germany, their ambiguous status as objects of both racial science and of quasi-ritual, phobic apprehension, their complicated, even contradictory positioning as pests (or "mere life"), as world-historical powerful forces allied to Bolshevism, and as contaminating or polluting threats to the *Volksgemeinschaft.* One would also have to address the attempt to "get rid" of them, first through expulsion or ghettoization, then through "extermination," as an intricate process that may well have been perceived by a significant group of Nazis as purifying, liberating, even elevating, and redemptive for the nation. How such an analysis itself would inform a reading of novels or other works of art, inquiring into whether and how their work and play, including their formal dimensions, come to terms with that genocidal process, would be the challenge of a historically and theoretically informed literary analysis. Eisenstein does not attempt such a reading. His argument appears to assume that there is only a choice between two options: a theoretical focus on structural trauma and a particularistic historicism isolating events or contexts and excluding theory, a choice that forecloses the difficult problem of articulating the relations between theory and historical inquiry other than in terms of mutual exclusion or derivation. Eisenstein's captivating and intellectually impressive reading furnishes, I think, a brilliant instance of the way a heady but reductionist and consumingly theoretical mode of discourse may induce the avoidance or subordination of both specific historical problems and the role of formal dimensions of art, taking one instead in the direction of a transhistorical ultraformalism or theoreticism.

Engaging the pressure exerted by the historical on the literary, along with the emotional power and the intellectual force of novels such as Thomas Mann's *Doctor Faustus*, in no sense excludes an appreciation of the intricate, at times experimental role of formal devices. I have insisted that my critique of "theoreticism," formalism, or a certain kind of transcendentalism in no sense implies a denigration of the importance of form, especially with respect to literature and art. Formal considerations help to prevent a simple reduction of the latter to symptomatic expressions of either transhistorical forces or historical contexts, while still raising the problem of the mediated, problematic relation of novels or other works of art to both transhistorical and historical considerations. Moreover, in their most challenging modalities, formal analysis and quasi-transcendental conditions may be approximated both to each other and to questions of framing and implicit assumptions that may themselves be subject to historical variation. The danger in a certain application of one or another critical theory, including Freudian or Lacanian psychoanalysis, is the avoidance, subordination, or transcendental-theoreticist fixation of formal analysis along with disavowal of, or disinterest in, the way specific and historically variable formal devices are crucial in literature and its effects, both cognitive and affective. But a different deployment of critical theory may provide a mode of understanding that does not necessarily obviate or diminish the importance of formal analysis (and of framing) but, depending on the way critical-theoretical and formal analysis are articulated as well as the way they bear on historical issues with their relation to contextualization, may further complex self-questioning processes of understanding.[25]

One psychoanalytically inflected concept that has arisen with respect to extreme limit events is that of traumatic realism, and it presents a mode of realism that is not amenable to either conventional techniques of representation or to self-sufficient formalistic analysis.[26] More broadly, literature and art might be read in a nonreductive way as providing a relatively safe but at times risky haven for exploring problems such as the manifold modulations of acting out (or compulsively repeating) and to some extent working over and through trauma and its symptoms. The reader's relation to the text itself engages transferential processes that also connect up with processes and problems in society and history. Moreover, from the perspective of a traumatic realism, ordinary reality is disrupted by disorienting, even shattering forces, notably including scenes of violence and abuse. As I intimated, one might also see certain forms of experimentation as engaging and enacting simulated posttraumatic symptoms and trying to play them out or even work them through in a kind of intricate "fort-da" game. One way of reading Samuel Beckett from this perspective is as staging analogs of the disempowered victim and his or her persecutor, approaching at the limit the plight of the *Muselmann*, the most abject and disconcerting inmate of the camps.

A thought-provoking suggestion, emerging, for example, from the work of Walter Benjamin, is that the discontinuities and paratactic devices of modernism resonated with the traumatic and posttraumatic shocks of modern life. These were touched on in the poetry of Charles Baudelaire but emerged most resoundingly with the major disruptions, deaths, mutilations, and "shell-shocked" survivors of the First World War, a catastrophic war whose effects were exacerbated in the atrocities to come. Responses to such developments and their aftermath played an evident role in the writings of key figures such as Sebald and Coetzee. But a particularly difficult "literary" case that may at least be mentioned is the famous use of ellipses by Louis-Ferdinand Céline that was bound up with an attempt to express the "immediacy" and the visceral unreflective quality of vernacular speech, especially in repeated moments of crisis. This attempt was a reaction to what Céline saw as the excessively cerebral, degenerate, effete nature of French society at the time, and in complicated ways it was related to his rabid anti-Semitism and advocacy of the Nazis. One may perhaps hazard the speculation that one thing that may have been happening in the gaps or silences of his gasping, at times elated ellipses, at least on a symbolic and "symptomatic" level, was the "unspeakable" yet, for some, exhilarating, breath-taking slaughter of Jews.

"As a Chinese proverb says, the stupid person, when a finger shows him something, looks at the finger."[27] The proverb could just as well have referred to an ultraformalistic approach. But, as I have insisted, the critique of a formalistic methodology does not negate the importance of form or the issue of how a text or artifact does what it does. Indeed, when it is not tantamount to a fixated gaze, being attentive to the pointing finger is itself a critical procedure that raises questions to a "meta" level and may induce one to question the questions and their framework or set of assumptions rather than taking them for granted. The elusive quality of literariness is arguably linked to form even if one thinks literariness cannot be identified in a purely formal manner or defined in a way that would no longer leave it in question. Here one has inter alia the problem of the tense, at times (as in Sebald) markedly hybridized interaction between texts and genres such as the novel or historiography. It should be obvious that a significant text does not simply fall within or illustrate a genre but in part rewrites the genre by testing its limits and at times by transgressing them.[28]

Perhaps in part because it has by and large not been housed in a professional discipline or subjected to highly structured codes, the novel is a genre that cannot be confined within restricted generic definitions and has throughout its history been actively engaged in interactions with other genres, both literary and nonliterary (not only historical research but journalism and the media). In the modern period the novel has been taken by a number of important theorists as especially important and even as having a distinctive relation to modernity. Lukács, for example, saw the novel as the form of the modern bourgeois period in terms of the individual hero at grips with larger social forces. Mikhail Bakhtin presented the novel as a dialogic and carnivalesque monster or grotesque being that legitimately transgressed its own borders and actively interacted with other genres. The novel has also been of special interest to some historians in terms of the problems of narrative structure, literary form, and the relation between fact and fiction in narration.[29]

Not only the novel but the literary in general has been seen as a special site for accessing experience, especially affect or feeling. Historians themselves will often be close to this view when they assign a literary work because it gives a "feel" for experience or life at a given time—what the French term *le vécu*. The interesting point or perhaps paradox is that literature or art in general conveys feeling in a fashion that does not detract from the role or importance of art's formal properties. We are moved not through content alone, which without formal constraints might even appear sentimental or maudlin, but by the way content is articulated, formed, and deformed. Or rather, even if we object to any opposition between form and content but see the two as inextricably intertwined, we may still find the capacity of literature or art to affect us emotionally as somehow requiring effective formal processes. The pathos of Conrad, Flaubert, Sebald, and Coetzee is bound up with the ways their texts do what they do, in other words, with dimensions of a text or artifact requiring formal analysis. And, especially in the aftermath of catastrophe or extreme disorientation, a style that itself attempts to address at times bewildering processes of repetition with at times traumatic change may both register the "voices" or echoes of the past and attempt stylistic variations that may be a more accurate rendering of certain complex processes, ranging from traumatizing experience to such possibly unsettling phenomena as secularization, the interplay of melancholia and mourning, the emergence of the postsecular (including the quasi-ritualistic and sacralizing), and the modalities of victimization, scapegoating, and prejudice.[30]

I have argued that a crucial problem for analysis at the intersection of history and literature is how a literary text comes to terms with the pressures of historical events and forces—an issue that cannot be treated in a one-size-fits-all manner. Certain texts as well as their readings may nonetheless signal the need for further inquiry into important contexts, for example, the context of losses or suffering undergone during the Second World War as well as both repetitions and variations in the way those losses have been articulated or represented (an issue active in the work of Sebald). One may also mention aspects of the colonial context, which, as Grandmaison's thought-provokingly controversial book indicates, have become an important concern for literary writing, critical reading, and historical research (notably with respect to such figures as Conrad, Coetzee, and to some extent Sebald). The lives and treatment of animals is another clear case in which literary, historical, and ethicopolitical concerns are at issue. In any event, questions of form and of framing may be acknowledged and even insistently explored while one nonetheless tries to work out a mutually provocative interaction between literary, historical, and theoretical analysis.

CHAPTER 2

The Quest! The Quest!

Conrad and Flaubert

Two famous exclamations bear an uncanny resemblance to each other and have almost become literary clichés: "The horror! The horror!" and "A lover! A lover!" The first, from Joseph Conrad's *Heart of Darkness* (1902), is of course Kurtz's final apostrophe to that "heart of darkness" to which he responds in extremely violent, ultimately genocidal ways. It is in fact just about the only substantive thing he does say, and my gloss on its meaning and consequences is as open to contestation as the gloss of numerous other perplexed and perplexing yet resounding phrases in the novel. Yet it appears to be the grounds on which Marlow bases his ecstatic, overblown, bombastically expressed estimation of the importance of the mysterious man who, unlike others, "had something to say."

The second phrase, from Gustave Flaubert's *Madame Bovary* (1856), is Emma Bovary's after her first adulterous love affair with Rodolphe, and it is an incantatory phrase that is in a sense repeated each time she deceptively seems to find a worldly incarnation of her ideal imaginary lover.[1] Emma is manifestly on a romantic quest to transcend her mediocre bourgeois surroundings and her tedious married life in the provinces. Marlow is on a quest to find Kurtz, and, despite what Marlow sees as Kurtz's hollowness within, Kurtz is even at one point homoerotically compared to "an enchanted princess sleeping in a fabulous castle" (42). Kurtz himself seeks ivory but is also on a quest, in a sense a metaquest for something worthy of a quest. Given the insubstantiality of Emma's romantic dreams, she is also on a quest for a quest, whose object must remain elusive and whose incarnations can never live up to the ideal.

The quest motif plays a significant role in structuring the two novels in both serious and ironic or self-parodic ways—two novels that are infrequently discussed together. Yet the role of the quest does not seem to have been thematized or extensively explored in the literature on these "classics" in which a quest figures so centrally, both with respect to the novel and to the author's own understanding of his novelistic enterprise. And, although Flaubert's novel was written earlier, there is a sense in which it seems to come after *Heart of Darkness*, at least with respect to its insistence in deploying and parodically excavating the quest motif.

The complex treatment of the quest motif, including the role of irony and parody, is one reason why *Heart of Darkness* is not the place one would go for a comprehensive account of colonialism or racism, just as *Madame Bovary* would not be one's foremost choice for an understanding of nineteenth-century France and French provincial life. Yet *Heart of Darkness* does extensively question the role of the civilizing mission, and *Madame Bovary* is at times a devastating inquiry into bourgeois marriage, romantic love, and the notion of the autonomous individual (most subtly through the decentering variations of free indirect style). Both novels may stimulate one to undertake more historical studies of the contexts that both serve as backgrounds to the stories they tell and are intricately inscribed in the texts themselves.

The nature of this inscription in the two texts differs at least in one important respect. In Conrad one might speak of an often misty, twilight, at times indeterminate mode of inscription of both characters and (often misty or fog-bound) environment. Indeed, much in the novel is left in the dark, as in the phrase depicting "life" in terms of "the stillness of an implacable force brooding over an inscrutable intention" (34). In Flaubert one might allude to a precise depiction that is disorienting or misleading in its very precision. The paradigm case of the latter is perhaps Charles's hat near the beginning of the novel, which is described in painstaking detail but whose representation or imaging is impossible to realize. (This prominent feature of various descriptions in the novel, notably of Emma Bovary as emblematized in the changing color of her eyes, is enough to place in doubt the prosecutor Pinard's reading of the text at the trial in pictographic or imagistic terms as a series of scenes, especially "lascivious" scenes.) The unimaginable or unpaintable description of Charles's hat is all the more disorienting in that it ends with an arresting non sequitur: "It was one of those headgears of composite order, in which we can find traces of the bear and the coonskin, the shako, the bowler,

and the cotton nightcap; one of those poor things, in fine, whose dumb ugliness has depths of expression, like an imbecile's face. Ovoid and stiffened
with whalebone, it began with three circular strips. Then came in succession
lozenges of velvet and rabbit fur separated by a red band; after that a sort of
bag that ended in a cardboard polygon covered with complicated braiding,
from which hung, at the end of a long thin cord, small twisted gold threads
in the manner of a tassel. The cap was new; its peak shone" (7). This haunting description may have been "inspired" by a graphic, but it would not
seem possible to go from the verbal account to a graphic representation of
the hat. One might belatedly read the description as a curious inversion of
recent, contestable notions of trauma whereby the traumatic event imprints
the brain (more specifically, the amygdala) with an eidetic image that cannot
be translated into language by verbalizing centers, thus presumably rendering
trauma unrepresentable or unreadable.[2]

Emma Bovary herself is rendered in a way that enables the reader to say
what she is not (a buxom blonde, for example) but not exactly what she is.
Precision of detail (the shape of Emma's hand or the color of her eyes) often
induces bewilderment or confusion, hence perhaps leading to a state of mind
in the reader similar to that produced by Conrad's own blurred impressionism, blockage of understanding, or patchwork motley. One might see the
two novels as convergent routes to a crisis of representation, which might
conceivably be construed as a posttraumatic effect, with aporia itself as the
textual figure of trauma.

Flaubert is in his own way on a metaquest for an impossible ideal that
would undercut the very conditions of representation—a book about nothing that would negate and transcend the mediocre yet disconcerting historical
reality he is forced to inhabit as a writer. This is perhaps the most significant
sense in which to take his well-known assertion, "Madame Bovary, c'est
moi." Flaubert elaborates his novelistic quest and recognizes its impossibility
in his correspondence. Conrad may not reach this level of self-insight, and it
is one reason he seems to be more a predecessor than a successor of Flaubert.
Or perhaps his reading of Flaubert was one factor in helping to shape the
path his writing would take if it were not to repeat Flaubert's quest in an
obvious way. In *Heart of Darkness* his style of writing could not seem more
unlike that of *Madame Bovary*. For it seems often to take the form of vague,
equivocal, inflated rhetoric if not insistent bombast, while in Flaubert there
is a deflation of rhetoric, an insistence on banal metaphors, and a hollowing
out of the kind of phrases Emma may at times utter or, in a patriotic and
technocratic register, Homais may intone. Yet the type of vaporous bombast
that seems frequent in Marlow and at times in the frame narrator may in

Conrad ultimately have the same disabling effect as the extreme deflationary antirhetoric the Flaubert-narrator employs. Indeed, excess and lack, hyperbole and understatement, are typically the supplementary and mutually reinforcing extremes of word and action in the face of a frustratingly banal or disempowering situation.

One almost deafening feature of *Heart of Darkness* is the incredible number of times "darkness" or its variants are repeated and repeated in the text, to the point of rendering the term all but meaningless. This is but the most blatant self-parodic feature of a novel that treats a very serious topic: European or even Western colonialism and its disastrous effects that are marked in but (*pace* Conrad at times) not limited to Belgium and the Congo. The very terms "darkness" and "heart of darkness" themselves do not have a stable referent in the novel: they apply to Africa and the Congo, but they also shift and come to apply to the "sepulchral city" of London—and even Europe or the "West" in general, as the journey up the Congo takes one back to the Thames and its "dark" vistas. At times the heart of darkness also assumes an ontological or quasi-transcendental status to signify the hole at the center of existence or the void in the symbolic order, evoking the traumatic death drive or Lacanian real. (A similar point might be made about the hollow core of Emma Bovary's existence that she tries to fill with romantic dreams— although in neither case should such a point divert attention from more specific contextual forces and constraints. In Emma one can never tell whether emptiness is in her from the outset and thinly veiled by romantic illusions or instead is an "accomplishment" of disillusioning experiences in life.)

The narrative structure of the two novels is, of course, different in an obvious way. In *Madame Bovary* there is only the intricate Flaubert-narrator, with any implied author seemingly erased. *Heart of Darkness* has an unnamed frame narrator, a character-narrator (Marlow), and, lurking somewhere in the shadows, Conrad as implied author. What one can ascribe to Conrad is always open to question in view of the complex narrative structure. Hence the idea that one may assert, on the basis of the novel, that Conrad is a thoroughgoing racist, as the noted novelist Chinua Achebe was inclined to do, is problematic at best.[3] At most one can argue that racism is intricately inscribed in the novel, with Marlow as well as others at times making racist as well as misogynist remarks or objectifying the black African in ways that are dissonant with respect to the indeterminate, at times misty impressionism prominent elsewhere in the text. In brief, the relation of the novel as text, and in certain ways its author, to ideologies and prejudices inscribed in it, is open to question. It is variably symptomatic or uncritical, probingly critical, and potentially transformative insofar as ideologies or prejudices are foregrounded and exposed to the possibly critical and even practical response of the reader.

Marlow as narrator says things that both verge on and diverge from racism. He questions the treatment of people of color (their use as beasts of burden or as target practice). Thus, for example, he states: "I could see every rib, the joints of their limbs were like knots in a rope, each had an iron collar on his neck, and all were connected together with a chain whose bights swung between them, rhythmically clinking" (15). "They were dying slowly—it was very clear. They were not enemies, they were not criminals, they were nothing earthly now, nothing but black shadows of disease and starvation lying confusedly in the greenish gloom. Brought from all the recesses of the coast in all the legality of time contracts, lost in uncongenial surroundings, fed on unfamiliar food, they sickened, became inefficient, and were then allowed to crawl away and rest. These moribund creatures were free as air—and nearly as thin" (17). These are very powerful and largely direct assertions despite the purplish alliteration of "greenish gloom" and the nonsuspensive, aggressively polemical irony in the allusion to creatures free as air and nearly as thin. Yet they may also be read as objectifications of the other who is not presented in recognizably human form or as having a voice. Moreover, Marlow at times says things about blacks that are clichés or stereotypes. For example, "they had faces like grotesque masks" (14); "a lot of people, mostly black and naked, moved about like ants" (15); "the man seemed young—almost a boy—but you know with them it's hard to tell" (17); "their head man . . . with fierce nostrils and his hair all done up artfully in oily ringlets" (40); "Restraint! I would just as soon have expected restraint from a hyena prowling amongst the corpses of a battlefield" (42). Of course, there are also the famous words of "the Manager's boy" as reported by Marlow: "Mistah Kurtz—he dead," words described as uttered "in a tone of scathing contempt" by the disembodied "boy," putting "his insolent black head in the doorway" (69). At times, however, you have reversals: "white men being so much alike at a distance that he could not tell who I [Marlow] might be" (16).

Marlow's own intimation of closest proximity to an African remains restricted, retrospective, and sublimely egocentric, as he recognizes with respect to his dead helmsman a "distant kinship affirmed in a supreme moment" (51). But this is, of course, not Conrad speaking in any unmediated way, although (as in the case of Flaubert) you cannot tell in the terms of the novel where exactly the implied author is on many issues.[4] It is at least arguable that in Marlow the text is often offering, with at least a critical twist, a European perspective that in the colonial context is barred from dialogue or even empathy with the colonized and is restricted at best to ambivalent, sometimes patronizing, sympathy. Anything pretending to a different kind of dialogue or empathy, where all parties are equally in play and at risk, might be seen as idealized or even mystified, given the conditions of "communication" in an extremely asymmetrical, exploitative situation. In any event, what seems to stand out clearly is that Kurtz is represented as the vehicle of excess, "brutality," and lack of restraint—what in the colonial company is perceived as unsound method. Yet the narrative itself seems evasive in specifying the precise nature of Kurtz's excesses or "unspeakable acts," and it is "reticent" or perhaps obfuscating concerning the practice of mutilation that Europeans perpetrated on Africans—a practice readily displaced onto putative African customs such as cannibalism.[5] There are the shrunken heads encircling Kurtz's house, but their provenance remains a mystery, however disconcerting their (intimidating? decorative? apotropaic?) use may be.

At times Conrad in his paratexts may even give way to a more or less avowed combination of disillusioned nihilism and an almost clichéd modernist strategy of suggestive nebulousness. Concerning his bleak view of humanity and society, he wrote, with a hint of social Darwinism: "Man is a vicious animal. . . . Society is fundamentally criminal—or it would not exist. Selfishness preserves everything—absolutely everything—everything we hate and everything we love. And everything holds together. That is why I respect the extreme anarchists.—'I hope for general extermination.' Very well. It's justifiable and more over, it is plain" (294–95, letter of February 8, 1899, to R. B. Cunninghame Graham). In it he even affirmed "a hopelessness darker than night" (ibid.). Sounding like Ford Madox Ford, he wrote to Richard Curle that "it is a strange fate that everything I have, of set artistic purpose, laboured to leave indefinite, suggestive, in the penumbra of initial inspiration, should have that light turned on to it. . . . Explicitness, my dear fellow, is fatal to the glamour of all artistic work, robbing it of all suggestiveness, destroying all illusion. . . . Yet nothing is more clear than the utter insignificance of explicit statement and also its power to call attention away from things that matter in the region of art" (302, letter of April 24, 1922). Of course, much hinges on whether a writer leaves in an indefinite, suggestive, illusion-generating penumbra the procedures and results of torture and colonial or sexual exploitation, on the one hand, or, on the other, the shadowlike illuminations of nature and erotic attraction. In his novelistic practice Conrad did not always treat matters in the same "glamourous," if not aestheticizing, manner. He even insisted with respect to his literary works: "Truly I don't believe myself that my tales are gloomy or even very tragic, that is not with a pessimistic intention" (303, letter to Richard Curle, April 24, 1922).

The preceding points relate to the variations in Conrad's self-understanding and to the way *Heart of Darkness* may be read simultaneously in different registers: as elusive impressionist or "modernist" writing, as (more or less critical if not traumatic) realism, and as self-parodic, carnivalized, at times self-explosive bombast.[6] The novel's irony moves in multiple registers from the "suspensive" or undecidable to the "cannibalistically" consuming and agonistic. These varied dimensions of the novel are perhaps signaled by the motley dress of Kurtz's Russian disciple, who "looked like a harlequin . . . covered with patches all over, with bright patches, blue, red, and yellow—patches on the back, patches on the front, patches on elbows, on knees, coloured binding round the jacket, scarlet edging at the bottom of his trousers, and the sunshine made him look extremely gay and wonderfully neat withal because you could see how beautifully all this patching had been done" (52). (This eye-dazzling description might conjure up Charles Bovary's hat.) The "modernist," more or less experimental dimension was at times stressed by Conrad as well as by his close friend and collaborator Ford Madox Ford. It was developed, by the important critic Ian Watt, in the direction of impressionism (underplaying the role of narrative and allowing for no discussion of the quest motif).[7] The critical realist dimension was, I think, important for those who in fact read the novel as an exposé of colonial abuses that presumably had effects in the anticolonial movement, notably with respect to King Leopold's administration in the Congo.[8] As noted in the previous chapter, this reading has been forcefully reiterated by Olivier Le Cour Grandmaison in his provocative, controversial, powerful book *Coloniser, Exterminer*. For Grandmaison, who pays little attention to problems of narrative structure or style (including the role of the quest motif that may, however ambivalently, draw narrators, implied author, and readers in the direction of Kurtz), Conrad's novel is a critically realistic account of colonization that is more reliable than empirical histories of the time that were often caught up in the ideology of empire, the white man's burden, and the civilizing mission: "The literature of Conrad, at least that which has held our attention, is a literature of radical and brutal disenchantment. That's why it was rebellious at its time; it remains so today, for it allows one to take the just measure of what was the conquest and colonization of Africa for the populations that were subjected to it."[9]

Conrad himself (like Flaubert, at times *malgré lui*) wrote things that would support at least a qualified critical-realist reading of *Heart of Darkness*. On December 21, 1903, he wrote to Roger Casement, at that time his close friend and a key figure in the anticolonial movement and, unlike Conrad, a publicly committed activist: "The fact remains that in 1903, seventy-five years or so after the abolition of the slave trade (because it was cruel) there exists in Africa a Congo State, created by the act of European Powers where ruthless, systematic cruelty towards the blacks is the basis of administration, and bad faith towards all the other states is the basis of commercial policy" (271).[10] In a letter of October 9, 1899, to Hugh Clifford, he took a linguistic turn: "The things 'as they are' exist in words; therefore words should be handled with care lest the picture, the image of truth abiding in facts should become distorted—or blurred. . . . However the *whole* of the truth lies in the presentation; therefore the expression should be studied in the interest of veracity. This is the only morality of *art* apart from *subject*" (296). Writing of *Heart of Darkness* in the preface to *Youth*, Conrad stressed the role of limited hyperbole: "*Heart of Darkness* itself is experience too; but it is experience pushed a little (and only very little) beyond the actual facts of the case for the perfectly legitimate, I believe, purpose of bringing it home to the minds and bosoms of the readers" (290). Yet he also wrote to Clifford: "You do not leave enough to the imagination" (296). And, in a letter of August 2, 1901, he sounded very much like Flaubert, as he wrote to the *New York Times* "Saturday Review": "In the sphere of an art dealing with a subject matter whose origin and end are alike unknown there is no possible conclusion. The only indisputable truth of life is our ignorance" (297). A Flaubertian note was again struck in a letter of February 8, 1899, to another politically active friend, R. B. Cunninghame Graham: "I look at the future from the depths of a very dark past, and I find I am allowed nothing but fidelity to an absolutely lost cause, to an idea without a future" (295). And to John Galsworthy he asserted: "The fact is you want more scepticism at the very foundation of your work. Scepticism the tonic of minds, the tonic of life, the agent of truth—the way of art and salvation" (298). Hence, the very quest Conrad would at times affirm was one set in a "sceptical" frame.[11]

Although the role of irony in *Heart of Darkness* is well recognized, the more self-parodic side of the novel has been little discussed and apparently has not been evident to many critics. Irony itself tends to be construed in rather restricted terms largely divorced from its more critical and carnivalesque dimensions—particularly when it is seen as unmitigated suspension or endless parabasis incompatible with direct statement or clear and trenchant judgment.[12] The role of self-parody and carnivalized bombast is not commented on in any of the critical selections included in the 2006 Norton Critical Edition. The famous statement by the frame narrator may be read as a primary instance of the serio-parodic type of inflated and perplexing (if not purple) prose that appears continually in the novel. In the words of the frame narrator:

The yarns of seamen have a direct simplicity, the whole meaning of which lies within the shell of a cracked nut. But Marlow was not typical (if his propensity to spin yarns be excepted) and to him the meaning of an episode was not inside like a kernel but outside, enveloping the tale which brought it out only as a glow brings out a haze, in the likeness of one of these misty halos that, sometimes, are made visible by the spectral illumination of moonshine. (5)

While the passage obviously invites a reading as a critique of "depth hermeneutics" of any sort, the intricacy of its playful if not mocking metaphor is bewildering, and the "spectral illumination of moonshine" does not promise much enlightenment. Indeed, the metaphor is so convoluted that it seems to dissipate by the time one reaches its final terms. Its parodic nature is intensified by the fact that, soon after enunciating it, the frame narrator apparently expresses the collective view of Marlow's auditors that "we knew we were fated, before the ebb began to run, to hear about one of Marlow's inconclusive experiences" (7). The reader may be led to wonder whether the misty halo or glowing haze of rhetoric applies not only to Marlow, as well as to Kurtz, but also to the writer of the text. Needless to say, those who take the novel as an instance (or even a univocal critique) of racism, sexism, and/or colonialism may be particularly closed to its ironic, parodic, and self-parodic dimensions. These dimensions do not eliminate its more "serious" sides and the problem of how to analyze and read the complex nature of its inscription of ideologies and historical practices, but it does complicate matters. The novel does convey or seem symptomatically to repeat the widespread idea that Africans and Africa represent an early stage of civilization, away from which the West has evolved ("we were travelling in the night of first ages, of those ages that are gone, leaving hardly a sign—and no memories" [36]). But this idea is at least destabilized by the explicit indication that the Thames casts its shadow on the Congo and that the "heart of darkness" is within the West, perhaps implying that the latter itself has often plunged from darkness to darkness and that theories of social evolution, notably in their social Darwinian form, are little more than projections of their proponents, if not "the spectral illumination of moonshine."

A primary locus of the "heart of darkness" is, to all appearances, Kurtz who combines a vague idealistic quest and a terroristic, seemingly sacrificial practice in his role as idol for the "savages," who bow before him and offer him unspeakable rites. And "all Europe contributed to the making of Kurtz," (49) whose mother was half-English and father, half-French. (That, of course, leaves half of Kurtz for distribution in the rest of Europe.) It is also noteworthy that what Marlow says of the British Empire resonates with what he says of putative cannibals over whom European powers ruled: "one knows some real work is done in there [areas colonized by Britain] (10)[. . .]Fine fellows—cannibals—in their place. They were men one could work with" (40). The distance between putative cannibals and beef-eating Britons seems imperceptible here.

Kurtz remains an even more shadowy figure than Emma Bovary. In many ways he (along with a good deal but not all of Marlow's or the frame narrator's narration) remains in a state of suspension as "eloquent phantom" (76) or empty signifier—a sublime object of hazy fantasy. He becomes what others project onto him and may deny in themselves. Tellingly, he is referred to primarily as a voice (67) in a text where only Europeans and not Africans have voices. The text itself is paradoxically a written account of an oral tale, with only the frame narrator as someone possibly writing but with Marlow telling a tale to listeners and with Kurtz as a potential narrator with something to say that largely remains unsaid or perhaps unsayable.[13] What Kurtz actually says is brief, stumbling, anticlimactic, or inconclusive. But we are told that he paints, plays music, writes and recites poetry—and he is eloquent, indeed a universal genius, a kind of Hegelian Absolute Spirit whose talents apparently also involve unlimited violence and the ability to intimidate, traumatize, and elicit the worship of subject people. Arguably, the hollowness at his center (his absent kernel?) is closely connected to his excess, and even the eloquence imputed to him amounts to largely unspoken words that cannot fill the abyss within and without but that flow from and cloak it rhetorically with a sublime and charismatic yet hazy aura. Marlow is "unable to say what was Kurtz's profession" (71), placing Kurtz in a category unlike that of others in Marlow's club of professional listeners or even the seaman Marlow himself. Marlow is told by a journalist that "Kurtz's proper sphere ought to have been politics 'on the popular side' . . . and, becoming expansive, confessed his opinion that Kurtz really couldn't write a bit—'but heavens! How that man could talk! He electrified large meetings. He had the faith—don't you see—he had the faith. He could get himself to believe anything—anything. He would have been a splendid leader of an extreme party.' . . . 'He was an—an—extremist'" (72). Marlow assents, and, in light of how few words Kurtz utters in the text, the reader has to believe him and the journalist on faith.

Yet Kurtz, of course, does write a bit. He has been commissioned by the International Society for the Suppression of Savage Customs to write "a report for its future guidance" (72). Marlow tells us: "It was eloquent, vibrating with eloquence, but too high-strung I think. Seventeen pages of close writing" (49). Yet all Marlow offers the reader is a disturbing yet somewhat deflationary summary of the report:

The opening paragraph, however, strikes me now as ominous. He began with the argument that we whites, from the point of development we had arrived at, 'must necessarily appear to them ["savages"] in the nature of supernatural beings—we approach them with the might as of a deity,' and so on and so on. 'By the simple exercise of our will we can exert a power for good practically unbounded,' etc. etc. From that point he soared and took me with him. The peroration was magnificent, though difficult to remember, you know. It gave me the notion of an exotic Immensity, ruled by an august Benevolence. It made me tingle with enthusiasm. This was the unbounded power of eloquence—of words—of burning noble words. There were no practical hints to interrupt the magic current of phrases, unless a kind of note at the foot of the last page, scrawled evidently much later in an unsteady hand, may be regarded as the exposition of a method. It was very simple and at the end of that moving appeal to every altruistic sentiment it blazed at you luminous and terrifying like a flash of lightning in a serene sky: 'Exterminate all the brutes!' (50)

The belated, genocidal postscript is of course well known to readers and has been made even further known by the title of Sven Lindqvist's quest narrative, which seeks the origins of Conrad's novella.[14] But its framing by Marlow's inflated prose, referring to Kurtz's own excessive language, which resonates with his excessive actions, both contrasts with the incendiary brevity of the exterminationist exclamation and paradoxically heightens its force that burns through and implodes the preceding high-flown rhetoric. Commentaries that address this exclamation typically omit (or forget) the telltale words that follow it in the text: "The curious part was that he [Kurtz] had apparently forgotten all about that valuable postscriptum because later on when he in a sense came to himself, he repeatedly entreated me to take good care of 'my pamphlet' (he called it) as it was sure to have in the future a good influence on his career" (50). The forgotten postscriptum might be better seen as in certain ways repressed or disavowed, and what is tempting to construe as its posttraumatic status is not unlike that of the genocidal dimensions of colonialism itself, at least in the century intervening between the novel's publication and the recent past.

Misogyny is not as simple or straightforward a propensity of the text as some have argued. Marlow does assert in stereotypically idealistic and chauvinistic terms: "They—the women I mean—are out of it—should be out of it. We must help them to stay in that beautiful world of their own lest ours gets worse" (48). Yet, just as they and noncombatants in general are not outside the fields of battle, mass murder, torture, and abuse, women are not simply *hors texte*. There are women working in the Belgian colonial office in their own small way as agents of colonialism and, one assumes, as exploited dependents of their men. There is Marlow's aunt who also plays a behind-the-scenes role in the empire by using her influence to get Marlow a position as captain of a steamer. And there are the stereotypical ebony-and-ivory pendants of the "savage and superb, wild-eyed and magnificent" (60) African woman, who remains without voice and who one assumes was Kurtz's black mistress, and the nameless fiancée, the Intended, who is the fading white lily who remains at home as Kurtz's spiritual support and, after Kurtz's death, Marlow's symbolic legacy. The novel's overdrawn penultimate scene takes place between Marlow and the unnamed Intended, whom Marlow feels obliged to visit if he is not to betray his unexplicated loyalty to Kurtz that leads him both to betray himself and to disclose his own complicity in the colonial enterprise. This loyalty is comparable to the type of loyalty evoked in many by various charismatic figures whose names are all too familiar in recent history.

Marlow supposedly detests lies and associates them with decay and death. Yet he must go against the grain and, despite his "dull anger" (76), lie to the Intended. Why? To cover Kurtz, to ease the pain for a woman whose age is starting to show, to cover himself and somehow underwrite his loyalty to Kurtz, which is simultaneously a compromised loyalty to colonialism and imperialism, to add to the elusiveness and perplexity that seem to be the most prominent mood of the novel? As he recalls Kurtz's last words—"The horror! The horror!"—he "pulled himself together" and tells the Intended: "'The last word he pronounced was—your name'" (76–77). One can obviously read this correlation of "the horror" and the Intended's never-spoken name as itself another ironic and self-parodic echo from "the heart of an immense darkness"—the words of the frame narrator that in fact end the novel a few lines later, after a reference to Marlow sitting apart, "indistinct and silent, in the pose of a meditating Buddha" (77). The penultimate scene of Marlow's meeting with the Intended seems inflated or overblown, like a meeting of potential lovers or of sympathetic souls who fail to connect—a meeting that borders on drawing room comedy bent burlesquely out of shape. It is reminiscent of the meeting of Frédéric and the aging Madame Arnoux in Flaubert's *Sentimental Education* or, in certain ways, of many of the nondialogues or alternating monologues that lead to frustration in *Madame Bovary* (for example, the exchange between Emma, seeking spiritual counsel, and the uncomprehending priest Bournisien, dispensing medical advice and idiotically encouraging a consultation with her husband; the saccharine romantic duet between Emma and Léon at their first meeting; or the *comices agricoles* scene alternating Emma's lyrical longings, Rodolphe's manipulative words of seduction, and the deflationary official speeches about cattle and manure).

One of the women working in the colonial office appears to Marlow "uncanny and fateful" and evokes an "eerie feeling" in him (11). Yet there seems in general to be little role for the uncanny in a novella where the world appears to be more fogbound and perplexing than out of joint and punctuated by pointed repetitions of a belatedly returning past or able to generate expectations that are then upset in a strangely disconcerting manner. Alternatively, one might say that everything (and so nothing) seems uncanny. Perhaps the one pronounced, distinguishable element of uncanniness is the state of Marlow's mind when he arrives back in London, the "sepulchral city." He finds himself "resenting the sight of people hurrying through the streets to filch a little money from each other . . . to dream their insignificant and silly dreams. They trespassed upon my thoughts" (70). He "felt so sure that they could not possibly know the things I know" (71).

Thus Marlow has come to believe that his at times traumatic experience in Africa has given him a special knowledge not shared by those around him. And yet he has in reality not acquired any new knowledge: he has uncannily "discovered" a "darkness" in the Congo that may be nothing other than the displacement of the "darkness" already there back home in England but that he comes to recognize or acknowledge only *après coup* or *nachträglich*. The uncanniness of the abortive apocalypse or the failed quest is, in seeming contrast, pronounced in *Madame Bovary* where the repetition compulsion runs rampant: Emma escapes her father's house by marrying Charles only to find even greater constraint in marriage; she escapes a mediocre husband and banality in marriage through affairs with men who are in fact less attached to her than her husband and bring her only heightened disillusionment; she seeks spiritual counsel from a priest who is the mirror image of the pompously technocratic pharmacist; and she follows a passionate romantic quest in life to find a suicidal outcome that, in a fatalistically uncanny manner, may have been within her from the outset.

I have intimated that the darkness at the heart of Conrad's novel seems multidimensional and ultimately indeterminate. It is a historical darkness in Africa and, more pointedly, in the Europe that colonizes and exploits it. It is a darkness at the core of elusive protagonists, not the least of whom is Marlow. It also seems to be an existential darkness, a quasi-transcendental void at the heart of things that may even have a nihilistic, genocidal force—a death drive or "real" that may either be somehow engaged and worked through to the point of counteracting its deadly effects or indulged and acted out in the manner Kurtz seems to display and to symbolize. The omnipresent darkness may also refer to an excessive, obfuscating infatuation with the beyond that the novella in part sends up and helps to dispel in a litany of invocations that may amount to hurling invectives at the ineffable.

I would mention one aspect of *Heart of Darkness* that I have not seen discussed to any significant extent, although I suspect it will soon be. This is the resounding silence that surrounds the elephant, where the novella is I think symptomatic and uncritical in its inscription of historical and contextual issues. (One might also mention the rubber that is bled from trees for commercial exploitation.) We hear much about ivory and the quest for it. But ivory is treated in the stereotypical fashion of a commodity whose source and production we know nothing about or perhaps ensconce in the protected reserve of the open secret. Ivory simply seems to be there, and the elephant is not discussed. We do not hear about hunting, poaching, trapping, killing, and the massive disruption of the social customs of not only human but also elephant societies, including intricate mourning rituals. If the novella, despite its qualifications, tells us very little about the actual ways of African societies other than in terms of European reactions and (mis)interpretations, it tells us even unqualifiedly less about nonhuman animals. Elephants remain unnamed yet are among the "brutes" to be killed, if not exterminated. Indeed, they seem to be utterly "derealized" in a novel in which realism otherwise plays a noteworthy role. The animal becomes little more than a commodity, not entirely unlike the colonized worker who at times is reduced to this status.

One of the few hints of colonialism in *Madame Bovary* is in the exotic name of Emma's dog *Djali* who runs off, never to be seen again, in the move from Tostes to Yonville. (In an apparent parodic gesture, Djali was borrowed by Flaubert from the name of Esmeralda's little goat in Victor Hugo's *Hunchback of Notre Dame* [*Notre-Dame de Paris* of 1831], an "exotic" source pointing in the direction of "gypsies" and their companion animals.)[15] Flaubert in his own way, most evidently as rentier, was complicit in the colonial enterprise and wrote about it elsewhere, notably in his *Voyage en Orient. Madame Bovary* structurally resembles Flaubert's other novels in that the quest is displaced and repeated in the treatment of exoticized alterity. One goes toward the alluring other or the romantic ideal to escape what one has at home (boredom, mediocrity, hypocrisy), but one finds, at least in terms of one's own experience, what one was fleeing, perhaps in an aggravated, even suicidal form. (One may think here of the syphilis Flaubert contracted on his own *voyage en Orient.*) As noted, Emma escapes her father's house to become married; she escapes marriage with a boring husband (whose role as a reduced model of herself she cannot see) to engage in adulterous affairs; she finds in her wedded family life an accentuated repetition of her unwedded family life; and she finds in her lovers less devoted and more self-centered partners than her husband—inferior copies that not only betray the ideal romantic splendor of her imaginary lover but even fall short of the love and devotion of her despised husband. In any event, "a" lover never becomes "the" quasi-transcendental lover.

Sartre has argued that the Flaubert-narrator himself has a quasi-transcendental relation to objects of narration that is ultimately nihilistic and genocidal—a narrating "for-itself" that "derealizes" or exterminates and imaginatively transcends the narrated "in-itself." In a sense, he finds in Flaubert a version of his own early self that he continually fled but never quite overcame. Sartre's version of Flaubert does relate to one dimension of Flaubert's novelistic practice and to perhaps his dominant self-understanding of his project in his letters. Flaubert does hate and seek to "exterminate all the brutes"—or at least to annihilate most of his characters along with their despicable world. Arguably, there is a nihilistic or nihilating relation of the Flaubert-narrator to his objects of narration whereby an objectifying, deflationary, distantly ironic style sucks the life out of them or, in more philosophical terms, negates and transcends them toward an impossible imaginary beyond—call it, if you will, purely formal or literary. One could argue that this is also one dimension of Conrad, at least in a minor key. Echoing certain comments in Conrad's letters, Marlow puts it thus: "Droll thing life is—that mysterious arrangement of merciless logic for a futile purpose" (69). Life as a futile passion—one thinks of the Sartre of *Being and Nothingness*. And death? A few lines after his pronouncement on life, Marlow states: "I have wrestled with death. It is the most unexciting contest you can imagine. It takes place in an impalpable greyness with nothing underfoot, with nothing around, without spectators, without clamour, without glory, without the great desire of victory, without the great fear of defeat, in a sickly atmosphere of scepticism, without much belief in your own right, and still less in that of your adversary" (70). Here one might be reading one of Flaubert's own dispirited letters or overhearing Antoine Roquentin on the denuded horror of existence (so close to the traumatizing Lacanian real) in Sartre's *La nausée*. Still, at least with respect to Conrad's (as well as Sartre's) novel, there is a parodic tinge to the inflated (or despairing) prose.[16]

Along with the other aspects of *Heart of Darkness*, the novel on some level remains a yarn, some sort of seaman's yarn, clearly in Marlow's narration and perhaps in Conrad's writing. There is a strong, if at times exaggerated, near-Gothic story line, and the novel can be both captivating and disturbing as a story. One can get caught up in it, a fact attested to by the way it often seems to be taken only seriously without any sense of its parodic or even ironic sides. The yarn is, I think, quite tangled by virtue of certain initiatives of the text, but its ability to catch up and entangle the reader is pronounced. In Flaubert the yarn threatens to become threadbare and unraveled. And the story may readily be experienced as boring—as Baudelaire noted, a banal tale of adultery in the provinces. Interest shifts from the story to other levels of novelistic and narrative practice—form, style, perspective, voice, and so forth. If this does not happen, there is a tendency simply to identify with characters in a positive or negative way—to be swept away with Emma or to take up the cudgels for Charles, perhaps even at present to identify with Homais, who is after all the big winner in the novel—a pompous self-promoter, a calculating exponent of technical rationality, a hedge-fund manager of provincial self-interest, a destructive dealer in toxic assets, the recipient of the Legion of Honor, and, strangely enough, the only professional writer in the story.

Homais, never seen "from the inside," is the utterly distanced object of the narrator's irony, in what may be seen as an act of disavowal, negating the ways Homais could be seen as like the Flaubert-narrator or even Flaubert the writer, for in his technocratic hyperbole Homais (who in one sense could be seen as an ultraformalist) also overwhelms, negates, and transcends his objects of discourse. Rodolphe, the manipulative seducer, is a less complicated object of narrative irony, sharply juxtaposed to the transfiguration he undergoes in Emma's desires, imaginings, and incantatory words. The most intricate relation is that of the narrator to Emma, even in her most self-deceptive illusions, for there is an impetus in her insistent if suicidal quest for transcendence that may be analogous to Flaubert's own quest for the book about nothing. Hence the irony in the following passage is blatant, given Rodolphe as its hollow referent, but irony is not the only tropical passion in this lyrical flight of the woman with whom Flaubert affirmed an identification.

> She repeated: 'I have a lover! A lover!' delighting at the idea as if a second puberty had come to her. So at last she was to know those joys of love, that fever of happiness of which she had despaired! She was entering upon a marvelous world where all would be passion, ecstasy, delirium. She felt herself surrounded by an endless rapture. A blue space surrounded her and ordinary existence appeared only intermittently between these heights, dark and far away beneath her. (131)

Identification at some level may be inevitable. But *Madame Bovary* is of critical interest for other reasons as well. I have mentioned the glaring contrast with *Heart of Darkness:* there is no named narrator or frame narrator but only the "Flaubert-narrator" and his shape-shifting permutations, including the use of free indirect style. The latter may be best seen as one crucial dimension of the overall problem of the role of modulations of narrative perspective and voice in the novel, which includes the way it inscribes history or context. As is well known, the novel begins with a first-person plural narrator and then, after a few movements, shifts to a third-person form of narration. This massive shift, a kind of narrative double-take (if not textual trauma) on the part of an elusive, carnivalesque mountebank, which may pass unperceived by the reader because of the seamlessly cosmetic effects of Flaubert's celebrated style, might be taken as an initial alarm, like the whistle of Marlow's ship that frightens the "natives," signaling more subtle narrative shifts, including those of free indirect style.

Marlow's style is often declamatory and literally, yet deceptively, dialogic with respect to his addressees, the style of a teller of tales, hemmed in somewhat by the frame narrator but still the primary vehicle in the telling of the tale. Vaguely reminiscent of the colonized Africans, Marlow's listeners by and large remain silent, not even Socratic "yes-men" but a captive audience with at times wandering (or sea-faring) minds.[17] The style of the Flaubert-narrator is in certain respects different. It is internally dialogized (as is that of *Heart of Darkness* at times, especially with respect to the silent Africans, perhaps indicating the double binds that pose a limit to colonial exchange). The role of literal dialogue in *Madame Bovary* is restricted and typically made up of mutually cancelling, cliché-ridden monologues. The relation to the reader, who may resist direct identification with characters (and hence counter the demoralization Flaubert himself sought as reader response), depends on an appreciation of the internal dialogization of the text. Free indirect style is often read as a form in which the thoughts or feelings of characters are expressed in the words of the narrator. This may at times happen, although this analysis is circular since the only way one has access to the former is through the latter. Free indirect style may be best seen as a modality of internal dialogization, with variable degrees of proximity and distance, empathy and irony between the narrator and objects of narration, including but not restricted to characters. (It may encompass various objects and even body parts.) And free indirect style includes nihilation as well as ironic deflation of its objects in a larger gamut of discursive possibilities. Here, for example, is an instance in which it is difficult to locate the thoughts or feelings at play in the struggle over the description of Emma's hand.

> Charles was surprised by the whiteness of her nails. They were shiny, delicate at the tips, more polished than the ivory of Dieppe, and almond-shaped. Yet her hand was not beautiful, perhaps not white

enough, and a little hard at the knuckles; besides, it was too long, with no soft inflections in the outlines. Her real beauty was in her eyes. Although brown, they seemed black because of the lashes, and her look came at you frankly, with a candid boldness. (16)

This passage is strangely disconcerting. It begins with what appear to be Charles's perceptions. Emma's nails as he sees them are surprisingly white; they are shiny and delicate at the tips. But with the last observation we are leaving Charles who is not one to recognize delicacy. And the description of her hand is taken from Charles, as a struggle for Emma's hand seems to ensue between the doltish husband and the more observant, sophisticated narrator. The idea that the nails are more polished than the ivory of Dieppe is a nice ironic touch since Charles's first wife, the cold, unlamented, ironically named Héloïse, was from Dieppe. (Héloïse dies conveniently, abruptly, and in free indirect style, once she learns of Charles's attraction for Emma: "She said, 'O God!' gave a sigh and fainted. She was dead! What a surprise!" [19]). In the passage on Emma's hand, the narrator proceeds to give Charles a veritable lesson in observing the beauty of this woman. The husband was completely wrong about the nails. In fact, Emma's real beauty is in her protean eyes that are brown but seem black, for some unexplained reason, because of the lashes. (Elsewhere Emma's eyes are blue.) Then, in a non sequitur (reminiscent of the passage on Charles's hat), we are told that "her look came at you frankly, with a candid boldness." How could this passage be in any way seen as the narrator expressing the thoughts or feelings of a character in the narrator's own words? The right to describe Emma, tantamount to the right to possess a fictional being, is taken from the husband and unceremoniously usurped by the narrator—a narrator who in a sense is one of Emma's lovers as well as her double in the quest for an impossible ideal or form of transcendence.[18]

A crucial aspect of Flaubert's disorienting precision in the inscription of history or context is the way dating is made possible only through passing marginal allusions. Moreover, temporality is multiple, and there is an inverse relation between the seeming reality of imaginary and actual towns or cities. The events of the novel seem to unfold in the period leading up to the Revolution of 1848, but the latter is not even mentioned. Perhaps Emma's suicide, with the aid of arsenic filched from Homais's storeroom, takes the place of what was for Flaubert a failed and misguided, even toxic political event. Nor is there any sign in the novel of the sometimes extremely violent colonial actions being undertaken by France in Algeria beginning in the 1830s. In the terms of the novel, news of these actions does not register in the repetitive life-world of provincial France.

Fictional towns—Tostes and Yonville l'Abbaye—appear to be very real and may even inspire empirical research into their "real-life" analogs. The composition of the small towns seems altogether representative of French towns at the time, including the proverbial hostility between the priest and the representative of secularism (*laïcité*)—here the pharmacist instead of the school master—engaged in a struggle for the hearts and minds of citizens. In contrast to the realistic depiction of the imaginary small towns, the real city of Rouen is largely a sketchy setting for Emma's adulterous trips to see Léon, while Paris is the analogue of the imaginary lover—a nebulous land of dreams at which Emma never arrives, except indirectly and ironically through her suicide: "What was this Paris like? What a boundless name! She repeated it in a low voice, for the mere pleasure of it; it rang in her ears like a great cathedral bell; it shone before her eyes, even on the labels of her jars of pomade [. . .] She wanted to die, but she also wanted to live in Paris" (49, 52).

The dominant temporality in the novel is repetitive, and the type of repetition often undermines projects (notably projects of escape) and deflates reverie that seems to stop or transcend time (for example, Emma's at the window or even Charles's in the café and, more trenchantly, toward the end of the story as he loses himself in mimetic contemplation of Rodolphe's face).[19] The figuration of the repetitive life led in the provinces could readily be understood in terms of Fernand Braudel's idea of *la longue* (or at least *la moyenne*) *durée*. Forces of modernization have a role, but they seem primarily to disrupt Emma's destiny, along with that of Charles. She is as much a victim of commodification as she is of more obvious romantic illusions, as the commodity fetish comes to occupy a role alongside that of the imaginary lover as a deceptive modality of excess that has suicidal consequences. At a certain point in the novel, commodities and lovers seem to swirl in the same all-consuming, destructive, and self-destructive vortex or black hole. Charles is not a doctor but a health officer (*officier de santé*), a rather lowly position in the medical hierarchy. And his upward mobility is not self-motivated but given impetus by his wife along with the pharmacist Homais. His operation on Hippolyte's clubfoot, intended to establish his reputation and assure his fame, is of course a disaster and causes a functional disability to become a horrible source of suffering and agony through gangrene and amputation. Modernization itself seems to take place in a downward spiral and to be subsumed in a compulsively repetitive temporarily.[20]

Here one may raise the imposing problem of reception. With it one approaches the relation of history and literature from the other end of the tunnel, so to speak—not in terms of how a novel inscribes its historical contexts, past and present, or even how it may anticipate or resist certain futures, but how it is read and used in various historical contexts that constitute its afterlife. These questions are not altogether discrete, for a study of reception is invariably inflected by a researcher's own responsive reading, from the extreme of sustained if imperfect objectification that effaces or represses one's own response and charts only how others have read the text over time to the kind of participatory, performative reading that deceptively autonomizes one's own response and transforms critical commentary into a pretext for improvisational or projective flights, often reprocessing the text in terms of a preferred, at times self-referential reading strategy. Situated somewhere between these extremes is an approach wherein one's own response is explored and perhaps made explicit as a reference point in charting or "mapping" the responses of others—individuals, institutions, groups, and even political entities such as nation-states or transnational movements and organizations. My own response is explicitly informed by the readings of others, and it attempts to engage those readings in critically dialogic fashion and to bring out aspects of texts that I think have not received the attention they warrant.[21]

Flaubert's trial may be taken as one crucial instance of reception that affected both the professional and the personal life of the author. In Conrad's case, something of an analog in a different register is the reading and use of *Heart of Darkness* in the anticolonial movement from his time to our own. Beyond these two salient instances of reception, one has an entire gamut of possibilities, including the way the books are or are not taught in classes, placed or displaced in canons, taken up or rejected in sociopolitical movements (such as feminism, antiracism, and anticolonialism), found or not found in libraries around the world, get translated into other languages, become elements of a general education or *Bildung*, play a role in a person's culture within a stratified society, have a greater or lesser importance over time and place, notably in comparison with other media such as film or television (indeed may become the bases of films or television productions), provide at least a set of touchstones in one's conversation or even sense of self, may amount to little more than shadings in one's cultural suntan, and are discussed and debated, with differences in focus or emphasis, by professional readers such as literary critics who exercise a greater or lesser influence as guides for larger publics, including students.

Reception has developed into an entire field or subfield whose more objectifying paradigms of research are often very close to those of conventional history. I have intimated that one crucial question is how reception intersects with responsive understanding, and whether and how such understanding helps shape the study of reception itself. In my own study of the trial of

Flaubert and its relation to *Madame Bovary*, I did not try to make my approach as objectifying as possible, although I did attempt to resist projective reprocessing and to situate my account in the context of Flaubert's own time and offer some idea of ensuing developments in the reading of the novel. And I did not see empirical questions as either irrelevant or as worthy of only an abstract, even quasi-transcendental reference to "the empirical" as a category that does little historical work and poses no real challenges to conceptualization, however provocative that conceptualization may be. Rather I tried to elaborate an interaction between what could, to a significant extent, be empirically substantiated as readings at the trial on the part of the prosecuting and defense attorneys (Pinard and Sénard) and what I was offering as a reading of the novel in a critical exchange with what I judged to be the most insightful and thought-provoking studies with which I was acquainted.

At the trial the prosecuting attorney offered a reading that, while limited, was more thought provoking than that of the defense attorney (Sénard), who strained to banalize the novel by reading it in conventionalizing and moralizing terms as a cautionary tale addressing what happens to a young woman educated beyond her social station—a reading effortlessly interwoven with a portrait of the impeccable moral character of its author. The prosecutor Pinard was genuinely troubled by the novel, notably by its telling reversal of relations in a phrase attributing to marriage what one might expect to be said of adultery, and vice versa: "*les souillures du mariage et les désillusions de l'adultère*—the stains (or pollutions) of marriage and the disillusionments of adultery.[22] I argue that this reversal attested to the overall strategy of the novel in signaling and even intensifying a legitimation crisis in which basic concepts and key oppositions (such as the autonomous bourgeois individual and the opposition between marriage and adultery or the sacred and the profane) had become radically problematic or even rendered insubstantial, with the result that the individual could not be seen as autonomous or sovereign and key oppositions could not structure a viable society or an integrated self, notably in terms of "family values" and religion. Yet in Flaubert's own dedication to art and his adoption of an "exigent" writing practice as a form of *askesis*, if not *kenosis*, emptying the empirical self through an impersonal, even self-punitive, "style," and his pursuit of an impossible, possibly sublime ideal—*un livre sur rien*—there is a specter of the postsecular or at least of a devotional practice that can go to obsessive extremes. To a greater or less extent, this orientation came into prominence in other writers and thinkers who helped establish Flaubert as a turning point in the history of the novel (inter alia and with differing evaluative emphases, Baudelaire, Blanchot, Beckett, Sartre, Barthes, Henry James, Coetzee, Sebald, and Conrad himself).

A crucial factor or force in the novel's own practice of problematization and destabilization was Flaubert's use of free indirect style, which itself might be read as a mode of "deconstructing" the putatively sovereign individual and displacing that ideological construct in the direction of an internally dialogized, not totally self-determining, heteronomous and at times dismembered or even seemingly evacuated "self." The role of free indirect style was sensed at the trial, where it produced anxiety, but it was not clearly perceived, and the tendency of the one most unsettled by it, the prosecutor Pinard, was to ascribe to the author in unmediated terms whatever took place in free indirect style. This ascription led to the simple conclusion that Flaubert condemned marriage and celebrated adultery (whereas the more cogent and disconcerting contention would be that he threatened to collapse the two as constituting a distinction with no real difference). The modulations of voice and perspective and the variations in irony and empathy were simply flattened in Pinard's own amalgamation of author, narrator, and character. As I have intimated, free indirect style should be related to the broader issue of complex, at times disorienting modulations or mutations of narrative voice and perspective, which in turn could be referred to a more or less reduced carnivalesque impetus (also at play to some extent in Conrad). In this respect the narrator was comparable to a juggler and a clown of multivoiced irony, parody, and self-parody, which could conceivably have critical or at least discomfiting effects for readers attuned to them.

Despite the opinion of Olivier Le Cour Grandmaison, I doubt whether one could construe Conrad's critique of colonialism to be as radical or even brutal as Flaubert's excavation of bourgeois society and civilization. But could one see Emma's imaginary lover along with her phantasm of Paris and her consuming desire for commodities as avatars of Conrad's elusively undecidable heart of darkness? And what about Flaubert's own quest for the notorious book about nothing? Does *Heart of Darkness* itself in some nontrivial sense become such a book? These questions should not divert attention from the more specific ways both *Madame Bovary* and *Heart of Darkness* raise questions about historical developments whose literary inscription may be agitated or even motivated by an impossible quest but that simultaneously point to events and experiences in which darkness, excess, violence, and destruction take accentuated forms that cannot be etherealized or endlessly suspended in a permanent parabasis. The critic's alchemy or postsecular longing cannot utterly transform iron into irony.

It should be evident that the intricacies of the relation between formal dimensions of literature and the possibilities or pressures of historical processes become insistent in both Conrad and Flaubert. Each has been seen as an innovative "modernist," with Flaubert commonly taken as marking a turning point in the novel, and Conrad as an ambiguous yet still paradigmatic phenomenon in the history of "modernism." The signal form of history or historicity in Flaubert is the very banality not simply of "evil" but of modern "bourgeois" life in general. It is banality itself that becomes traumatizing, at times serving as a thin veneer covering suicidal, nihilistic, or even genocidal inclinations. In this respect, it is but a small step from Emma Bovary to some of Flaubert's more exorbitant creations such as Saint Julien l'Hospitalier or Saint Anthony. Flaubert at times turned to pure style or pure art (the two often conflated, as they have subsequently been) and appeared to find in it a form of redemption. But any redemptive move was riddled with self-questioning and doubt. And Flaubert himself never formalized style into a methodology for either writing or criticism. In Conrad the turn to art or style was also a pronounced move, but it became perhaps even less sufficient as a saving grace than in Flaubert. And the pressures of history in the accentuated form of colonialism and its aftermath were to some extent thematized rather than, as in Flaubert, left in the margins of the narrative. In each writer the quest as both formal and thematic dimension became in significant ways displaced to a "meta" level as a quest for a quest. This formally and historically necessary displacement subsequently became a signature feature of "modern" writing in its more experimental or ambitious modalities and was taken up, queried, or parodied by those who came after and often looked back to Flaubert and Conrad, notably W. G. Sebald and J. M. Coetzee.

❧ CHAPTER 3

Coetzee, Sebald, and the Narrative of Trauma

The approach to trauma, including its rendering in narrative, has long been accompanied by a paradox or double bind: the traumatic experience is unspeakable yet calls for endless speech. This uncannily familiar situation is well evoked in the Wittgensteinian subtitle of a book by two French psychoanalysts: *Whereof One Cannot Speak, Thereof One Cannot Stay Silent.*[1] The similarities and differences between not only testimonies but all attempts to address or "represent" traumatic experiences and events are determined by the manner in which this paradox or double bind is negotiated, from the aporetic gaps and muted signs of seemingly symptomatic performance to the attempts at some articulation of, or work on and through, problems in ways that may intensify or at times mitigate the haunting presence of the past.

In narrative these problematic negotiations are undertaken most prominently in the structure of narration, including the modulations of narrative perspective and voice, as well as in the words and actions of characters, who may at times seem to come close to, even merge with, narrators if not writers, or perhaps diverge from them in ways that destabilize expected forms of differentiation, distance, and irony. Narrative may inevitably bear traces of a quest, but in a markedly traumatic or posttraumatic context the quest resists a return to a putative normality and may well be devoid of a well-defined goal. Anything like a grail or a redemptive sign of grace becomes elusive, phantomlike, at best evanescent.

W. G. (Winfried Georg "Max") Sebald and J. M. (John Maxwell) Coetzee are two much-discussed writers who may be compared with respect to the recurrently insistent issues I have raised. Their extremely sophisticated approaches to questions of language and literature are signaled by their suspicion of naming and categorizing as well as by their combination of strong criticism of other writers and orientations, with a frequent turn to internal dialogization (in the phrase of Mikhail Bakhtin) or self-contestation and self-questioning in their essays, in their narrators or modes of narration, and in certain characters (notably Elizabeth Costello). They even share a desire for the pseudonymous, indicated by their preference for initials instead of proper names. Indeed, the convergences and divergences between Sebald and Coetzee offer a vast nexus of problems for possible discussion and debate.[2] They are both, in their own views, members of a generation "born later," coming after the perpetration of atrocities and living in the aftermath and the heavy shadow of events they did not directly "perpetrate" but for which they nonetheless bear a sense of responsibility if not guilt—better stated, an anxiety-ridden, rather bewildering disquiet that concepts such as responsibility and guilt (as well as the more ritualistic notions of stigma and stain) specify and localize in a questionable fashion.

Recently, the Holocaust and colonialism have been related historically and analytically in various ways, perhaps most pointedly in the argument that colonialism, especially in conjunction with racism, may have paralleled and at times prepared for the Nazi genocide. This argument may raise doubts about the assertion of uniqueness as indicative of an overly Eurocentric frame of reference.[3] But, if one were to offer a simplistic equation, one might say that the Holocaust is to Sebald what colonialism and apartheid are to Coetzee, although both are also concerned with the abusive treatment of nonhuman animals, which Elizabeth Costello compares with the Holocaust, thus raising for the reader, as well as for her interlocutors, the problem of analogies.[4] More basically, her orientation helps to bring up the issue of experiencing the evil of practices one is convinced are radically wrong to the point of drawing analogies one senses may be intemperate.

Both Sebald and Coetzee are "serious" academics as well as writers, writing critical texts and teaching for considerable periods of time. Sebald (here unlike Coetzee) was a relatively "late bloomer" as a writer of literary texts. Both emigrated from their "homelands" and wrote from a discomfiting, "deterritorialized" position at the margin or in the borderlands. Indeed, both are ill at ease in using their "mother" tongues, which have been appropriated for oppressive, even atrocious purposes, a problem more manifest in Sebald but not absent in Coetzee.[5] Their styles share an understated quality even when addressing issues evoking hyperbole, found at times in the responses or analogies of their characters (most famously perhaps in Elizabeth Costello, who is herself a writer). One aspect of the uncanniness of their texts is this subdued stylistic unsettlement in the face of the excessive and overwhelming. Costello's writing is compared to James Joyce's, but there are relatively few pyrotechnic passages in Coetzee, or in Sebald, for that matter. The more immediate model, as Coetzee humbly acknowledges, is Kafka, and Sebald at times seems like a student of Kafka, among other predecessors (notably Flaubert and Benjamin)— someone who has undertaken archival research both in documents and in the recesses of memory.[6] The latter point brings up the way both Sebald and Coetzee are occupied, even preoccupied by the question of realism, indeed traumatic realism, in relation to formal techniques and various distancing devices without which literature would not be literary. Yet what may be most interesting in both, however differently, is the way a mutual pressure is exerted, at times to a near breaking point, between the demands of historical and sociopolitical reality, on the one hand, and the exigencies of form and formal experimentation, on the other. Whatever the shifting sands between history and literary form may be in Coetzee and Sebald, the movement is not fixed by a rigid boundary marker or a notion of discrete realms. Sebald may employ an associative, at times dreamlike linkage of fact and fiction in a manner more pronounced than in Coetzee, but his conjunctions are never simple amalgamations, and texts that may be weighted in one direction or another still leave the reader off-balance concerning their genre. The inserted, seemingly documentary, black-and-white photograph or graphic is the most blatant instance of the archival artifact in a Sebald text, but its function is never simply documentary, and the reading of text and photograph may create both a sense of mutually informative signification and a puzzlement at times approaching vertigo, to invoke the title of Sebald's first long prose work.[7] Sebald states that 90 percent of his photographs (at least in *The Emigrants*) are "authentic,"[8] but that makes the reader uncertain about the sometimes elusive other 10 percent.[9] Not only because of the graphic elements but also the frequent, at times abrupt segues and detours, the eye (and the mind), confronted with a page of Sebald, does not know where to settle, and the reader is both fascinated and distracted by the various modalities of juxtaposition. Narrative flow is disrupted, shards of often enigmatic, at times traumatic actuality are inserted (one may recall inter alia the photograph of the massive heap of herring framed by standing men in *The Rings of Saturn*),[10] and the reader's train of thought (like Sebald's) may wander along associative paths and the byways of essayistic ruminations evoked by traces of the past, with closure becoming all the more elusive.

Another semiautobiographical comment Sebald makes about the appeal of photographs is worth quoting since it offers nonreductive insight into the orientation toward the past and its dead that informs his writing.

> Death entered my own life at a very early point. I grew up in a very small village, very high up in the Alps [in Bavaria—DLC], about three thousand feet above sea level. And in the immediate post-war years when I grew up there, it was in many ways quite an archaic place. For instance, you couldn't bury the dead in the winter because the ground was frozen and there was no way of digging it up. So you had to leave them in the woodshed for a month or two until the thaw came. You grew up with this knowledge that death is around you, and when and if someone died, it happened in the middle or in the center of the house, as it were, the dead person went through their agonies in the living room, and then before the burial they would be still part of the family for possibly three, four days. So I was from a very early point on very familiar, much more familiar than people are nowadays, with the dead and the dying. I have always had at the back of my mind this notion [recurrent in Sebald—DLC] that of course these people aren't really gone, they just hover somewhere at the perimeter of our lives and keep coming in on brief visits. And photographs are for me, as it were, one of the emanations of the dead, especially these older photographs of people no longer with us. Nevertheless, through these pictures, they do have what seems to me some sort of a spectral presence. And I've always been intrigued by that. It's got nothing to do with the mystical or the mysterious. It is just a remnant of a much more archaic way of looking at things. (*Emergence of Memory*, 39–40)

Hence, for Sebald the heralded indexicality of the photograph is itself ghostly but presumably not mysterious or mystical, for it emanates from the dead and is the medium of a spectral, absent presence (as is the case with the Sebald-narrator, a kind of photographic negative with respect to Jacques Austerlitz, for example).[11] At least one prominent role played by both Sebald and Coetzee as writers is that of the witness—the witness simultaneously to history and to the contemporary challenges and possibilities of literature. The writing of neither is restricted to bearing witness and giving testimony, but they are nonetheless compellingly called and even hauntingly caught by the insistence of the real (both the historically real and the less determinate, transhistorical Lacanian real—the presumably decentering, shattering, traumatizing hole or void in human existence). They are also more than mindful of the playful possibilities and the pitfalls of their callings as writers. I would also maintain that in neither writer does the witness stand in for the dead God or sublime seer and assume a prophetic or martyr-like voice. Their writing tends to be difficult to classify, notably in terms of the opposition between the secular and the religious or even in terms of the more recent notion of the postsecular. Issues in and around the religious, the spiritual, and the postsecular may be seriously (or playfully) broached, but the approach remains tentative, exploratory, and at times ironically inflected. Sebald often explicitly resists quasi-religious or "mystical" appropriation.[12] And Coetzee's epiphanies are at best ambiguous or equivocal, as I shall try to indicate with respect to his approach in *Elizabeth Costello* and *Disgrace*, the texts, along with the earlier *Lives of Animals*, on which I shall focus.[13]

Sebald has been taken in postsecular directions, notably in Eric L. Santner's *On Creaturely Life*.[14] In reading Sebald, one can sense the appeal of this approach and in general value the sustained attentiveness evident in Santner's insights (a quality he emphasizes in Sebald's work), even if one questions a perhaps overly restrictive linkage of Sebald with the German-Jewish tradition (importantly including, for Santner, Franz Rosenzweig), a tradition that had an evident appeal for Kafka, Benjamin, and Santner himself. Without in any sense denying the importance of Kafka and Benjamin for Sebald, I would nonetheless reiterate the point that, as Santner realizes, the forces bearing on Sebald's work render it overdetermined, including the role of non-Jewish writers such as Bernhard, Flaubert, Mann, and Nabokov, among others, as well as of historical phenomena, notably the Nazi genocide, colonialism, and such diffuse processes as rampant destruction, victimization, and abuse, including the treatment of animals.[15] Moreover, the evanescent epiphanic moment or opening in Sebald often seems to be the tenuous accompaniment of a sense of extreme disempowerment and near fatalistic melancholy, at times bordering on despair, about an entropic course of history that subsides, via its mounting ruins, into the cycles of nature. Here it would be Benjamin's Angel of History—seen as a traumatized, bewildered, immobilized witness, propelled by the blowback of a catastrophic history (a post-traumatically disordered, spectral spectator)—more than the messianic intimations, the momentary attempts to redeem the commodity, and the problematic intersections with Jewish mysticism that would appear to be Sebald's saturnine muse.[16] To recur to another Benjaminian topos, ruins (or perhaps better: rubble) from catastrophes form the inclined path from history or culture to nature that is also ruined. Or, as Sebald himself puts it in rather deflationary, decidedly nonprophetic terms:

> I think [Walter] Benjamin at one point says that there is no point in exaggerating that which is already horrific. And from that, by extrapolation, one could conclude that perhaps in order to get the full measure of the horrific, one needs to remind the reader of beatific moments of life, because if you existed solely with your imagination in *le monde concentrationnaire*, then you would somehow not be able to sense it. And so it requires that contrast. The old-fashionedness of the diction or of the narrative tone is [*sic*] therefore nothing to do with nostalgia for a better age that's gone past but is simply something that, as it were, heightens the awareness of that which we have managed to engineer in this century.[17]

I have started to touch on the question of divergences between Sebald and Coetzee, which should not be invoked to deny their affinities. This question may be further explored with reference to Coetzee's own interesting brief discussion of Sebald in the former's collection of essays, *Inner Workings: Literary Essays 2000–2005*.[18] Coetzee is himself struck by the pronounced sense of melancholy, possession by history, and the feeling, perhaps the conviction, that humanity may have been a passing yet ruinous, too often demented excrescence that will sink back into the mire of an ecologically damaged nature. He is also intrigued by Sebald's distinctive style, which made an immediate impression on generally captivated readers. He notes that Sebald's second prose fiction, *Emigrants* of 1992 (with an English translation in 1996), "brought him wide attention, particularly in the English-speaking world, where its blend of storytelling, travel record, fictive biography, antiquarian essay, dream, and philosophical rumination, executed in elegant if rather lugubrious prose and supplemented with photographic documentation of endearingly amateurish quality, struck a decidedly new note (the German reading public was accustomed by this time to the crossing and indeed trampling of boundaries between fiction and nonfiction)" (145). This complex assessment is more the work of the literary critic than the writer offering an appreciation, much less homage, to a fellow writer. And the praise is muted both by the reference to "lugubrious prose" (rather than, say, impossibly mournful prose in keeping with the rendering of lamentable, catastrophic, possibly irremediable experience) and by the unexplicated reference to the German reading public that had been subject to the trampling of boundaries between fiction and nonfiction not only in unspecified writing but, arguably, in the fictions and phantasms purveyed by the Nazi regime. The implication would seem to be that Coetzee prefers crossings that do not trample the nonetheless unsettled boundaries between fiction and nonfiction, although it is not clear whether he is charging Sebald with the trampling he deems customary for the German reading public.

Coetzee's observations immediately following the above quotation resonate with its tonality and its low-keyed critical temper:

> The people in Sebald's books are for the most part what used to be called melancholics. The tone of their lives is defined by a hard-to-articulate sense that they do not belong in the world, that perhaps human beings in general do not belong here. They are humble enough not to claim they are preternaturally sensitive to the currents of history—in fact they tend to believe there is something wrong with them—but the tenor of Sebald's enterprise is to suggest that his people are prophetic, even though the fate of the prophet in the modern world is to be obscure and unheard. (146–47)[19]

As I intimated, I think "the tenor of Sebald's enterprise is to suggest that his people" are less prophetic than seemingly eccentric, often symptomatic accentuations of prevalent tendencies and possibilities to which we may be insufficiently attentive. Coetzee seems to indicate as much when he observes that research in Sebald—"burrowing in archives, tracking down witnesses"—itself only confirms what melancholia and attendant symptoms already bear witness to: "there is no cure, no salvation." Melancholia leads to "compulsive activity, often consisting of nocturnal walking, dominated by feelings of apprehension" (146). To Coetzee's remarks I would add that literature here seems to turn to historical research itself in a compulsive manner that repeats what is already known or at least sensed, and the writer formulates what on one level appears to be a terminal logic of aporia and impasse. Ambulatory mania might itself be seen as the symptomatic analogue of the insomniac activity that writing itself may become, especially when it is immersed in stranded objects, delineates the interminable expanse of proliferating, typically far-from-romantic ruins, and returns obsessively to a haunting past that will not pass away.

Coetzee debatably states that "*The Rings of Saturn* (1995) comes the closest among Sebald's books to what we usually think of as nonfiction. It is written to tame the 'paralyzing horror' that overtakes its author—that is to say, its 'I' figure—in the face of the decline of the eastern region of England and the destruction of its landscape." Coetzee goes on to point out parenthetically that "of course the 'I' in Sebald's books is not to be identified with the historical W. G. Sebald. Nevertheless, Sebald as author plays mischievously with similarities between the two, to the point of reproducing snapshots and passport photographs of 'Sebald' in his texts" (148–49). It is noteworthy that the "of course" that of course dismisses simple identification is followed immediately by a "nevertheless." The proximity or perhaps the distortive similarity—but not the identity—of author, writer, and narrator, even at times character, not only the shifting first-person Sebald-narrator in *The Emigrants* or *The Rings of Saturn*, but the somewhat more differentiated Jacques Austerlitz (from whom the Sebald-narrator nonetheless often seems to have the minimal distance of a diaphanous medium) and the so-called historical W. G. Sebald (an elusive if not phantomlike figure in any case) would seem much closer and less manifestly interrupted by explicit formal devices than in Coetzee, such as the role of "focalizers" (for example, son John in *Elizabeth Costello*). Yet both Sebald and Coetzee are insistently concerned with the problem of the relation between historical reality and literature as well as fiction. In both writers this relation is variable, unstable, and impossible to fix with certainty.

There is indeed much "nonfiction" in *The Rings of Saturn*, combined in at times bewildering ways with literary turns.[20] One might perhaps read the title in terms of an endless journey or ambulatory writing pilgrimage that circles melancholically and at times dizzyingly around the ruins of history and its sediments in contemporary life. This repetitive circling, with the narrator often in a twilight state between waking and dreaming, has no "dialectical" impetus or movement of "overcoming," much less redemption. It is at most broken by uncanny, evanescent epiphanies, such as that provided by the momentary appearance of a duck (89), of rays of sun "making a fan-shaped pattern as they descended, of the sort that used to appear in religious pictures symbolizing the presence of grace and providence" (241), or even "the almost supernatural apparition" of "a pimp in a white suit," wearing "gold-framed sunglasses" and "a ludicrous Tyrolean hat" (82). But the epiphanies are momentary or may even seem like parodic pop-ups, and a state of grace or a providential presence is at best a thing of the past whose modern residues do not come trailing clouds of glory. The writer's own textual labor—what Flaubert famously termed *les affres du style*—is analogized to the torturous activity of the silk weaver or even the silk worm, which is discussed in manifold ways, from the ruthless cruelty of the Dowager Empress Tz'u-hsi of China, who had daily blood sacrifices to the gods of silk (151) to the use of silk worms by Nazis in the Third Reich, including their snow-white relation to "the best and cleanest of all possible worlds" (292) and the extermination of the worms in a killing operation by suspending cocoons over a boiling cauldron for upwards of three hours (294).[21] At one point the narrator observes that "my rational mind is nonetheless unable to lay the ghosts of repetition that haunt me with ever greater frequency" (187). And, in post-traumatic fashion, he approximates the disorienting feeling of numbness to that of repetition, wondering whether repetition is "some kind of anticipation of the end, a venture into the void" (188). Sebald's own stylistic repetition of repetition introduces variations that are not simply symptoms and may even counteract compulsiveness, if only in limited ways.

The writing of *The Rings of Saturn* may be reminiscent of the later Flaubert, but it is Joseph Conrad, especially in his relation to Roger Casement, who inter alia receives extended treatment. Sebald apparently feels an affinity not only with Flaubert but also with the Pole who wrote in English yet retained a Polish accent and had an uncomfortable relation to both his "native" and his adopted cultures as well as an apprehensive sense of a "guilt-ridden" colonial enterprise—an implication in an addled history that Sebald seems to understand as similar to his own relation to the Nazi genocide. Sebald refers a few times to Conrad by his Anglicized name but then turns, in a telling alienation effect, to the Polish "Korzeniowski." He asserts that "the madness of the whole colonial enterprise was gradually borne in upon Korzeniowski" (117). He adds that, during his journey, "Korzeniowski began to grasp that his own travails did not absolve him from the guilt he had incurred by his mere presence in the Congo" (120), which may downplay the involvement and the relative lack of active political resistance in Conrad's relation to a nonetheless criticized Belgian colonialism. Sebald notes as well that "back in Léopoldville, Korzeniowski was so sick in body and in soul that he longed for death. But it was to be another three months before this man, whose protracted bouts of despair were henceforth to alternate with his writing, was able to depart homeward" from Africa (121).

Roger Casement may be an even more pronounced object of Sebald's empathic interest. His depiction of Casement is strongly etched and forceful, stressing the importance of Casement's trenchantly critical report on the Congo and "his unconditional partisanship for the victims and those who had no rights" (128). He also stresses Casement's espousal of the oppressed not only in Africa but in Britain with respect to "the white Indians of Ireland" (129). He notes that Casement's homosexuality, which was an embarrassment to many Irish partisans, may well have "sensitized him to the continuing oppression, exploitation, enslavement and destruction, across the borders of class and race, of those who were furthest from the centres of power" (134).[22] He concludes his discussion by noting dryly that Casement was, "as expected," found guilty of high treason and hung, and the remains of his body, exhumed from a lime pit in 1965, were "presumably scarcely identifiable any more" (ibid.). Earlier in the section Sebald asks with respect to the dead in the Battle of Waterloo, evoked by the Lion Monument in Brussels ("the very definition of Belgian ugliness, in my eyes" [123]): "Are we standing on a mountain of death? Is that our ultimate vantage point? Does one really have the much-vaunted historical overview from such a position?" (125).

Perhaps an even better candidate for the status of nonfiction in Sebald is the collection of critical essays in *On the Natural History of Destruction*.[23] This bitterly elegiac "history" in the mode of endless lament most approaches a muted concept of working through the traumas and disasters of the past in its discussion of Alexander Kluge, only to swerve away from Kluge in an insistence on the futility of hope and the irreparable nature of history:

> Despite [Kluge's] ironic style, the prospect suggested here of an alternative historical outcome, possible in specific circumstances, is a serious call to work for the future in defiance of all calculations of probability. Central to Kluge's detailed description of the social organization of disaster, which is preprogrammed by the ever-recurrent and ever-intensifying errors of history, is the idea that a proper understanding of the catastrophes we are always setting off is the first prerequisite for the social organization of happiness. However, it is difficult to dismiss the idea that the systematic destruction Kluge sees arising from the development of the means and modes of industrial production hardly seems to justify the principle of hope. (64)

One might ask why Sebald refers to the "principle of hope," the term of Ernst Bloch, or even the somewhat sinister "social organization of happiness," when defiant determination against the odds would seem more in keeping with his account of Kluge's thought. Later in the text Sebald seems close to Peter Weiss, whom he discusses at times in a participatory if not projective manner, emphasizing, more than Weiss himself, the latter's Jewish background and insisting on "the endemic perversion of cruelty inherent in the history of mankind" that cannot be redeemed "in the last chapter . . . since our species is unable to learn from its mistakes" (189–90). Arguably paying insufficient attention to the role of resistance, including political resistance, in Weiss, what Sebald detects in Weiss's *Ästhetik des Widerstands* (*The Aesthetics of Resistance*) is "not only the expression of an ephemeral wish for redemption, but . . . an expression of the *will* to be on the side of the victims at the end of time" (190). Indeed, Sebald's own perspective in *The Natural History of Destruction*, which at times uses the same seemingly amalgamating terminology of annihilation and disaster for the German victims of aerial bombing and the Jewish and other victims of the Nazi genocide, however much open to criticism on the level of historical and critical analysis, may be understood as the way the past might well be subjectively experienced by a German "born later" with an inclination to align himself with the victim.[24]

Coetzee discusses most extensively Sebald's *After Nature* (1988), which is made up of three long poems.[25] He notes that in the first two poems, which treat Mathias Grünewald, the sixteenth-century painter, and Georg Wilhelm Steller, the eighteenth-century intellectual who abandoned theology to engage in scientific cataloguing, "scholarship takes second place to what [Sebald] intuits and perhaps projects upon" his subject, notably the "claim that Grünewald, though married, was secretly homosexual" (151). Here Coetzee plays the role of the historian or historically oriented literary critic who explicitly compares what is found in a poem with the results of presumably more reliable research to argue that "it is thus best to think of Grünewald and Steller as personae, masks that enable Sebald to project back into the past a character type, ill at ease in the world, indeed in exile from it, that may be his own but that he feels possesses a certain genealogy which his reading and researches can uncover" (151–52). The type of history in Sebald would thus seem to be basically intuitive and projective, with research serving as a means to provide directions that may be contravened or superseded if they do not lead to the desired, or perhaps the compulsively constrained, results.

The third of the poems, "Dark Night Sallies Forth," is "more overtly autobiographical," and "Sebald, as 'I,' takes stock of himself as individual but also as inheritor of Germany's recent history. In images and in fragments of narrative, the poem tells his story from his birth in 1944 under the sign of Saturn, the cold planet, to the 1980s" (152). Pari passu, this could be said of all of Sebald's works, written under the sign of Saturn and enacting, if not at points acting out, equivocal relations between autobiography, history, melancholic obsession, and literature. I have stated that the prose work that is probably closest to nonfiction, while remaining preoccupied with the themes and impasses characterizing the more literary texts, is *On The Natural History of Destruction*, which is the complement of *After Nature* in its delineation of what is to come after history, as the world subsides in seemingly fatalistic fashion into the *posthistoire* brought about by massive destruction—be it that of the aerial bombing of German cities or the Nazi genocidal annihilation of Jews and other victimized groups. Indeed, Sebald's perspective combines extreme precision with respect to historical details and a transhistorical sense of a vortex-like consumption of history in a movement or retrovirus of devastating catastrophe—what might be seen as the plummeting of historical reality into the black hole of the traumatic Lacanian real. Sebald might even be seen as rewriting Walter Benjamin's *Trauerspiel* book with mourning explicitly and insistently becoming impossible and even looping back into endless melancholy.[26] Precision of detail would almost seem not to invite but instead to foreclose the type of specificity that might both test transhistorical apprehensions and at times even indicate the possibility of locating or generating alternatives to the one-way journey backward of the Angel of History. I have referred to Sebald's momentary epiphanies or "beatific" breaks in the clouds, which—however much read against the grain—may facilitate his appropriation for postsecular readings that insist on the pervasiveness of trauma, catastrophe, haunting, and compulsive repetition yet also point to the messianic chips of time that fleetingly and accidentally present themselves in an altogether aleatory fashion—acts of grace or gratuitous acts that might themselves be seen, from a less ecstatic or more doubting perspective, not only as necessary points of contrast but also as symptomatic complements of despair and disempowerment. The latter estimation would seem close to Coetzee's, when he notes, toward the end of his essay, that Sebald's discussion in *After Nature* of Altdorfer's painting *The Battle of Arbela* discloses "a panorama of slaughter on a huge scale rendered in detail of hallucinatory, vertigo-inducing minuteness." Indeed, "the painting ought to precipitate another of his melancholic collapses. Instead it leads to the rather unconvincing transcendence with which the poem ends: an opening out of vision beyond horizons of unending warfare, East versus West, to a new future" (154). Here Coetzee seems to see "unconvincing transcendence" as an empty utopia. Yet it is, of course, consubstantial with the accidental, aleatory epiphany that it appear utterly arbitrary and comes miraculously (like a certain form of divine grace) when it will. It may never seem convincing, but it may be as compelling to a certain kind of melancholic-messianic sensibility as are the haunting past, ambulatory mania, associative or paratactic segues, and the chiaroscuro tonalities and opacities of insomniac writing.

Eric Santner raises the question of humor in Sebald and notes that "one rightly wonders whether there is room for humor in the bleak world of historical suffering his work seems to live and breathe." Yet Santner himself rightly points to an affinity between Sebald and Kafka, "a writer with a considerable, if unusual, sense of humor." Santner finds Sebald's Kafka-like sense of humor "just at those points of creatureliness . . . where the *nonsensical* aspect of . . . 'signifying stress' becomes manifest to us, the point where we catch a glimpse of the mechanical stupidity of our jouissance" (146–47). I think the sense of humor evoked here, which unexpectedly conjoins Bergson and Žižek, goes in the direction of the "funny-peculiar" and the bemused, quizzical, or anxious smile (if not grimace) rather than what might evoke laughter. Or, perhaps more basically, Santner may be stressing humor's putative relation to the "mechanical" quality of the repetition compulsion, which he problematically maintains is "precisely that excessive 'inhuman' vitality that sets us apart from the animal and in some sense first makes us distinctly human" (191). In any case, could one possibly relate the "unusual" sense of humor Santner postulates—so close to the uncanny, the absurd, the ironic, and the ridiculous—to the kind of "unreduced" laughter Bakhtin stresses, which touches on the grotesque and can prompt the hearty belly-laugh that shakes the entire body? They seem quite distant if not incommensurable. Santner dwells on the pervasive melancholic immersion in stranded objects, the cringe of the creature rendered abject by the sovereign superego or the bureaucratized social agency, the more fundamental, transhistorical if not universal abjection of structural trauma or the Lacanian real with its stifling, anxious, yet presumably exhilarating, human-making excess akin to a born-again sense of original sin, and at the very least the deservedly stressed bond between vulnerability and solidarity. (The latter is tellingly evoked by Santner in an image-laden passage he quotes from *The Rings of Saturn*, which the Sebald-narrator concludes by seeing himself "become one" with a cowering, terrified, paralyzed, then panicked hare that leaps out of its hiding place, with "its eyes, turning to look back as it fled and almost popping out of its head with fright" [*Rings of Saturn*, 234–35, quoted in Santner, 160]—an image that may uncannily recall photographs of Kafka.) In Bakhtin, laughter is a powerful Rabelaisian force that unseats the sovereign, at least symbolically, and is typically associated with eating and drinking as well as with functions and sounds one shares with other animals. It does not necessitate a turn to a generalized notion of abject creaturely life and of "the" animal as the instinct-bound opposite of excessive human drives. Yet these alternatives, if they are indeed alternatives, may not quite fit all one finds in Sebald (or in Santner).[27]

One need not simply direct attention to the way Sebald recurs time and again to the joke humans are constantly playing on themselves in their seemingly compulsive destruction of one another, other animals, and nature in general. Sebald's texts may reach the point of at least bursts of laughter when he elaborates things—lists, names, series of objects, geographical locations—to a surrealistic extreme that becomes vertiginous (as in the seemingly endless, run-on paragraphs of *Austerlitz* or in the maddeningly enchanting description of the trip of Ambros Adelwarth and Cosmo Solomon to the Holy Land, followed by Adelwarth's discomfiting dream, in *The Emigrants* (135–45).[28] One may also refer to the temptation for the impatient or inattentive reader to do a pratfall as s/he stumbles over the narration with its proliferation of place names and incidents, perhaps confusing one text with another or a character, referred to in the first person, with the Sebald-narrator. There are as well Sebald's at times comic, fleeting allusions (the recurring butterfly man, the [postsecular?] pimp in the white suit, or the incongruously named Susi Ahoi, the Chinese optician in *Vertigo* whose touch produces an eerie feeling [97], for example). And one might mention cases of senseless repetition and abrupt transition approaching slapstick (such as the way Fritz, Luisa's first true love in *The Emigrants*, suddenly dies from a stroke while playing the *Freischutz* overture for garrison officers [214–15]). Along with evanescent moments of beauty, these interludes also relieve somewhat what might otherwise seem like a *monde concentrationnaire*.

My account implies that it would be a mistake to see Sebald simply as a melancholic bricoleur, despite the importance of melancholia and parataxis in his approach. The complexity of his understanding of melancholia and his critical orientation to dubious (not all) conceptions of mourning and working through is particularly evident in what might be seen as a key text not only concerning its ostensible objects of analysis but also with respect to Sebald himself: "Constructs of Mourning: Günther Grass and Wolfgang Hildesheimer."[29] Sebald's preference for Hildesheimer is unmistakable, but his reasons are simultaneously historical and literary, perhaps ethical and political as well. He views Grass in terms similar to those he applies to others in the so-called Gruppe 47, particularly Alfred Andersch, whom he scathingly treats and implicitly contrasts with Jean Améry, in essays included in *On the Natural History of Destruction*.[30] For Sebald, Andersch did not make a sincere attempt to come to terms with the past and his own implication in it. Instead he resorted to obfuscation in a self-interested fashion, strove to turn the page and be forward-looking, and advanced the cause of an exclusionary *Literaturbetrieb* (or postwar literary establishment) that even based its solidarity on a shared experience of the war (which of course excluded Jews), hence blindly repeating on the level of the institution of literature certain dubious features of the presumably rejected Nazi movement itself. Despite his very belatedly acknowledged, unknown-to-Sebald, participation as a very young man in the Waffen-SS, Grass may not be comparable to Andersch (who abandoned his Jewish wife only to reclaim a relationship with her after the war when it would help to validate his credentials as a "good German"). But Grass, for Sebald, nonetheless obscured "the real aspects of the story of the Danzig Jews" in his 1974 *Tagebuch einer Schnecke* (translated as *Diary of a Snail*) in which, as Sebald notes, the empirical history in Grass's account was in any event largely taken not from Grass's experience but from a monograph by the historian Erwin Lichtenstein (215n). More important, in *Campo Santo* Sebald observes that Grass's "snail-like theme of melancholy . . . functions as an alibi to counter the programmatic intention of mourning," which would be necessary to engage the history of Danzig's Jews (110).[31] And he sees whatever mourning there may be in Grass as "laboriously constructed" and "the performance of a historical duty" (115). He argues that "the story of Hermann Ott that forms the backbone of the *Diary*, and is used by the author to offer the reader's receptive imagination many consoling ideas, will not ultimately stand up to critical examination. . . . The implication . . . in everything we learn about Hermann Ott, is that there really were Germans of a better kind, a thesis that stakes its claim to a high degree of probability through the combination of fiction with the documentary material. . . . As we can read in [Heinrich] Böll, they ["Germans of a better kind"] confined their effective activities to saying a Good Friday prayer which [quoting Böll] 'even includes the unbelieving Jews.' German literature of the postwar period sought its moral salvation in these fictional figures" (109–10).

By contrast, Sebald reads Hildesheimer's *Tynset* of 1965 as an allegory of the Nazi genocidal treatment of Jews and finds in its experimental paratactic techniques the echoes of posttraumatic effects. (Hildesheimer, while not a Holocaust survivor, was Jewish and a translator at the Nuremberg trials.) Sebald even finds that *Tynset* "seems to have been created from the heart of mourning itself" (115). And he pinpoints in the text (which Hildesheimer refused to term a novel) rituals poised between melancholy and mourning that provide some relief but not release or salvation—rituals such as the narrator's nocturnal reading of telephone directories and timetables as well as his dreams of a country beyond Dürer's sea of *Melancholia*. Sebald notes that the first-person narrator of the lengthy monologue "is never clearly perceived as a character, only as a voice" and that, following trails of complicity and fellow-traveling that emerge from his random phone calls, he conveys to upright fellow citizens messages so urgent that they leave home in haste (115–16). Sebald does not make the seemingly obvious point that the directories and timetables may also be repeatedly read by the insomniac, ambulatory narrator to note and commemorate what had been murdered, mutilated, destroyed, or distorted in the Nazi past. Sebald insists that "we are dealing here with something far from nihilism in the usual sense of the word; it is more like an approximation to death . . . to which melancholy clings like [quoting *Tynset*] 'the fat weed / that roots itself in ease on Lethe wharf,' a provocative gesture of resignation" (121). Comparing Hildesheimer to Kafka, he adds that "the area that melancholy thus sets out to explore stretches out before us in *The Castle* as a snowy, frozen landscape, and its exact counterpart is Tynset, a place in the north of Norway that the narrator ventures to visit. Tynset is the penultimate stage on his journey. After it comes Röros, which [quoting *Tynset*] '[lies] like a last camp on the way to the end of the world, before that way is lost in inhospitable regions, a territory so incalculable, so menacing, that its exploration has been postponed year after year, until the camp has become the eternal autumn quarters inhabited by aging explorers who have lost sight of their goal; have forgotten it, and now look vaguely for the geographical origins of a melancholy . . . that they have long been seeking, but on which they can never lay hands'" (121–22)—a quandary that might be read allegorically as a commentary on the contemporary political left. I would add that it is appropriate if ironic that Röros may be very close to the Svalbald (not the Sebald!) Global Seed Vault (or "doomsday vault") near the north pole in Norway, which is the postapocalyptic multinational repository of seeds that presumably may restart vegetation in the wake of a world-destroying catastrophe. Sebald himself, in this essay in *Campo Santo*, resists the almost overwhelming temptation to embrace fatalism and melancholy but instead traces the unfixed interactions between a marked saturnine response, which for many has become Sebald's distinctive signature, and its intricate links to forms of mourning that do not bring either closure or redemption but nonetheless have a necessary (yet not sufficient) role in working through the relations between past, present, and future.[32]

An obvious question to which I have alluded is that of Coetzee's own subject-position or "voice" as he writes about Sebald. Sebald is a companion spirit if not a doppelgänger for Coetzee, and, at the very least, he offers options or perhaps temptations that might well have a strong appeal for Coetzee. At a certain level, Coetzee is also being "autobiographical" in writing about Sebald, in both historical and literary ways. That this is at least arguably the case does not undermine the interest, cogency, or even validity of his observations and critical insights. If anything, it lends them heightened forcefulness in that they have a possibly critical, self-reflexive or self-referential side that itself is intimately bound up with the question of the relation between the historical and the literary.

How to define the literary is of course a vexed issue.[33] One definition or at least marker is self-referentiality and its relation to the larger problem of form, including the role of critical distance and romantic or postromantic irony (including with respect to the "self" and its involvements). A related definition is to see the literary in terms of the uncanny or strangely disconcerting that itself resists definition, categorization, or delimited generic classification, making the literary a dimension of all writing that is most accentuated and explicitly placed in the foreground or played out in certain (not all) texts termed literary. Along with these considerations comes the role of rhetoric not as mere adornment but in terms of both tropes and broader considerations of style, composition, address, performativity, voice, and the relation to the historical, actual, and empirical. Coetzee's own discussions of the literary and what might be called the task of the writer touch on all these issues, as does his essay on Sebald itself.

A more comprehensive discussion of Coetzee on the literary and its relation to the historical would require an extensive discussion of his critical essays, which is beyond the scope of my analysis.[34] There is a pervasive playfulness in Coetzee's texts, which at times reaches laughingly comic proportions (for example, in the fraught, star-crossed relation or nonrelation between Elizabeth Costello and Paul Rayment in *Slow Man*).[35] But the playful does not exclude the "serious" engagement with stressful issues such as apartheid, colonialism, or the treatment of other animals. Indeed, literature becomes, in the phrase of Thomas Mann, a form of serious play. And it is expectably the case that the relation of the historical and the literary is explored in the novels as well as in the essays, notably in *Elizabeth Costello*, with its initial chapter or "lesson" on realism and its engagement with a multiplicity of related problems, including the Holocaust and the abusive treatment of animals, which Costello compares with one another, thus raising not only the problem of analogies but that of the relation between history and literature. More basically, her orientation helps to bring up the issue of experiencing the evil of practices one is convinced are radically wrong to the beleaguered point of being led to make comparisons or draw analogies one senses may be problematic and intemperate. The abuse of animals and the Holocaust have perhaps their most prominent role in *Elizabeth Costello*, but in that novel there are also multiple reminders of colonialism and its postcolonial aftermath, which come to a somewhat surrealistic head as Elizabeth, an Australian, is asked by one of her examiners before "the gate," at the end of the story when an inquiry is held into her beliefs: What about the Tasmanians? Elizabeth is at first nonplussed, thinking the questioner is referring to a contemporary development in Tasmania of which she is unaware. But she then comes to realize that the question concerns the pressure of the past on the present where the problem of aborigines is still contentious.[36] As we shall see, she addresses the question on a general level, saying she has not been called to give voice to the Tasmanians but if she were she would be open to them and even to the voices of their persecutors (202–4). In "Lesson 5: The Humanities in Africa," Elizabeth visits her sister Blanche, a nun in Africa, who is a force in converting indigenous peoples in Nigeria to evangelical Christianity in a fashion that leads her to downgrade the importance of the humanities and the model of

Greece and even to uphold a view of religious piety that makes the sacrifice for Christ the center of life, as in the case of Joseph, a craftsman who repetitiously makes crucifixes featuring an anguished Christ, something that for Elizabeth seems to be a diminution and straight-jacketing of his talents. In a less sharp-edged way, in "Lesson 2: The Novel in Africa," she also encounters the more commercial and "glitzy" sides of postcolonialism on a pleasure ship whose cruises include a cultural suntan provided by presentations from famous or once famous writers, including Elizabeth and a former lover and, for her, former writer turned entrepreneurial showman, Emmanuel Egudu, Nigerian proponent of the so-called oral novel that presumably makes the novel the vehicle of indigenous oral traditions. In the case of David Lurie in *Disgrace*, the role of apartheid and of the postapartheid regime in South Africa is an omnipresent if at times spectral presence that is addressed in many implicit yet insistent ways that permeate and punctuate the story of Lurie, his daughter Lucy, and their interactions with others.

Animals make frequent appearances in Sebald, but I think they are for the most part treated as aspects of a consuming vision of ecological disaster, both man-made and quasi-fatalistic, and when they appear in more discrete and relational terms, it is often in a deranged or demented state brought about by human abuse or at least dubious behavior. Prototypical here is the captive obsessive-compulsive raccoon of which the Sebald-narrator, near the beginning of *Austerlitz*, remarks: "The only animal which has remained lingering in my memory is the raccoon. I watched it for a long time as it sat beside a little stream with a serious expression on its face, washing the same piece of apple over and over again, as if it hoped that all this washing, which went far beyond any reasonable thoroughness, would help it to escape the unreal world in which it had arrived, so to speak, through no fault of its own" (4). I have intimated that Sebald's own narrative practice might at least at times be seen as analogous to the behavior of the raccoon in light of its seemingly compulsive, repetitive descriptions of hopeless scenes from the perspective of a contemplative yet disconcerted bystander, listener, or onlooker—in a sense a benumbed, incapacitated witness at the dilapidated, even shell-shocked zoo of history. (Captivity in zoos is one problem that eats at Sebald, including, in *The Natural History of Destruction*, the devastating effects of bombing on animals in zoos.) This impression of transfixed, often horrified witnessing is intensified by the juxtaposition on facing pages of two photos enframing large animal eyes, seemingly a raccoon's and an owl's (or perhaps two kinds of owl), with the former surprisingly larger than the latter, and two sets of clipped human eyes, one apparently Wittgenstein's and the other of an older man, presumably the painter Jan Peter Tripp.[37] Wittgenstein repeated the near proverbial saying that the eyes are the mirror of the soul, and here the eyes seem to reflect nothing. Yet Sebald's descriptions of animals are hauntingly compelling, and they may well evoke an empathic response in readers or even induce them to see other animals not as mere objects of use or even as abject recipients of divinely delegated, at times merciful human dominion but as making both demands for nonabusive treatment and claims for justice that have often gone unheeded.

Animals have a marked prominence in Coetzee's stories, especially *The Lives of Animals, Elizabeth Costello,* and *Disgrace. The Lives of Animals* was of course inserted as "lessons" 3 and 4 of *Elizabeth Costello* with both gains and losses in the transition. One loss was the set of commentaries accompanying *The Lives of Animals,* which have the value of allowing the reader to have access to the responses of an important set of thinkers across various disciplines: an introduction by Amy Guttman and commentaries by Marjorie Garber, Peter Singer, Wendy Doniger, and Barbara Smuts. None of the commentators addresses the problem of the relation between history and literature, including problems of narrative. And they at times share an unexamined anthropocentrism in the manner in which they discuss problems. Guttman begins with the debatable assertion that "John Coetzee displays the kind of seriousness that can unite aesthetics and ethics" (3). (One might rather contend that he, both seriously and playfully, explores the often tense relations between the two.) Like Elizabeth Costello, Guttman stresses the opposition between the heart and reason. Apparently slated to be a reluctant respondent to Coetzee at Princeton, where the *Lives of Animals* was first given as the Tanner lectures, Singer offers what might be read as a "more-meta-than-thou" account in the form of a fictional discussion of the text with his daughter who is cast in the Costello role, while he takes up that of the philosopher, indicating his disappointment that Coetzee resorted to irony and fiction to avoid arguing and taking a stand on the issues. In the process, the Singer-persona makes some presumably decisive human/animal contrasts, asserts the higher value of human life over that of other animals, and plays a zero-sum endgame (in a pinch, would he save his daughter or his dog?). Smuts observes that *The Lives of Animals* indeed addresses the treatment of animals, but, after misleadingly maintaining that Costello does not refer to "real-life relations with animals" (108), she chooses not to discuss the text but to use it as a pretext for discussing her own interesting and important work (as well as life) with animals (or, in her term, "nonhuman persons").[38] Doniger opposes cultural relativism, or at least diversity, to abstract universalism and anthropologically reviews some of the different ways humans relate to animals, often in terms of the anthropocentric problems of human purity, contamination, and power, including ways of incorporating the power of the seemingly other. In her own voice, she also makes some provocative assertions about animals, for example, that they, notably dogs and horses, "understand the feelings of other animals" and "have compassion," even that animals have languages to which we should learn to attend (103–5). Garber focuses on the literary and ends with a seemingly rhetorical question about whether "all along [Coetzee] was really asking, 'What is the value of literature?'" (84). Her approach itself has the value of stressing the significance of the literary and its insistence in the work of someone like Coetzee, for whom it is quite important. But it might be interpreted as implying that there is one key if not essential issue and that a concern with the literary and its value must preempt other concerns—a perspective that easily leads to an ultraformalistic, quasi-transcendental, if not postsecular, view of the "literary."

Garber's is close to the approach taken by Derek Attridge in his important book, *J.M. Coetzee and the Ethics of Reading*, although Garber plays down what the literary work can achieve in the "real world" while Attridge stresses the nature of the literary work as itself an event and an object of commitment, stretching a good point to mount a defense of a rather circumscribed "ethics" of reading and writing.[39] In spite of his acknowledged indebtedness to Derrida for whom either/or choices and accompanying binary oppositions were, on basic levels, typically misleading, Attridge arguably takes a deconstructive approach in markedly formalistic directions, separating the historical from the literary, seeing at best only allusive or ironic relations, and emphasizing the literariness of the literary, even in the absence of any definition of the latter.[40] Hence he asserts:

> It is when we take all the Costello pieces together that their abiding concern with the creation of literary works, with what it means to commit oneself to a life of writing, emerges most clearly. Although individual pieces may appear to focus on issues not particularly related to this question (issues determined by the nature of the invitation to which Coetzee is responding), such as animal lives or the value of the humanist tradition, the figure of Elizabeth Costello (or in one case Robinson Crusoe [in *Foe*]) is always central. Coetzee is pursuing the difficult path he broached in *The Master of Petersburg,* with its dark exploration of the cost of fictional creation, and alluded to at the very end of *Boyhood* (written as he was beginning the Costello pieces) when the young John contemplates the burden of the storyteller's vocation. (200)

What I would question in the above account is not the reference to Coetzee's (or anyone's) "abiding concern with the creation of literary works" and the commitment it requires, although what that commitment entails,

notably concerning the understanding of literature, the literary, and its relation
to other issues, is open to debate, and allusions to "cost" and "burden" may be
somewhat histrionic in a world where, as Coetzee is well aware, other abiding
concerns and commitments may have rather heavy costs and burdens. What
I find problematic is the type of centering that becomes exclusivist, dichoto-
mizing, and invidiously hierarchical, reducing certain problems to the level
of the *merely* contingent. The "Costello pieces" are concerned with writing,
feminism, animals, the status of the humanities, and much else besides, and,
even while affirming the key role of the literary in Coetzee's writing, one
may question whether there is a zero-sum game being played among these
concerns. There are indeed performative differences, as Attridge points out,
between the initial delivery of *The Lives of Animals* in a rather disconcerting
lecture format, its role as a novella accompanied by commentaries, and then
as a novel's chapters or "lessons" (in the more serio-parodic, didactic term).
But such pertinent considerations do not imply the need for a certain kind
of centering, an overly decisive division and hierarchical ordering of claims,
or a "transubstantiating" idea of "the literary," even if one recognizes the
great—indeed the transformative or performative—power of form that may
be particularly pronounced in literary writing.

Attridge refers to Cora Diamond, who is known as a feminist concerned
with the issue of animals and "animal rights." Attridge commends her as a
philosopher who is attuned to the primacy of the literary in literature, in
contrast to "most of the respondents in *The Lives of Animals*" who "take the
arguments as *arguments*" rather than as "*arguings*, utterances made by individuals in concrete situations" in a literary text that must be read above all
as literature conveying "the full ethical force of the fictions themselves"
(197–98). Of course, Coetzee is not making arguments on his own behalf
in an unmediated manner, and, while the opposition between arguments and
arguings may not resolve all problems, the positioning of the arguments in
the text is indeed a crucial formal issue.

The excessive emphasis on the literariness of the literary may undercut
the ethical and political import of the text, and it cannot control how a
reader will respond to it, including the reader who is sensitive to formal
issues, such as those bearing on the differences between author, narrator,
and character, along with the importance of how issues or arguments are
staged in a text, involving the voice, subject-position, and situation of those
making and responding to them. But it is altogether possible that a reader of
The Lives of Animals or *Elizabeth Costello* may take Costello's arguments, with
their hesitations, self-doubts, and self-disparagements, to be more forceful
and compelling than a rather restricted notion of the ethics of reading and

writing, especially when the latter is sharply set off or bracketed technically from the issues discussed in a text. And the Coetzee-narrator, along with Costello's son John, who plays the crucial role of focalizer (the character through whom other people, problems, entities, and so forth are seen), may seem unable to fully contain Elizabeth Costello, the pathos and power of her personality, and the force of her concerns if not her arguments.[41] Son John has manifest difficulties in containing and coming to terms with his mother, whom he both loves and finds exasperating. It is noteworthy that the ending of the story resonates with its beginning where the son awaits the arrival of the "aged," "flabby" mother. The story ends with these words: "They are not yet on the expressway. He pulls the car over, switches off the engine, takes his mother in his arms. He inhales the smell of cold cream, of old flesh. 'There, there,' he whispers in her ear. 'There, there. It will soon be over'" (69).

Is the son's gesture loving, patronizing, or both? In any case, with these words the novella is in fact over, and the reader in retrospect awaits its reincarnation in the novel *Elizabeth Costello*. The reader assumes that Costello's life will also soon be over. Is this ending too resonantly concordant, perhaps even a bit too facile in the nature of its self-referential turn?

One temptation offered by the insertion of *The Lives of Animals* into *Elizabeth Costello* is to read both texts predominantly, if not exclusively, as experiential feminist sagas of the woman writer and thereby lose sight of the issues that concern Costello, notably with respect to the lives of animals—the very issues that help to make her an imposing or at least discomfiting figure. I think this occurs in the decidedly anthropocentric passage from Cora Diamond that Attridge commends (even though for him the story is ultimately "about" the saga of the literary writer, particularly Coetzee himself):

[Elizabeth Costello] is a woman haunted by the horror of what we do to animals. We see her as wounded by this knowledge, this horror, and by the knowledge of how unhaunted others are. The wound marks her and isolates her. . . . So the life of this speaking and wounded and clothed animal is one of the "lives of animals" that the story is about; if it is true that we generally remain unaware of the lives of other animals, it is also true that, as readers of this story, we may remain unaware, as her audience does, of the life of the speaking animal at its center. . . . If we see in the lectures a wounded woman, one thing that wounds her is precisely the common and taken-for-granted mode of thought that 'how we should treat animals' is an 'ethical issue,' and the knowledge that she will be taken to be contributing, or intending to contribute, to discussion of it. (quoted 198)

One would have to be a particularly obtuse reader to remain unaware of "the life of the speaking animal" in *The Lives of Animals*. (Indeed Costello refers to herself as not "a philosopher of mind but an animal exhibiting, yet not exhibiting, to a gathering of scholars, a wound, which I cover up under my clothes but touch on in every word I speak" [70–71].) And I doubt that the understanding of the treatment of animals as an ethical issue constitutes a taken-for-granted mode of thought or that this mode of thought is one thing that particularly wounds Costello in comparison, say, with the way animals are in practice treated in factory farms, slaughterhouses, food consumption, and experimentation. But I may be wrong or perhaps sounding too much like Elizabeth Costello myself. In any event, I do think that centering attention on the experience of the "wounded woman" runs the risk of becoming diversionary. It underplays the widespread influence of feminist criticism, and it overplays the extent and influence of critical animal studies, including the constitution of the treatment of animals as an ethical as well as a political issue related in multiple ways to other issues, both feminist and ecological. There is also a danger in taking the witness for the victim, at least when it shifts attention from the victim and either becomes hyperbolic about the wounds of the witness or emphasizes them in a manner that may divert attention and concern from that to which the witness is in fact bearing witness. But the basic point, which warrants the greatest emphasis and cannot be repeated too often, is that gender is a crucial issue, but a zero-sum approach to the problems of the woman writer and the other-than-human animal is both unnecessary and self-defeating.[42]

In a brief talk on "The Novel Today," printed in 1988 in the small journal *Upstream* and not, to the best of my knowledge, reprinted in a collection,[43] Coetzee provides a synoptic statement of his conception of the relation between historical discourse and the novel. It is tempting but too simple to read it as a charter for radical constructivism and ironic, suspensive, aesthetic formalism, a reading that does not do justice to the contextual constraints under which it was written or the problem of its relation to Coetzee's novels and other critical writings. Indeed the tone of the talk is beleaguered in a manner reminiscent of the state of mind (but not the beliefs or convictions) of Elizabeth Costello, for Coetzee was being attacked for what some, including Nadine Gordimer, saw as apolitical, ahistorical, aesthetic escapism.[44] Coetzee responds with the assertive view that the novel and the discourse of history, as well as the discourse of politics which he construes as a "sub-discourse" of history (3), are essentially different. He sees historical discourse as colonizing the novel in South Africa at the time, and he positions the novel in a subaltern position as a minority force of resistance and rivalry in relation to history and politics (or their discourses). (His understanding of the relation of historical discourse and history is unclear, and he seems to see history only as a projective figure of historical discourse.) He also affirms a binary opposition between history and the novel in what may perhaps be understood in a contextual manner that seems to make his argument a response in an ongoing "dialogue" or heated exchange, but he expresses it in generalized if not absolute terms. He concludes by affirming (somewhat ungrammatically, at least in the printed transcription): "In particular, I do not see why the consent to be anyone's handmaiden, nor do I see why there should, here and now, or anywhere at any time, for the sake of anything, be agreed to be a moratorium on the kind of reservations I am expressing" (4–5). As intimated, the reservations are expressed in terms of a binary opposition whereby the novel "cannot be both autonomous and supplementary" (3). Yet his understanding of supplementarity seems conventional rather than Derridean, for it marks a position of stable subordination (as colonized other or as handmaiden). If one thinks of supplementarity in less stable, more relational, and mutually provocative terms, one might turn to a more generous both/and logic whereby one would indeed resist any subordination of the novel to historical discourse (or vice versa) but still argue for a (relative) autonomy of each and a supplementary relation between the two that itself could not be postulated as a simple fact but as an empirically variable relation and a normative project. In certain circumstances such a project might indeed involve a critique of a subordination of the novel to historical discourse, including the idea that the value of the novel is simply to offer a "feel" for experience and to fill in the gaps in the more "reliable" documentary record. One might also argue that the difference—or rather differences—between historical discourse and the novel are important, complex, and at times difficult to specify but not accept Coetzee's rather apodictic assertion that "difference is everything" (4). One might also agree that historical discourse (or historiography) is not tantamount or transparent to reality and that "the categories of history are not privileged just as the categories of moral discourse are not privileged" without conflating historical discourse and history or affirming an unqualified, anthropocentric, radical constructivism whereby "history is nothing but a certain kind of story that people agree to tell each other" (4). In any event, I doubt whether "The Novel Today" provides a sufficient basis for analyzing the relations between literature and history in Coetzee's own novels, notably including the ones I discuss here.

The Lives of Animals and Elizabeth Costello should of course be read together, and the similarities and differences between the two, including formal differences, deserve more extended treatment than I can offer. I would, however, point out that animals do not disappear in the other "lessons" or chapters of *Elizabeth Costello*. Indeed the first "lesson"—"Realism"—which treats the very problem of reality, history, and literary form—includes a veritable bestiary, with references (in noninvidious order of appearance) to the seal, Daisy Duck, the cat, the shark, the mouse, the goldfish, the (dying) whale, the steed, Mickey Mouse, the cockatoo, fish and fowl, the bitch in heat (with an allusion to Molly Bloom), the queen bee (another possible allusion to Molly Bloom), the lioness, the ape (unnamed Red Peter), the flea, the parrot, the dog, the hive (can the bee be far behind?), the monkey, the calf, the bird, the fish, and the python. Of course the list itself, in which I have just indulged, plays a prominent role in the discussion of realism in literature as a phenomenon that intensifies a sense of reality and may well disorient it.[45]

Coetzee employs realistic devices, is concerned with real problems, and periodically bares the realistic device. With a wry sense of humor, he almost parodically begins the first "lesson" with the problem of beginnings:

> There is first of all the problem of the opening, namely, how to get us from where we are, which is, as yet, nowhere, to the far bank. It is a simple bridging problem, a problem of knocking together a bridge. People solve such problems every day. They solve them, and having solved them push on.
>
> Let us assume that, however it may have been done, it is done. Let us take it that the bridge is built and crossed, that we can put it out of our mind. We have left behind the territory in which we were. We are in the far territory, where we want to be. (1)

Although it does not take him to the far territory, one bridge Coetzee has to consider is that from *The Lives of Animals* to *Elizabeth Costello*, and one of the things he does is to provide information about characters that was not available in the earlier work, for example, the exact birth date of Costello (1928), the fact that she has been married twice and that she has two children, one by each marriage. (This bridging information comes in the very paragraph that follows the two I quoted.) In the next paragraph we have a fictional fact that readers of *The Lives of Animals* already knew. Costello made her name with *The House on Eccles Street* (1969), here specified as her fourth novel, and we now learn that there is even an Elizabeth Costello Society, based in Albuquerque, New Mexico, which puts out the quarterly *Elizabeth Costello Newsletter*. (Would that this society existed, for, given its location, it would find in me a frequent visitor, even if I had to subscribe to its newsletter.)

"We skip," as Coetzee writes a couple of paragraphs later and quite a few times thereafter, as I shall have to begin skipping a great deal. I would simply observe in a lapidary fashion that Coetzee, in the texts on which I focus, attempts to bridge or to negotiate, at times playfully, the relations between historial/social/political reality and the literary, prominently including the formal, without being either reductive or binaristic. But, before turning to the novel's ending, I shall quote a few more passages that (as historians used to, and may still at times be wont to, say) almost seem to speak for themselves. First a passage in which there is a divergence between son John as focalizer and the Coetzee-narrator, who seems to be speaking or writing in his own "voice" or from his own situated subject-position (appropriately enough in light of the assertions in the quotation):

> Realism has never been comfortable with ideas. It could not be otherwise: realism is premised on the idea that ideas have no autonomous existence, can exist only in things. So when it needs to debate ideas, as here, realism is driven to invent situations—walks in the countryside, conversations—in which characters give voice to contending ideas and thereby in a certain sense embody them. The notion of *embodying* turns out to be pivotal. (9)

This passage does not imply full agreement on the part of the Coetzee-narrator, for what it omits is the work and play of the text, including the role of the narrator, in positioning and inflecting what is "embodied" in characters and situations. The next two passages bring, I think, fuller agreement between John as character or fictional narrator/focalizer and the Coetzee-narrator (as well as the "historical Coetzee"?). The first is from son John who objects to a restricted feminist reading of his mother's work, as he shares a postcoital bed with a woman scholar he has just gotten to know. He insists, via ostensibly rhetorical questions and with immediate misgivings about rhetorical appropriateness, that Costello is "now after bigger game . . . such as measuring herself against the illustrious dead. Such as paying tribute to the powers that animate her. For instance" (25–26). The second is from the lecture Costello herself delivers in this first "lesson," and it refers, with a telling self-referential twist, to Red Peter and to the story in which he appears, Kafka's "Report to an Academy":

> We don't know. We don't know and will never know, with certainty, what is really going on in this story: whether it is about a man speaking to men or an ape speaking to apes or an ape speaking to men or a man speaking to apes (though the last is, I think, unlikely) or even just

a parrot speaking to parrots. . . . The lecture hall itself may be nothing but a zoo. . . . I am not, I hope, abusing the privilege of this platform to make idle, nihilistic jokes about what I am, ape or woman, and what you are, my auditors. That is not the point of the story, say I, who am, however, in no position to dictate what the point of the story is. There used to be a time, we believe, when we could say who we were. Now we are just performers speaking our parts. The bottom has dropped out. We could think of this as a tragic turn of events, were it not that it is hard to have respect for whatever was the bottom that dropped out— it looks to us like an illusion now, one of those illusions sustained only by the concentrated gaze of everyone in the room. Remove your gaze for but an instant, and the mirror falls to the floor in shatters. (19–20)[46]

Of course, these words would not be accepted by many groups in the world, either today or in the past, and even those with "liberal" views and doubts about ultimate foundations, notably in the profession of anthropology, have recently been urging us to take seriously and respect expressions of religious belief and piety, however "fundamentalist" or particularistic they may seem.[47] Costello's words help to delimit a specific group, one that is indeed concerned with such issues as the literary and its bearing on "real-world" problems—one that may even have a more or less guarded interest in the so-called postsecular. The last quote I am about to offer is from son John and, particularly in its own postsecular skid, can be taken at best with a very large grain of salt. Indeed, John here suspiciously seeks closure, which he finds only in falling asleep, and his affirmation may be less earned than the one Coetzee objected to in Sebald.

Not all the monkeys in the world picking away at typewriters all their lives would come up with these words in this arrangement [to wit, the words "sleep that knits up the raveled sleeve of time"]. Out of the dark emerging, out of nowhere: first not there, then there, like a newborn child, heart working, brain working, all the processes of that intricate electrochemical labyrinth working. A miracle. He closes his eyes. (27)

Should one see this as an affirmation of the birth of the purely literary as a performative miracle that itself creates a decisive gap between man and monkey—an affirmation suspiciously having a sleep-inducing virtue and conveyed through a hackneyed reference to Shakespeare (who else?) as well as through an organic analogy to the birth of a child that did not exactly come out of nowhere?

"The Problem of Evil" (chapter 6) begins with a reference to the analogy Costello makes earlier between the Holocaust and the abuse of animals, specifically their treatment in slaughterhouses. It also refers to criticisms she received for making this analogy, for example in the pages of *Commentary*, for "belittling the Holocaust" (156). The chapter then turns to the lecture she is to give at a conference in Amsterdam, largely based on a discussion of Paul West's novel *The Very Rich Hours of Count von Stauffenberg*.[48] For Costello the novel is "obscene" and dangerous in the way it conveys evil by bringing the reader into the chamber where Hitler's executioner follows the Führer's command to excruciatingly torture and slowly strangle the officers who conspired to kill Hitler on July 20, 1944. For her, West dangerously and objectionably sympathizes with the Devil (or radical evil) in a manner that jeopardizes both the writer and the reader of his novel. ("Certain things are not good to read *or to write*. To put the point another way: I take seriously the claim that the artist risks a great deal by venturing into forbidden places; risks, specifically, himself; risks, perhaps, all. I take this claim seriously because I take seriously the forbiddenness of forbidden places. The cellar in which the July 1944 plotters were hanged is one such forbidden place" [173]).

In responding to this criticism, (the historical) Paul West (who, unlike his counterpart in Coetzee's novel, does not remain silent) argues for the necessity of a certain kind of rendition if one is to convey an event by "sympathizing, empathizing with the people who went through it," including perpetrators such as Hitler's executioner. He sees Coetzee not as agreeing with Costello but as making her "a sacrificial animal . . . carefully set up to be destroyed" in the novel.[49] West does not explicate what he means by a sympathetic, empathic rendition. But I think his view of Costello as Coetzee's "sacrificial animal" is problematic at best. One might rather argue that the relation of the Coetzee-narrator to Costello varies both from chapter to chapter and at times within chapters, with different degrees of critical, at times ironic distance, and proximity—proximity in terms of empathy or compassion that cannot be seen as tantamount to identification. (Here one has the question of what Costello herself means by the "sympathetic imagination." It is unclear whether it is equated with identification or allows for alterity.) In the chapter on "The Problem of Evil," the narrator by and large does not present Costello's view ironically but as something to be taken seriously (as she clearly takes it), although he notes, in a passage written in free indirect style, that "ineluctably she is arguing herself into the position of the old-fashioned censor" (165)—the very position she sees her sister Blanche, a rather dogmatic nun, as occupying in the preceding chapter (or, in another register, the position of Claude Lanzmann on Holocaust representation in general and trying to understand perpetrators in particular).[50] But I think the implication of Coetzee's figuration of Costello in this chapter is that, while her views on the rendition of radical evil in literature are not to be easily dismissed, her reading of West's novel is largely if not entirely projective (one way to read Costello's own reference to her making the book her own "by the madness of [her] reading" [174]) as well as to "an obsession that is hers alone and that he [West, whom Costello is surprised to find is a participant at the conference and in the audience at her lecture] clearly does not understand" (177). Costello herself reflects on her complicity as a person and as a writer in the accusation she addresses to Paul West: "a violence was done to her but she conspired in the violence" through her very act of "excited" reading (181). It is significant that she provides nothing approximating a close reading of West's novel or even of limited sections of it. She simply conveys in general terms her reader response unsupported by references to what the text of the novel does or does not do. My own reading of (or response to) West's novel, which will have to remain as schematic as Costello's, is that its portrayal of the executioner and his actions is in some sense empathic but not tantamount to identification, and certainly not a vicarious sharing of the type of malicious glee that Costello sees in her own abusive torturer, the longshoreman (Tim or Tom) who comes to react violently to her refusal of the sexual encounter she seems to have led him to believe would occur, indeed who appears to enjoy more his violence than he would have enjoyed sex with her (166–67).

In the last chapter (or lesson), which is followed by a postscript, Costello is on trial before the gate in what the text unkindly designates as "Kafka reduced and flattened to parody" (209). This scene is a dreamlike invocation, a kind of rejoinder to son John's intimation, concerning how it will soon end. To pass by the gate into whatever lies beyond it, Costello must give a confession before the board of examiners (as must David Lurie, in *Disgrace*, to be reinstated by the committee that examines him for conduct unbefitting a professor). Costello is nonplussed by this demand and unable to comply (as is Lurie). The only thing she can enigmatically testify to is a belief in frogs, and she finds that "her first impression was right: a court out of Kafka or *Alice in Wonderland*, a court of paradox" (223).[51]

Still, it is noteworthy that in the final chapter Costello seems significantly different from the person who is beleaguered but forceful in the "lessons" or chapters 3 and 4, printed separately as *The Lives of Animals*. She refuses adamantly to state her beliefs to the board of inquiry and instead modulates through many more or less indecisive reflections on belief, including an idea, both neoromantic and perhaps, in its linguistic turn, postmodernist, that she herself finds difficult to take seriously: the idea that she is simply the vehicle and amanuensis for higher powers that speak through her. Her indecision, which, contradicting the examining board, she refuses to see as confusion, seems most intense at what seems to be her encounter with death or its imaginary aftermath, and her appeal to frogs allows her to see something "she can believe in: the dissolution, the return to the elements; and the converse moment she can believe in too, when the first quiver of returning life runs through the body and the limbs contract, the hands flex" (320). Yet this appeal to death and what would seem to be mere life is a minimalist statement of belief at best. Earlier in the novel she did put forth quite strong beliefs (or convictions—at least concerns) about animals and the unacceptable ways they are treated in procedures such as slaughtering, factory farming, experimentation, and captivity in zoos.[52] Why does Costello before the gate not restate these "beliefs"? It might seem that her refusal or resistance marks her determination not to buckle under in the face of the board and to subordinate art to the demands of a censorious politics, going against the grain of her argument in chapter 6 and reminding one instead of David Lurie before his investigative board. Yet much in Coetzee indicates that the relation of art or literature to politics as well as to ethics cannot be reduced to the problem of censorship.

There is yet another twist to the tale in the final paragraph of the final chapter, where Elizabeth has a vision at the gate. "At the foot of the gate, blocking the way, lies stretched out a dog, an old dog, his lion-coloured hide scarred from innumerable manglings. . . . Beyond him is nothing but a desert of sand and stone, to infinity" (224). Costello does not trust her vision "in particular the anagram GOD-DOG. *Too literary*, she thinks again. A curse on literature!" The man behind the desk observes rather dryly and anticlimactically: "'All the time,' he says. 'We see people like you all the time'" (225). I would simply note Costello's impatience with turns that are too literary and the appearance of the dog center stage on the threshold between this side and the infinite desert on the far side beyond the gate. (I am tempted to read this scene as the parodic, immanent, deconstructive underside or counterstatement to the transcendentally oriented Abraham-and-Isaac story, where the typically forgotten, victimized sacrificed animal is situated offstage. This staging is followed by many commentators, including Kierkegaard.)[53]

The Postscript takes the form of a letter from Elizabeth, wife of Hofmannsthal's Lord Chandos, to Francis Bacon, stereotypical exemplar of empirical inquiry and a plain style. The letter could be read as a displaced plea or testimony in lieu of the confession that Elizabeth Costello refused to give to the board of examiners. Here Coetzee does approach rhetorical pyrotechnics along with a more subdued indication of possibilities beyond or at least alongside the type of melancholy and disempowerment often found in Sebald. The final words of Elizabeth C. to Lord Bacon are filled with pathos, even pathetic: "Drowning, we write out of our separate fates. Save us" (230). One expects no response to this call. Yet here are some of the penultimate words of Elizabeth C., in part addressed to her husband, Philip, Lord Chandos, not a Francis Bacon but someone whose own problems with language would make response at best unlikely.[54]

> All is allegory, says my Philip. Each creature is key to all other creatures. A dog sitting in a patch of sun licking itself, says he, is at one moment a dog and at the next a vessel of revelation. And perhaps he speaks the truth, perhaps in the mind of our Creator (*our Creator*, I say) where we whirl about as if in a millrace we interpenetrate and are interpenetrated by fellow creatures by the thousand. But how I ask you can I live with rats and dogs and beetles crawling through me day and night, drowning and gasping, scratching at me, tugging me, urging me deeper and deeper into revelation—how? *We are not made for revelation*, I want to cry out *nor I nor you, my Philip*, revelation that sears the eye like staring into the sun. (229)

It may be superfluous to add that a crucial question, which is at least one of the questions posed by Coetzee, is how to deal with problems in a world in which we find that we are not made for revelation.

It is questionable whether *Disgrace* provides more than tentative, exploratory answers to this question. It is perhaps to be read in good measure as a negative experiment that explores options that, at least with respect to its seemingly central character, David Lurie, do not appear to open onto possible ways of working through the past without denying or transcending it in quest of revelation. Lurie is a self-proclaimed disciple of William Wordsworth, but his heart leaps up when he beholds not so much rainbows in the sky or fields of daffodils fluttering and dancing in the breeze but instead pretty young women whose sight incites Eros to fire his aging loins.

In his *J. M. Coetzee and the Ethics of Reading*, Derek Attridge offers a reading of *Disgrace* that runs parallel to his reading of *Elizabeth Costello* and *The Lives of Animals*. In line with the recent turn to the postsecular, Attridge looks to "grace" as a "term present in a ghostly way through much of the text" (178). Grace "comes, if it comes at all, unsought, but the paradox of the theological concept of grace which I'm borrowing is that it is not a disincentive to good works, but a spur" (180). (The relation of grace to good works has been a hotly debated, even conflict-ridden issue. And can one simply borrow a theological concept?) The "ghostly" presence of grace presumably indicates that "a political challenge [is] staged in this novel, and in all Coetzee's novels to date . . . to find a way of building a new, just state that is not founded on the elimination of unpredictability, singularity, excess. . . . We might call it, should it ever come into existence, a state of grace" (191).

Attridge does not explicate how unpredictability, singularity, and excess contribute to "a new, just state" or "a state of grace." Would anything like a just state involve, say, unpredictability in health care or excess in the accumulation of wealth, with an increasing gap between rich and poor? If so, in the United States we are at least on the verge of a just state or even a state of grace. And what does singularity—and especially the stress on singularity—entail?[55] Attridge would seem to be working on a grand scale if not invoking quasi-transcendental notions of unpredictability, singularity, and excess that could be argued to elude my more terre-à-terre questions. But the further issue is how such notions evoke religious genealogies and bear on political and historical issues as well as on Coetzee's texts. A state of grace might be suggested by what may well be a prevalent, straightforward, sacrificial if not redemptive reading of the final scene of *Disgrace* in which Lurie offers up a crippled dog. It may also be suggested by Elizabeth Costello's assertion that she is vegetarian not from moral conviction but from "a desire to save [her] soul" (*Lives of Animals*, 89). But her response may be somewhat ironic as a rejoinder to an ingratiating but inquisitive questioner, the president at Appleton College where her son teaches and she gives a lecture and seminar on animals (evoking a self-referential allusion to Coetzee giving the Tanner lectures at Princeton).[56]

Although Attridge does not go in this direction, it is interesting to note that unpredictability, singularity, and excess, notably in modes that resist symbolization and representation, have been widely taken to characterize trauma, which has also been seen by some commentators as a modality of sublime experience if not of a state of grace.[57] One could also discuss the trio or trinity Attridge finds constitutive of a just state or even of a state of grace in terms that suggest other possibilities than those he stresses. In one sense, singularity might be seen as signifying the inescapable responsibility of the ethical agent that cannot be transferred to another. In Kierkegaard such responsibility was related to the ultimate vis-à-vis with the Hidden God and escaped or was in excess of any "Hegelian" dialectic. Hence singularity need not be taken to be identical with but rather in excess of particularity in relation to universality.

Singularity might also be construed as bound up with a call or address that is directed at the singular being, even if one brackets the issue of the source of the call, including a source such as the totally other or the Hidden God. Whether the call reduces to relative insignificance the role of more communal and institutional relations, for example, in a church or some other existential group, is a moot issue, although Kierkegaard himself arguably saw the religious and in certain respects the aesthetic but not the ethical as beyond the aegis of normatively regulated social relations. Moreover, Abraham's decision to sacrifice Isaac was not an ethical but a supra-ethical decision that placed a religious command before or beyond the ethical relation. It was "mad" but in a way that also raised the possibility that Abraham was mad and misread that madness as a sign of a word sent by God. The prior question, especially for a nonbeliever, is whether what is taken to be the religious relation should preempt or be conflated with the ethical one (for example, in terms of grace or gratuitous generosity). In still another but perhaps not unrelated sense, singularity conjoined with unpredictability and excess might be taken as pointing to original sin and the "fall" understood as the basis of imperfectability in the human being, a perspective at least tentatively affirmed by Coetzee himself. This view gives a traumatic event an originary status with respect to the human, although (as with the Lacanian real) it may be construed not mythically as a punctual event but as a reiterated dimension of at least every excessive "sin" or transgression.

A further issue is what exactly constitutes the disgrace and its source. The novel seems to be structured around a series of "disgraces" that in important ways remain multivalent and do not imply either a lost or a future saving grace, particularly one achieved through redemptive sacrifice, abjection, and victimization. Indeed the novel contains many indeterminate or suggestive dimensions that the reader is tempted to fill in with a determinate or specific interpretation or even referent (for example, the extent to which the novel is about contemporary South Africa in general or the controversial Truth and Reconciliation Commission in particular, the status of Melanie as "coloured" person or Jew, the precise rationale of Lurie's response to the committee of inquiry, the true reasons for Lucy's determination to stay on the farm, what exactly Petrus stands for, and so forth—issues that do not receive definite resolution). There is, of course, the background disgrace of apartheid, which is not explicitly discussed although it is a pervasive object of allusion. It hovers like a cloud over the events of the novel and problematically manifests itself in key incidents. There is also David Lurie's position as a disgraced professor, a failed husband and father, and a seemingly washed-out scholar who turns to composing a rather confused opera based on Byron's forlorn lover, the ample and aging Teresa (notably her "cat-on-a-roof," erotic arias [185] along with the "so-hot" plaint of Byron's neglected daughter Allegra)—an opera that in all probability will never be brought to completion. But Lurie refuses to recognize the "disgrace" imputed to him because of his affair with a student, at least in the terms demanded by members of the university committee of inquiry. He especially rejects all talk of repentance or confession and insists on a purely secular framework, thereby opening his gesture to a reading as an implicit critique of the Judeo-Christian discourse infusing the Truth and Reconciliation Commission and the emphatic, uplifting words of Bishop Desmond Tutu. He even refers to professors as "clerks in a post-religious age" (4), although a parareligious or postsecular age might be a more fitting term. Indeed, the quasi-religious cloak or shroud that has descended on the professor is one thing that Lurie's reaction, so problematic in other respects, helps to demystify. His only mock-confessional scene with respect to his student Melanie takes place with her pontificating father and embarrassed yet compliant mother, and, given his overly theatrical prostration and its recipients, it is difficult to take it as a serious act of contrition or even apology rather than as an ironic, even narcissistic, gesture (171–74). It might even be read as another parody of the quest for "truth and reconciliation."

The TRC and those involved in it are never mentioned in the novel, but it is an obvious if problematic allusion. There is of course no one-to-one corre-lation between the TRC and the committee of inquiry in *Disgrace*. Both have their internal conflicts and differences in orientation that go in somewhat different directions, in part because of the different kind of problem each addresses, with the accusation of "human rights abuse" in the case of Lurie and Melanie seeming to be an exaggeration and perhaps a critique or parody of "human rights discourse" both in the TRC and in general.[58] The "severest penalty" (51) and "a statement that comes from the heart" and will "express contrition" (54)—in Lurie's eyes a demand for "confessions, apologies [and] abasement" (56)—are demanded by Farodia Rassool with the apparent sup-port of other, less assertive women members of the committee.[59] The men on the committee investigating Lurie seem largely concerned with finding a compromise that will allow him to keep his position at the university (hardly comparable to the TRC's seemingly impossible quest to find a way to keep a society together after the fall of an oppressive regime, traumatic violence, and internecine conflict). As Desmond Swarts puts it: "We would like to find a way for you to continue with your career." In a manner that perhaps indicates that the color line is not an issue for the men on the committee, Swarts is echoed by Easily Hakim: "We would like to help you, David, to find a way out of what must be a nightmare." Lurie remarks: "In this chorus of goodwill . . . I hear no female voice" (52). In response to Lurie's rhetorical question asking if the committee has "in mind a ban on intimacy across the generations," Swarts offers perhaps the most sober and apposite response: "No, not necessarily. But as teachers we occupy positions of power. Perhaps a ban on mixing power relations with sexual relations" (52–53)—a ban that would extend beyond the teacher-student relation in ways Swarts may not envision.

The final resolution of the committee requires from Lurie an acknowledgement "without reservation [of] serious abuses of the human rights of the complainant, as well as abuse of the authority delegated to [him] by the University" along with a sincere apology and an acceptance of "whatever appropriate penalty may be imposed" (57). He adamantly rejects this "package" with an array of rationales and motivations that include a formal-legal demand to play by the book whereby he would plead "guilty of the charges brought against me" (54) without concern for the specific nature of the charges, a neo-perhaps mock-romantic-existential appeal to the "rights of desire" and the call of Eros, the seeming arrogance of the obdurate if not atomistic individual against the hypostatized "institution" (shades of Ayn Rand among others, including Meursault, the protagonist in Camus's *L'Étranger*), and perhaps what the French would term a generalized "je m'en foutisme." On leaving the inquiry, he responds to the question of a girl with a recorder ("Are you sorry?") with a quip that makes its way into the student newspaper: "I was enriched by the experience" (56).

From a historical perspective, the novel provides at best only a rather sketchy, dire picture of postapartheid South Africa, especially in rural regions. Lurie himself soon recognizes the suspect pathos in his responses to the committee and even intimates that he was looking for a way out of his teaching position, which he did not find to his liking. His expulsion from the university is also the pretext or perhaps the subtext of his attempt to renew contact with his daughter, as perhaps may have been his affair with his student Melanie. The final, blatantly incestuous, somewhat bemused sexual scene with Melanie takes place in Lurie's daughter's bed (29). One may also note that Lurie's initial way to have "solved the problem of sex" (1) with another woman of color, the seemingly pliable but ultimately inflexible Soraya, part-time prostitute and full-time mother and wife, comes crashing down when, to her chagrin, he forces her two separate worlds to collide—a kind of premonitory playing out of what he later sees as a clash of civilizations with respect to the rape of his daughter—a rape that may also cast a dark shadow back on his constrained, exploitative relation to Melanie.

Lurie's daughter Lucy is like David in not accepting her seeming disgrace that is a disgrace largely in Lurie's own rather self-centered eyes. Lucy insists that her rape is a private affair that she will keep secret and handle in her own way. As she puts it: "As far as I am concerned, what happened to me is a private matter. In another time, in another place, it might be held to be a public matter. But in this place, at this time, it is not. It is my business, mine alone." She specifies: "This place being South Africa" (112). To David (she never calls him father) Lucy says: "You don't understand what happened to me that day. . . . Because you can't" (157). Lucy's statement is not purely descriptive but performative—an assertion that she refuses even the possibility of understanding from Lurie.

Lucy is raped by blacks who appear suddenly on her farm, with the apparent knowledge if not complicity of Petrus, her steward, soon to be her landlord. Petrus (like Lucy and Lurie himself) will also not admit to what another demands: that, as Lurie insists, an unjust act—indeed an outrage, however much historically conditioned that act may be—has been committed and must be punished or even avenged. The black rapists, however, remain cardboard figures who suddenly appear and disappear but are not developed as characters with a sociopolitical and personal history or a present. They are perceived from the narrow perspective of Lurie who is, in one important sense, not only a father reduced to impotence and incapable of protecting his daughter (perhaps in his own eyes his most pronounced disgrace) but a stereotypical white man who wants to protect a white woman from stereotypical black men figured as rapists. The rape by blacks might even be read as a reversed enactment of the kind of outrages by white offenders under apartheid, offenders often not brought before the TRC for a variety of complex reasons.

With respect to the rape of his daughter, Lurie on a personal level is close to the point of confession: "'And?' Her [Lucy's] voice is now a whisper. 'And I did nothing to save you.' That is his own confession" (157). One may note the shift from quotation to the narrative voice, but here, as at times elsewhere, Lurie's and the narrator's voices seem to be in the closest proximity. Lurie is himself victimized and traumatized by his treatment at the rapists' hands, locked in a bathroom with his hair set on fire. Socially and politically, however, he construes the rape in terms of a clash of civilizations.

The boy, Pollux, who accompanies the two black men turns out to be Petrus's young brother-in-law and is presented as disturbed and vengeful to the point of genocidal desire in relation to whites, after he is struck by Lurie for peeping at Lucy (207). Petrus is ostensibly the new black South African on the rise who is turning the tables on the whites in a strategy of reversal whereby he will come out on top. He offers to make Lucy his third wife and provide protection—an offer she, to the horror of her father, is inclined to accept. ("'This is not how we do things.' *We*: he [Lurie] is on the point of saying, *We Westerners*" [202].)

Lucy is, however, an enigmatic figure, partially developed as a character yet with a blank silence at her core. She is a lesbian, but this fact plays little role in the novel and remains underdetermined, even a kind of enigmatic, floating signifier, at most something that presumably marks her out as a better rape victim than a virgin. She has returned to the land and is, in Lurie's eyes, letting herself go—a kind of earth mother figure, who is becoming "ample" if not heavy (paralleling Byron's Teresa in Lurie's opera), even going to seed in a gesture that may indicate the subsidence of culture into nature or even the way her rape symbolizes the rape of the land in South Africa. She bears the name of the first woman—not Eve but Lucy—whose remains were discovered in Africa in 1974. She asserts herself against her self-centered father who can see the rape only through his own eyes and in his own terms:

> You behave as if everything I do is part of the story of your life. You are the main character, I am a minor character who doesn't make an appearance until halfway through. [One may have here a little self-referential gesture, although Lucy appears about a quarter and not half-way through the novel.] Well, contrary to what you think, people are not divided into major and minor. I am not minor. I have a life of my own, just as important to me as yours is to you, and in my life I am the one who makes the decisions. (198)[60]

Yet Lucy's self-affirmation seems to involve not only the acknowledgment of vulnerability but the acceptance, even the affirmation, of abjection and exposure to the risk of repeated rape, which she even sees as perhaps "the price one has to pay for staying on" in South Africa (158). Despite the possible sacrificial interpretation of her words, it is significant that she does not appeal to the vocabulary of either salvation or grace in commenting on her attitude toward the rape and its aftermath. She is most disturbed by the "personal hatred" (156) acted out in her rape and, bloodied by it (we are not told why there is blood), even conjectures that "maybe, for men, hating the woman makes sex more exciting," even making sex "a bit like killing" (158). Lurie admits to himself that, with respect to the rape, "he can, if he concentrates, if he loses himself, be there, be the men, inhabit them, fill them with the ghost of himself. The question is, does he have it in him to be the woman?" (160). At this point for Lurie, as for Lucy, the blackness of the rapists is not at issue, only their maleness.

Lucy is convinced that what Petrus wants from her is not sex but property, and, in a sense, she is willing to insert herself into the social structure that Petrus represents. Yet she, as a white woman, is also a disruptive force in the new South African countryside. She is supported in her determination to stay on the land and keep her secret by her white friend, the ostensibly unattractive Bev (with whom Lurie, almost in spite of himself, has an affair).[61] Lucy is also determined to keep the baby resulting from the rape and not to have (we learn in passing) another abortion (198). But we never hear from Petrus's first wife, who remains another stereotypical figure without a voice or a point of view.

It might well be misleading to construe Lucy's assertion of privacy as an affirmation of the essential unrepresentability or absolute resistance to symbolization of her trauma insofar as this interpretive gesture would divert attention from the historical conditions and constraints to which the rape attests, possibly converting it into an avatar of the transhistorical "real" if not an emblem of the (negative) sublime. Without implying the expectation that one can fully express or overcome what occurs in a traumatic experience such as rape, one might maintain that Lucy's sense of privacy, as she herself intimates, is public in that it is situated in a specific context and points to a social crisis marked by the unavailability of interlocutors who would be empathic witnesses—interlocutors clearly not to be found in the police or even in the courts where her rape might be symbolically repeated in intrusive forms of interrogation, although she does have an interlocutor in her friend Bev, with whom she has apparently discussed the rape. In a sense, she may find other "interlocutors" or witnesses in her renewed relations with animals. (The large dogs she boarded, reminiscent of those trained to keep blacks in line, are shot by her rapists.) We do not know about the aftermath of her life on the farm and whether she is prey to repeated rape or to continuing post-traumatic symptoms, such as her sleeplessness and thumb-sucking, which she may or may not find ways of attempting to work through.

The rape and its aftermath serve to drive Lurie and Lucy further apart, and there is no "truth and reconciliation" in adversity even between victims who are father and daughter but who are also situated differentially in a problematic history of oppression. At one point they seem to share a sense of humiliation if not disgrace, although they perceive it very differently.

'How humiliating,' he says finally. 'Such high hopes, and to end like this.'

'Yes, I agree, it is humiliating. But perhaps that is a good point to start from again. Perhaps that is what I must learn to accept. To start

at ground level. With nothing. Not with nothing but. With nothing.
No cards, no weapons, no property, no rights, no dignity.'
   'Like a dog,'
   'Yes, like a dog.' (205)

Even if one moots the question of seeing oneself as utterly abject and the
idea of trauma or catastrophe as entailing a nihilating, ground-zero, apocalyptic attempt to begin again—themes that themselves are not unfamiliar
within the Judaic and Christian traditions and their contemporary avatars
(including Agamben's and Žižek's treatment of the *Muselmann*)—why see
the dog as a being without dignity? And why has Lurie earlier both appealed
to the threadbare traditional topos that differentiates between human
and animal in terms of the ability anxiously to envision death and even referred to humans as "a different order of creation . . . not higher, necessarily,
just different" (74)—in a context where difference always seems to entail
invidiousness? These questions bring up another disgrace broached in the
novel, the disgraceful treatment of other animals. This issue is for Lurie concentrated in the way in which dogs killed in shelters are disposed of. Lucy's
own view of animals belies her momentary polemical acceptance in heated
argument of the dog as the prototype of a being without dignity, and Lurie
himself will at least problematize his earlier radical separation of human and
other animals.

Lucy has sent Lurie to her friend Bev to assist her in her attempt to
ease the death of unwanted dogs. And it is in this context that Lurie seems
to feel emotion that has not been evident in him to that point. He comes
to realize, at least to some extent, that the decisive differentiating criteria
invoked to separate the human from the animal are illusory. He observes,
for example, that "the dogs in the yard smell what is going on inside. They
flatten their ears, they droop their tails, as if they too feel the disgrace of
dying" (143). But it remains unclear whether he shows compassion for
other animals or instead identifies with the dogs in a manner that remains
self-centered. In any case, he tries to save "the honour of corpses" (146) by
burning the dogs instead of leaving them in a garbage heap and subjecting
them to a compacting process. But he refuses to name a dog with a with-
ered hindquarter to whom he has become attached and to whom Bev refers as *Driepoot* (215). Here one is led to question the quasi-transcendental
correlation of naming with violence, for it would be difficult not to read
the refusal to name as a disavowal of bonding and commitment as well
as a prevalent way of facilitating the killing of another being. Here not
naming is a prelude to violence. Moreover, it is difficult to see how the

dog, without a name and a burial site, can be mourned. One may add that Lurie, in his narcissistic outrage, is unable to work through his daughter's rape and his humiliation. He does extend himself by intervening in the way dead dogs are treated, especially the practice of beating with shovels the bags containing rigidified bodies to make them more convenient for processing. Yet the act of incineration is itself at best equivocal since it does not lead to gathering the ashes and mourning the loss of the animals. Indeed the term surprisingly used for killing the dogs is *Lösung*, which recalls not only Nazi euphemisms in general but particularly *Endlösung*, the "final solution."

The ending of *Disgrace* invites a reading of it in postsecular terms as a sacrificial gesture—indeed as a quest for redemption (*Erlösung* in German) or even a state of grace:

> He opens the cage door. 'Come,' he says, bends, opens his arms. The dog wags its crippled rear, sniffs his face, licks his cheeks, his lips, his ears. He does nothing to stop it. 'Come.'
>
> Bearing him in his arms like a lamb, he re-enters the surgery. 'I thought you would save him for another week,' says Bev Shaw. 'Are you giving him up?'
>
> 'Yes, I am giving him up.' (220)

Both in terms of the text and even in larger ethical and political terms, does Lurie have the right to these final words? As he recognizes, the dog is not his. Hence the obvious inference, which he does not draw, is that the dog is not his to give up. Still absorbed in his "I" both as possible short-term savior and as sacrificial "giver," he seems to situate himself in a beckoning, quasi-sacrificial bystander position, with the dog analogized to a lamb. There is no intimation of where he goes from there, although one cannot anticipate anything promising. An ending wherein he names (or accepts a name) and takes the dog with him would have indicated a type of concern for the animal that was not entirely self-centered. The name "tripod" is already available. In making this point, one imagines the possibility of a significant modification in David Lurie but need not expect miracles, operatic epiphanies, or uplifting passages into a redemptive beyond (or, for that matter, a sacrificial state of grace). Lurie, in "giving up" the dog, also seems to be giving up on himself, perhaps giving up, period. (Is he also giving up on the future of South Africa?)

But, instead of rewriting the ending in a way that might seem gratuitous or petulant, perhaps it would be preferable to offer a counter-reading of it not as a straightforward valorization or endorsement of a sacrificial gesture but as a figuration of that gesture in a stereotypical form that makes its insubstantiality and ineffectiveness almost self-evident. In other words, the ending might be read not as a validation but as a critique or at least a questioning of sacrifice, especially in the setting in which it occurs in this text.[62] Here one might also recall the insistently nonsacrificial and nonanthropocentric words of Lucy before Lurie invokes the very Christian idea of different orders of creation—Lucy's words that shed another light on her allusion to the dog as lacking dignity and may remind one of both Elizabeth Costello and Elizabeth Chandos: "There is no higher life. This is the only life there is. Which we share with animals. That's the example that people like Bev try to set. That's the example I try to follow. To share some of our human privileges with the beasts. I don't want to come back in another existence as a dog or a pig and have to live as dogs or pigs do under us" (74).[63]

CHAPTER 4

Historical and Literary Approaches to the "Final Solution"

Saul Friedländer and Jonathan Littell

In what some may see as an unorthodox move, I propose to discuss together two recent prize-winning works of epic proportions that have received much attention: Saul Friedländer's two-volume historical study *Nazi Germany and the Jews*[1] and Jonathan Littell's novel *Les Bienveillantes*,[2] the former of which focuses on victims and the latter on perpetrators of the "final solution." I do not maintain that these works are exemplars of historical and literary approaches to the Nazi genocide. Yet they are two significant instances of such approaches, each of which has been successful with both professional commentators and the general reading public. The acclaim among professional historians for Friedländer's masterwork has been more widespread than has the nonetheless impressive, often positive reception of Littell's novel, and quite a few historians have seen Friedländer as innovative in literary as well as historiographical ways. Still, Littell's novel has had a broader array of professional commentators, including historians and literary critics as well as psychoanalysts and journalists, among others. It was a cause célèbre in France, where it received two important literary prizes, and it has been translated into many languages.[3]

Although it contains enormous quantities of historical documentation, Littell's novel is an ambitious literary undertaking that cuts across many genres: the fictional memoir, testimony, the historical novel, the literature of excess and radical transgression, traumatic realism or even hyperrealism, the picaresque, and the grotesque. In contrast to certain appreciations of Friedländer's work, those praising Littell's do not, to the best of my knowledge, make claims for formal innovations in the novel but look instead to its employment of existing orientations, especially in terms of their application to the perspective of the perpetrator as narrator and to the integration of historical processes.[4] One issue is the extent to which Littell's novel may itself be seen as an insufficiently framed (or excessively participatory) writing or even acting out of phantasms with respect to Dr. Maximilien Aue, a relatively upper-level but not quite inner-circle Nazi and SS officer, who is also a "passive" homosexual. Aue, Littell's first-person narrator-protagonist, attains the same rank as Eichmann (*Obersturmbannführer* or lieutenant-colonel), but his motivation and psychology appear to be more complicated than the latter's. Indeed, Aue ruminates extensively and engages the reader in a dialogic relation from the very outset, or rather a manipulative, pseudodialogic relation aimed at generating complicity and even subordination rather than critical exchange (somewhat similar to Nazi policy toward certain Jews such as members of Jewish councils). He even wants to evoke an identification in the reader whereby the latter acknowledges that, in Aue's position and historical context, he or she would have been led to commit the same atrocities. ("I am guilty, you are not, that's fine. But all the same you ought to be able to say to yourself that what I did, you would have done as well" [26].)

One may recall a comment made by Saul Friedländer before the publication of his *Nazi Germany and the Jews*, concerning Himmler's October 1943 Posen speech, which complicates one's understanding of Eichmann as well as other elite perpetrators and committed Nazis (a comment that has certain echoes in Aue's remarks concerning abyssal excess):

> Here, the perpetrators do not appear anymore as bureaucratic automata, but rather as beings seized by a compelling lust for killing on an immense scale, driven by some kind of extraordinary elation in repeating the killing of ever-huger masses of people (notwithstanding Himmler's words about the difficulty of this duty). Suffice it to remember the pride of numbers sensed in the Einsatzgruppen reports, the pride of numbers in Rudolf Höss's autobiography; suffice it to remember Eichmann's interview with Sassen: he would jump with glee into his grave knowing that over five million Jews had been exterminated; elation created by the staggering dimension of the killing, by the endless rows of victims. The elation created by the staggering number of victims ties in with the mystical *Führer*-Bond: the greater the number of Jews exterminated, the better the *Führer*'s will has been fulfilled.[5]

Does Littell, at least as implied author, identify with Aue, his admiration for bureaucratic efficiency, and his excesses? One cannot ascribe views expressed in Aue's narration, or his various desires and initiatives, directly to Littell, even as implied author, but Litell's relation to them is at best unclear or ambiguous. In interviews he maintains that he based Aue largely on himself, and he does so in terms that seem to conflate empathy with identification. As Littell states in response to the question "How did you prepare to get inside Max's head?": "I drew on my own way of seeing things. I based him mostly on myself, not anybody else."[6] Even if taken as a hyperbolic provocation, this assertion is noteworthy because Littell in interviews is a novelist who reflects critically on his own writing practice.

In an exchange with Peter Scowen, Littell refers to his own experience of extreme, traumatic events and draws from it dire and seemingly fatalistic conclusions:

After university and a stint as a literary translator, Littell joined an international aid organization that did work in Bosnia, Chechnya, Afghanistan and other war zones. "I went to Bosnia when I was 26 and I quickly figured out this is what the world is like, and whatever I do or think or hope or whatever is just completely irrelevant to all that," he says.

"It doesn't mean you shouldn't do things well. I deeply believe that when you do something, you should do it as well as possible within your capacities. But if you do look at the world around us, it's pretty awful. So one should do justice to that."[7]

In another comment, Littell contestably asserts:

In general I am much less interested in victims than I am in perpetrators. That's because they are the ones who are doing something and changing the reality. It's very easy to understand the victim: Something terrible happens to him and he reacts accordingly. But in terms of trying to understand something, there is nothing to examine. The perpetrator is more complicated to understand, along with the apparatus that activates him. By means of the attempt to give a voice to the perpetrator, lessons can be learned that will affect the way we look at the world today.[8]

As Littell himself elaborates in an interview where he rejects the analogy between his work and Tolstoy's *War and Peace*, his access to that "awful" world takes a specifically literary turn:

There is the concept of literary space explored by Maurice Blanchot. When you're inside it, you never know that you are. You can be sure you're writing "literature" but actually fall short, or be tormented by doubts although literature has long been present. A book by a crazy person can prove to be literature when that of a great writer is not, for ambiguous and hard to explain reasons. One is always full of doubt. One doesn't know [. . .]

A book is an experience. A writer asks questions as he tries to make his way through the darkness. Not towards the light, but further into the darkness, to arrive at a darkness even darker than his starting place. It is most certainly not the creation of a preconceived object. Which is why I have to write in one go. Writing is a throw of the dice. You never know what's going to happen when you write.[9]

One may perhaps see in this alluringly perplexing, risk-laden, albeit by now rather familiar notion of literature an evocation of sublime awe and an uncanny entry into a heart of darkness. In a conversation with his editor, the writer Richard Millet, Littell expands on his relation to Georges Bataille and Maurice Blanchot:

Blanchot, for me, is inseparable from Bataille. I read the two together. I came to Blanchot through Bataille, as did many. If there are two authors who truly define my way of thinking [façon de penser], of writing and of seeing things, it is principally these two. . . . It is these three [with the addition of Samuel Beckett] who pose the question of exigency in literature and what for me is crucial.[10]

In trenchant terms having a tense relation to his own problematic attempt to integrate historical processes into his novel, Littell sets forth his dichotomous understanding of the "domains" of history and politics in contrast to that of literature:

Here one has the fundamental cleavage between the domains of history and politics, on one side, and on the other, that of literature. When one is in life, thus eventually in history and politics, one is entirely in the domain of necessary compromise. Literature is the other side. It is the absolute escape hatch where one can find oneself again in the domain of limitless desire. One is alone, thus one does what one likes, in literature. One is again, as when one was an infant, free to indulge [exaucer] all one's desires, in a fashion that is certainly virtual, through writing, but all the same to do so.[11]

While Friedländer, as we shall see, insists on the voices of victims as bearing witness, Littell presents the perpetrator as witness and understands the articulation of his narration in terms of punctuating voice, especially the voice of the perpetrator.[12] It is striking that, with respect to his dichotomy between history and literature, Littell has a quasi-transcendental conception of the exigency of the literary in terms of the absolute, limitlessness, and entering further into a darkness, a darkness that may in fact be accentuated, not clarified or mitigated, by a superabundance of minute, at times recondite historical documentation. This approach relates to his idea of what is most distinctive about the historiography of Nazism and the genocide: "the more one *knows*, the more the obscurity [or dark side: *la part d'ombre*—perhaps evoking Blanchot's *La part du feu* or Bataille's *La part maudite*, both published in 1949] becomes impenetrable."[13] Littell seems to relish this apparent paradox, as he relishes the obscurely ambiguous relation or *"zone d'ombre"* between himself and his Nazi narrator Aue.

Of course, at least in terms of critical literary and historical reading, the more important question is not Littell's intentions or self-understanding, however arresting they may be. It is rather how the text does what it does and whether its way of doing—its *façon de faire*—has a significantly critical dimension. For example, does the text construct or figure Aue in ways that offer spaces where some perspective other than the narrator's may emerge and invite or allow for questions to be posed to the perpetrator's more or less complex orientation? Are there textual markers or procedures that provide the reader with critical distance that signals the way complicity with the first-person narrator may be resisted, disrupted, or overcome?[14]

There are some markers, but they may not be sufficient to counteract effectively the ways the text brings about the complicity of the reader, in effect saying, "there but for the grace of a different context go you." The text may even appear to write, if not act out, phantasms rather than situate them in a manner that offers critical perspective on them. As Julia Kristeva aptly observes: "The absence of distance between the narrator and the perpetrator [*le bourreau*] makes it difficult, if not impossible, to locate the least distance in relation to the anti-Semitic and nihilistic universe, while the feminine position of Max, victimized and magnified, attenuates the sadism of the perpetrator that he is: the insolently pathetic drag queen [in English in the original] makes one forget the SS. And the whole contributes to miming the grip of Nazi ideology on the reader, in modern times uninhibited, even if he ferrets out certain unconscious psychosexual keys."[15] I would add that an easily overlooked but crucial point is that Littell offers scant opportunity for victims to speak or even for exchanges between Nazis and Jews (say, in the context of Jewish councils), thus adopting in Aue's narration the Nazi unilateral objectification and appropriation of the persecuted other who remains silenced and obscure or obfuscated. (Here the contrast with Friedländer is pronounced.)

Context and circumstance are important. And one may argue that understanding perpetrators is important epistemologically, ethically, and politically, including the "empathic" recognition of possible ways one may be inclined to engage in extreme acts. But there is a difference between two orientations: on the one hand, acknowledging the possibility of one's own involvement in perpetration along with the fact that one can never be fully confident about how one might respond to certain situations, and, on the other hand (what I find more pronounced in Littell), universalizing and essentializing historically specific conditions by presenting Aue as everyman.[16]

There are aspects of *Les Bienveillantes* that may plausibly be read as alienation effects that would signal the possible role of self-questioning and serve to frame the narrative in a critical way. Aue as narrator is blatantly implausible and has been aptly termed a Zelig figure who seems to have participated in virtually every major incident of the war and the genocide. One may also see a kind of alienation effect in the extremity of his sexual "perversions" and the excess with which he acts out phantasms. Notable in this respect is his incestuous *passage à l'acte* with his twin sister Una and then, once she and their mother block further sexual relations, Aue's own "passive" homosexual, hyperbolically promiscuous performances, identifying with his lost love, and finally enacting a masturbatory *Walpurgisnacht* in the house his sister has left before he tries to rescue her from the invading Russian army. Yet even Aue's erotic excesses, such as sodomizing and bloodying himself with the branch of a tree during his extravaganza at Una's house, do little to unsettle or question the stereotype of the "passive," even self-punitive homosexual or its correlation with Nazism. It is difficult to suppress the feeling that there must be a sense in which one is encountering a distorted joke, a *canular* that is peculiar or ludicrous. The burlesque seems to be at play in a scene near the end of the novel where Aue finally meets Hitler in his bunker and is awarded a medal (880–81). During the ceremony he is disgusted by Hitler's fetid breath and bites the *Führer*'s nose (a gesture toned down in the original French version in which Aue "tweaks" [*pince*] the nose and that Littell insisted be restored to "bites" in all translations). This scene of course recalls many burlesque scenarios involving Hitler, from Charlie Chaplin to Mel Brooks. Yet the scene accentuates even further the hyperbolic excesses that are more ecstatically sordid and gruesomely grotesque than ambivalently carnivalesque (or, if one prefers, more in the manner of Bataille than of Bakhtin).[17] Aue states that he is unable to say why he bit Hitler's nose, but, immediately before his *passage à l'acte*, he is almost scandalized when he perceives the nose as non-Aryan, "Slav or Bohemian, almost Mongolo-ostic" (880–81). From all appearances (and with all-too-obvious psychoanalytic implications), Aue bites Hitler's nose to cut it down to size because it does not look sufficiently Aryan.

For the most part, Aue's narration is dead serious or at times cynical and ironic, even (in the eyes of fellow Nazis) idealistic, in a fashion that is by turns self-centered, dryly factual, blasé, or occasionally disconcerted about engaging in genocidal behavior with one's eyes wide open. Charged by Himmler, after the German defeat at Stalingrad in the winter of 1942–3, to inquire into conditions in the camps, he harbors doubts about the efficacy of killing or starving inmates whose labor was necessary for the war effort. He also takes refuge in reading, sharing Littell's tastes, for example, Blanchot, "plunging into this other world, entirely made up of light and thought" (546). Like Littell, Aue is also an avid reader of Flaubert, whose *Sentimental Education* he pores over during his flight from invading Russians (852).[18]

Aue's own sentiments and motivations are at times complex or inconsistent, at least as they are recounted thirty years after the war by an elderly ex-Nazi now living in safety and, in a transparent irony, directing a lace-making factory. Many readers have observed that the novel contains an overwhelming amount of historical detail that might well, and in fact has, found its way into many works of history, where Littell himself found it by undertaking impressive research and arriving at a remarkable degree of erudition.[19] Still, it is difficult to conceive of any competent reader taking the memoir-like novel as fact and being duped in the way readers were taken in by Binjamin Wilkomirski's *Fragments: Memories of a Wartime Childhood*.[20] For many, the implausibility of the latter was apparent only belatedly, while the implausibility of Aue's narration is blatant and explicitly intended by Littell. SS officer Aue is for the author a stylized composite figure or, more precisely, a kind of "scanner" who is not embodied in any historical Nazi, although he manifests an omnipresent and almost omniscient relation to history similar to that of a superadministrator (a kind of Eichmann raised to the nth power) and knows or encounters a vast array of historical figures. Present even at Himmler's October 6, 1943, speech at Posen, similar in content for him to the more famous speech of October 4 except for the former's "less informal, less sardonic, less slang-laden" tone (611), Aue affirms that the reason Himmler was so atypically explicit and unambiguous about the genocide was to fully implicate the Nazi elite and eliminate any possible plea of ignorance about the "final solution"—an approach causing discomfort in some of his high-ranking audience (613).

The mythological substructure of the novel is also explicit: the story of Orestes who desires his sister Electra and kills his mother Clytemnestra who herself had killed his father Agamemnon. Orestes is pursued by the Furies, the Erinyes, who are commanded by Athena to renounce vengeance against Orestes, and then become the Eumenides, the Kindly (or benevolent) Ones. There are some parallels to the myth in *Les Bienveillantes*, and myth has a structural role in the organization of the narrative. Aue goes well beyond love and desire for his sister. And, after he receives a bullet on the Eastern Front that leaves a hole in his head, he has a hallucinatory experience and wakes up finding his mother and his stepfather, both of whom he may want to kill, in fact slaughtered. It seems likely that, but not altogether clear whether, he actually murders them. In any event, he is pursued in the final sections of the novel by two relentless policemen, Weser and Clemens who, in one of many Nazi/Jew minglings, bear the names of two Nazi killers of Jews in Dresden.[21] They are the most literal parallels to the Furies but never become "kindly ones," and even when the aged Aue seems to find a refuge in his lace factory and in writing his memoirs, the last lines of the novel inform the reader that the "kindly ones" have found his trace again. (Both Clemens and Weser have, however, been killed by this point [893].) The status of "kindly one" is manifestly also that of Aue's best friend Thomas Hauser, who extricates Max from prosecution for a homosexual act, gets him into the SD (*Sicherheitsdienst*, the SS intelligence agency under Reinhard Heydrich), and becomes a protector or helper figure for the rest of the novel. His last act of helping is involuntary and fatal, as Aue kills him to steal papers that provide Aue with an alibi, enabling him to escape being apprehended at the end of the war. Still, the less direct, more general and controversial analogs of "*les bienveillantes*," many of whom remain alive and well at the novel's end, are arguably the SS themselves who presumably do avenge the *Volksgemeinschaft* yet appear at times to have a "kindly" solidarity with their victims. Indeed, Aue himself might be seen as one of the *bienveillantes*, a perpetrator doubling as a victim bearing witness and pursuing himself, in what might seem an overly "kindly," only occasionally fury-laden fashion.

A crucial point about the mythological substructure is that it ties together the unfolding of the genocide and Aue's personal erotic history in a linkage that is both freely associative and somehow fated. Aue even muses about the determinative or fateful force of words in different languages, finding *Endlösung* ("final solution") "such a beautiful word" (580). His seeming fate (which in a sense victimizes him) is to act out a compulsive desire for his sister and a homicidal desire for his mother in a manner that parallels his animus toward Jews, who are figured in terms of ambiguous relations with Nazis, intimated not only by the shape of Hitler's nose but by Aue's vision of Hitler as a Jew wearing the shawl of a rabbi and carrying ritual objects (802).[22] The grain of truth here is the relation of German and Jew as in some sense enemy brothers, with Nazi genocidal action having as one dimension the denial in oneself of anxiety-producing forces (money grubbing, industrialization, desire for world power, erotic attraction to the exoticized other, and so forth) that one projects and localizes onto the hated, disavowed other as scapegoat.[23] Hitler himself asserted that the Jews could not be the chosen people because the Germans were. But the nature of the relation of perpetrator and victim in *Les Bienveillantes* is an underdeveloped, confusing, at times obfuscating form of amalgamation or ambiguity. Aue himself expectably downplays the role of anti-Semitism in a way that uses comparison, for example, with colonial excesses, not in a critically analytic attempt to further understanding but in a self-serving fashion reminiscent of relativizing gestures, functioning to lessen the significance of the Holocaust during the *Historikerstreit* in the 1980s (615–16).[24]

A basic issue is the manner in which, intentionally or not, the intertwining—or even twinning—of Aue's personal erotic excesses with genocidal excesses as parts of the same "fated" story threatens to make the genocide itself an effect of fate and not of the complexities, including the constraints, of human action in history. Insofar as this is the case, history is absorbed into the transhistorical and the mythological, and tragic fate may be reinforced by a questionable construction of psychoanalysis as itself a tragic account of a fatalistic death drive or a universal nihilating "real"—a construction not found explicitly in the novel but that arguably has an affinity with Littell's narrative and that may postulate a monstrous core as the essence of the human being (a view formulated, for example, by Slavoj Žižek).[25] In the figuration of history as a derivative of fate and myth (or of a fatalistic transhistorical "theory") the problem of the articulation of history and literature is dissolved rather than addressed. Obscured in the process is the understanding of psychoanalysis that is not an unqualified, transhistorical or even quasi-transcendental affirmation of a tragic fate (or of a variant of original sin) but a mode of critical analysis that foregrounds the role of sometimes violent repetition compulsions but does not imply the necessity of acting them out in an unmediated manner. Rather, without denying their force, it indicates how they may be counteracted, modified, and worked though by means of various forms of sublimation and transformation, including responsible social and political action. A certain kind of novel and, in a different key, a certain kind of history, may be components of this larger process of working through, while not entirely transcending, the constraints or pressures of a haunting past or an oppressive present.

It is significant in this respect that, when Pierre Nora asks Littell about what Nora terms the "psychological, incestuous, masochistic, sexually passive vein of Aue," Littell has no real answer, suggesting that this dimension is a "*zone d'ombre*" for him in a manner that may indicate a compulsive enactment of phantasms. Littell can only attempt to distinguish his work from that of others, such as Luchino Visconti's film *The Damned*, by appealing to the "historical stratum to which I remain attached very closely, as closely as possible in any case. . . . Why are there precisely all these other aspects? I would be incapable of answering you. It's like that. If it were not like that, I would perhaps have written a history book but not a novel."[26] The "other aspects" may be there to intensify the sense of abyssal excess in the Nazi genocide, although one may question the way the "perverse" eroticism and the atrocities are articulated in the novel.

Twins and twinning are prevalent motifs of Littell's novel. I shall simply mention one of them that has already been commented on by Antoine Compagnon—that between the fictional Thomas Hauser and the historical Otto Ohlendorf.[27] This twinning may be emblematic of the relation between fiction and history more generally in the novel, insofar as both are subsumed under the larger mythological category of fate, especially tragic fate. Here responsibility for action would at best be mythologically imputed (à la Oedipus), and one may act with one's eyes wide open but still be blind to the larger forces controlling one's destiny. Aue's relation to Ohlendorf is adulatory, and the intelligent, sophisticated, seemingly nonfanatical but committed and decisive Ohlendorf seems the closest model among actual Nazis to Aue, at least in terms of Aue's ego ideal of what it is to be a good Nazi. Ohlendorf tells Aue that he had preferred a more "rational" solution to the problem of the Jews but that the *Führer* was forced by the incompetence of others to commit a "necessary error" in ordering a "radical solution" (208). The calm, composed, coffee-drinking Ohlendorf was head of *Einsatzgruppe* D, responsible for the mass murder of some ninety thousand men, women, and children in the southern Ukraine. With reference to the "terrible" order for annihilation (*Führernichtungsbefehl*), he is presented as reversing Nazi and Jew in appealing both to the Biblical command to strike down Amalek (here the Jew) and (via Kierkegaard) to the supraethical, faith-based, arrested injunction to sacrifice Isaac: "We had to consummate Abraham's sacrifice" (211).

As Compagnon points out, the novel really does not fathom the complexity of the motivation of Aue, Ohlendorf, or Hauser, despite Littell's forceful claim that historians have hit a wall on the problem of motivation.[28] In Littell's words:

> The issue of the perpetrator is the main issue the historians of the Shoah have been exploring for the last 15 years. The only remaining question is the motivation of the killers. Having read the works of the great researchers, it seems to me that they have hit a brick wall. This is very clear with Christopher Browning. He has created a list of potential motivations and has no way of arbitrating between them. Some prioritize anti-Semitism, others ideology. But in the end, they don't know. The reason is simple. The historian works from documents, and so from the words of the perpetrators, which are themselves an aporia. And where can one go from there?[29]

Apparently one goes from historical to novelistic truth. "Max Aue is a roving X-ray, a scanner. He is not, indeed, a plausible character. I was aiming not for plausibility but for truth. You cannot create a novel if you insist solely on plausibility. Novelistic truth is a different thing from historic or sociological truth."[30] What constitutes novelistic truth for Littell remains in the dark, as do the other-than-dichotomous relations between the historical and the literary, whereby one may argue (as I would) that the literary imagination may transform or go beyond "historical truth" without necessarily transcending or falsifying it. *Les Bienveillantes*, I think, transcends historical truth by the role it attributes to fate and threatens to falsify it insofar as it indiscriminately amalgamates or reverses perpetrator and victim. And it is unclear whether Littell's novelistic project aims at elucidating motivation, even partially, or instead insists, or even remains fixated on, the incomprehensibility of the presumably incomprehensible.

In a couple of passages, however, Aue himself addresses the problem of possible motivation of elite Nazi perpetrators in a manner that recalls Friedländer's observations about Himmler's Posen speech and brings out the dubious nature of at least certain forms of excess, transgression, and a quest for the absolute. Aue affirms:

> Since childhood I was haunted by the passion for the absolute and the transcendence of limits; now this passion had led me to the edge of common graves in the Ukraine [where Jews were shot and dumped during "killing" actions]. I always wanted my thinking to be radical; well the State, the Nation also chose the radical and the absolute; how could I, at this very moment, turn my back and say no, ultimately preferring the comfort of bourgeois laws and the mediocre assurance

of the social contract? That was obviously impossible. And if radical-ity was the radicality of the abyss, and if the absolute revealed itself as the bad absolute, it was nonetheless necessary—I was intimately per-suaded—to follow them to the very end, with my eyes wide open. (95)

The killing of the Jews at bottom serves no purpose. . . . It has no economic or political utility, no practical goal. On the contrary it is a rupture with the world of economics and politics. It is waste, pure loss. That's all. And thus what is happening can have only one meaning: that of a definitive sacrifice, which definitively binds us together and prevents us, once and for all, from turning back. (137)

Here a sacrificial orientation, associated with Bataille's notion of *dépense* (useless expenditure or pure waste) and creating a deadly solidarity in going to the limit, is ascribed to at least certain perpetrators. When Aue, in his of-ficial capacity under Himmler as investigator of work in camps, bemoans the counterproductive nature of killing or starving a needed work force, he turns pragmatic and seems not to appreciate the appeal of *dépense*, the antiutilitar-ian, the "definitive sacrifice," transgressive radicality, excess, and the quest for an absolute, however abyssal or destructive. He unreflectively incorporates a tension, if not a contradiction that did exist, perhaps both between groups of Nazis and within Nazis either at a given time or over time. Himmler himself apparently could turn from the fascination with transgressive abyssal excess in his Posen speech to trying to negotiate, toward the end of the war, a trade of Jews for trucks (which, for Friedländer, was not intended seriously by the Nazis [vol. 2, 621–25]),[31] and then in late 1944, he could make a hesitant move to cease deportations of Jews, which Hitler would not countenance, as well as more successful initiatives in 1945 to save Jews released from camps (647–48).

Saul Friedländer is, of course, very interested in victims and appreciates the complexity of their responses along with the difficulty of trying to understand them, including the traumatic and posttraumatic dimensions of their experi-ence. For Friedländer, Holocaust historiography, even when it studies victims, does not really attend to their "voices" and typically suppresses the jarringly disconcerting effect of attending to them.[32] The turn to Friedländer, after the hyperbolic initiatives of *Les Bienveillantes*, in both its detailed documentary and its phantasmatic excesses, is a sobering experience. Friedländer's two volumes are long, but his subject is immense, and his prose is understated and subdued. He nonetheless wants to unsettle the reader through an unassum-ing narrative, punctuated by the "voices" of victims whose experience and expression of suffering and abusive treatment should be enough to disturb.

Here is how he puts his objective in perhaps the most explicit passage of the introduction to the second volume of *Nazi Germany and the Jews*.

> Disbelief is a quasivisceral reaction, one that occurs before knowledge rushes in to smother it. "Disbelief" here means something that arises from the depth of one's immediate perception of the world, of what is ordinary and what remains "unbelievable." The goal of historical knowledge is to domesticate disbelief, to explain it away. In this book I wish to offer a thorough historical study of the extermination of the Jews of Europe, without eliminating or domesticating that initial sense of disbelief. (xxvi)

The use of "disbelief" here may be puzzling.[33] Friedländer certainly does not mean disbelief in the sense of negationists who want to use the very unbelievability or extreme nature of aspects of the genocide to evoke suspicion in the reader, the kind of incredulity that casts doubt on testimonies or the voices of victims. Nor does he go in an explicitly "postsecular" direction that validates notions of what may be taken as "beyond belief," such as the miracle, the sublime epiphany, or the "tremendum," however negative or abyssal, although elsewhere he has appealed to a notion of the negative sublime as perhaps necessary for analyzing certain excessive and even opaque aspects of what is evoked in Himmler's Posen speech: "For further analysis, we would need a new category equivalent to Kant's category of the sublime, but specifically meant to capture inexpressible horror."[34]

It is debatable whether Friedländer asserts the uniqueness of the Shoah, but he does affirm a sharp opposition between Jews and other victims.[35] Framing his comments as a summary of "different levels of anti-Jewish ideology," he states with marked emphasis:

> *The Jew was a lethal and active threat to all nations, to the Aryan race and to the German Volk.* The emphasis is not only on "lethal" but also—and mainly—on "active." While all other groups targeted by the Nazi regime (the mentally ill, "asocials" and homosexuals, "inferior" racial groups including Gypsies and Slavs) were essentially *passive* threats (as long as the Slavs, for example, were not led by the Jews), the Jews were the only group that, since its appearance in history, relentlessly plotted and maneuvered to subdue all of humanity. (xiv)

Friedländer insists on the distinctive nature of the Jews among victim groups:

> In many ways Auschwitz illustrated the difference between the Nazi concentration camp system in general and the extermination system

in its specific anti-Jewish dimension. In this multipurpose camp with a mixed population of inmates, the non-Jewish inmates soon became aware of the fundamental difference between their own fate and that of the Jews. The non-Jewish inmate could survive, given some luck and some support from his national or political group. The Jew, on the other hand, had ultimately no recourse against death and, as a norm, remained utterly defenseless. (508)

He quotes Yisrael Gutman as observing: "The Jews were pariahs in the concentration camps and were regarded as such by other inmates" (508).

Friedländer provides a detailed, nuanced approach to the so-called gray zone of perpetrator-victims, especially with respect to the still controversial issue of the role of Jewish councils. He carefully traces the various responses of councils and their members to what was a shared impossible situation, from the megalomaniacal "King Chaim" Rumkowski of Lódz, often criticized at his own time as well as later, to the anguished collaboration of Adam Czerniaków of Warsaw, who, when he finally realized that his actions were abetting the killing of children he had tried to protect, took his own life. He also qualifies the frequent opposition between the heads of the councils in Lódz and Warsaw by again quoting Yisrael Gutman, who argues that Rumkowski "created a situation of social equality in the ghetto" while Czerniaków who, in Gutman's words, "was indisputably a decent man, came to terms with scandalous incidents in the Warsaw ghetto" (63). Friedländer's own most comprehensive assessment comes in the introduction to the second volume:

> In her highly controversial *Eichmann in Jerusalem*, Hannah Arendt put part of the responsibility for the extermination of the Jews of Europe squarely on the shoulders of the various Jewish leadership groups: the Jewish Councils, or *Judenräte*. This largely unsubstantiated thesis turned Jews into collaborators in their own destruction. In fact any influence the victims could have on the course of their own victimization was marginal, but some interventions did take place (for better or worse) in a few national contexts. Thus, in several such settings, Jewish leaders had a limited yet not entirely insignificant influence (positive or negative) on the course and decisions taken by national authorities. This was noticeable . . . in Vichy; in Budapest, Bucharest, and Sofia; possibly in Bratislava; and of course in the relations between Jewish representatives and the Allied and neutral governments. Moreover, in a particularly tragic way, Jewish armed resistance (at times Jewish communist resistance groups, such as the small Baum group in Berlin), be it

in Warsaw or Treblinka and then in Sobibor, may have brought about an accelerated extermination of the remaining Jewish slave labor force (at least until mid-1944) despite the acute need for workers in the increasingly embattled Reich. (xxiii–xxiv)

For Friedländer, the "war" against the Jews was at least distinctive in that it entailed in principle the "extermination" of each and every Jew—man, woman, and child. Without denying the significance of the genocidal animus against Jews, one may nonetheless ask, in critically analytic and comparative terms, whether redemptive anti-Semitism is best seen in the larger context of racism, violence, and victimization that may take a quasi-ritual or even sacrificial turn, involving a desire for purification and regeneration, and sweep in other victimized groups such as "Gypsies," people of color, and other social "undesirables," for example, the "mentally ill" or "handicapped."[36] One may also question the extent to which the opposition between the active and the passive assists in understanding either the distinctive nature of the animus against Jews or its "totalizing" force. Partisans were seen as an "active" threat, and Jews were at times spuriously identified with them to justify "extermination." And extremely oppressed, often traumatized Jews, at the limit helpless *Muselmänner*, were reduced to a state of "passivity." In any case, it is significant that Friedländer does not further elaborate the active/passive opposition in the body of his long text.[37] To the extent Jews were seen as a threat, the bases of the perception were largely phantasmatic and ideological, as Friedländer is well aware, yet in ways demanding further inquiry, even if partly speculative, that Friedländer only partially enters into, relying in good part on the notion of "redemptive anti-Semitism."

What is clear is that Friedländer is cutting against the grain of a banalizing approach in which the very narrative of the historian would participate by treating the Nazi genocide in the terms and tone of business as usual. He treads a fine line, for his own tone of sustained reasonableness and sobriety, as well as his avowed quest for an "integrative and integrated," (xv) "thorough" (xxvi) history of the Holocaust as "a totality defined by [the] convergence of distinct elements" (xv), along with a seeming avoidance of theoretical reflection, can contribute to a conventional historiography that employs the same style and the same procedures for all events, including genocides. At a certain level, Friedländer would defend the role of certain historiographical conventions with respect to all subjects (as would I), conventions such as the provision of footnotes when necessary to specify sources, accuracy in recounting details, empirically substantiating assertions that are intended as factual, and not misconstruing what one argues the sources allow, indicating, if necessary, when statements are hypothetical, counterfactual, or speculative. He might also be critical of certain mixtures or amalgamations of fact and fiction, as he was in his *Reflections of Nazism: An Essay on Kitsch and Death.*[38] I believe that he might agree with many of my critical comments about Littell's novel. Whether he would agree with other dimensions of my account is a more open question. Despite the altogether invaluable contributions of *Nazi Germany and the Jews,* it may lend credence to Littell's claim that, with respect to the motivation of perpetrators, even great researchers have "hit a brick wall." To be more precise, Friedländer seems to stop before the "wall" and to provide only restricted ways and means of coming to terms with it, largely in his important concept of "redemptive anti-Semitism," which might benefit from greater theoretical elaboration.

An appeal to a precognitive "quasivisceral reaction," or to "the depth of one's immediate perception of the world," is problematic, and "disbelief" is probably not the term that best does justice to Friedländer's concerns. Moreover, not all knowledge or explanation is necessarily domesticating, although it may well challenge the quasi-visceral, immediate perception, and, in general, various forms of habitus or what is taken for granted and goes without saying. I have suggested "empathic unsettlement" as a term indicating an ethically and historically defensible response in a historian or other student of extreme events and experiences.[39] Friedländer seems to want more, not shock perhaps and not secondary trauma, but some uncanny disorientation that brings the historian or commentator more intimately, indeed immediately and viscerally, into the vicinity of the victim. Without simply subscribing to "the more we know the less we understand" paradox, he wants to maintain the unease of the uncanny or the role of the inexplicable and the excessive (in the sense of what overwhelms the imagination and even conceptualization)—or at least to counteract (as I would) the tendency of conventional narrative to airbrush or buffer the traumatic rather than convey some sense of its unsettlement. His very resistance to theory and his reliance on a direct and at times simple yet often effective use of language may itself be a manner of staying close to, if not keeping faith with, the "voices" of victims rather than giving greater conceptual or theoretical perspective on them.[40] It is also possible that Friedländer thinks that the deluge of images of horror has eroded the feeling of disbelief and that he, in a specific sense, would like to restore that feeling or response. But if that is indeed what he intends, the meaning and the specific sense of "disbelief" at issue might have been more fully developed. At present the problem may be not the "eliminating or domesticating of that initial sense of disbelief" but the fact that one's initial sense is not to feel "that's unbelievable" but to file away one more scene of atrocity without allowing it to register in any emotionally or critically significant manner. The very appeal to a sense of disbelief may in a curious way be nostalgic, harkening back to a time when certain forms of excess presumably did generate disbelief, perhaps in keeping with the prevalent (and appropriate) elegiac tone of the narrative.

In any event, I think that Friedländer finds the darkness in dimensions of the Shoah to be dark enough without needing further darkening, whether in literature or in history. (Here one may recall W. G. Sebald's apposite comment: "I think [Walter] Benjamin at one point says that there is no point in exaggerating that which is already horrific.")[41] Friedländer was himself a hidden child whose parents were killed at Auschwitz, thus someone with a subject-position that may warrant proximity or even intimacy with the victim's voice in a manner that would be more questionable in someone (like myself) whose subject-position is quite different.[42] Friedländer does not go into the question of subject-positions in his magnum opus, although he has touched on the problem elsewhere. As I have indicated, he tends to steer clear of more theoretical issues, even at the risk of underconceptualizing a very "rich" account (if that term is suitable in light of the subject matter). In the introduction to the first volume, he does raise the question of transferential relations between the historian and his subject(s). In the introduction to the second volume there is another reference to transference that apparently simply occurs in immediate response to the victim's voice: "Often the immediacy of a witness's cry of terror, of despair, or of unfounded hope may trigger our own emotional reaction and shake our prior and well-protected representation of extreme historical events" (xxvi). The concept does not arise again in the principal text treating the years of extermination where it might seem especially pertinent.

In a thought-provoking article, Amos Goldberg affirms the undisputed excellence of Friedländer's masterwork and even sees in it an original literary form closely integrated with the sustained and sensitive effort to give voice to victims.[43] Yet he sees the form as often close to melodrama in the way it stages certain effects, without indicating whether or how Friedländer transforms that well-established genre. (Like Peter Brooks, Goldberg construes melodrama as a mode of representing excess but one that restabilizes a disturbed order, allows for an unproblematic opposition between the good and the bad, fosters empathy only with the victim, and, in Friedländer, is subordinated to the authoritative narrator, thus working against the generation of a sense of disbelief that is the author's intended objective.) Goldberg affirms the value of Friedländer's desire to convey to readers the disbelief the latter thinks was the primary response of bewildered victims who were perplexed and radically disoriented by what was happening to them. Yet Goldberg argues that a closer study of the writings of victims gives a more accurate and fuller understanding of their complex responses. He also sees an asymmetry between Friedländer's elaboration of an overall perspective for perpetrators in terms of redemptive anti-Semitism and the absence or lack of such a conceptualization in the case of victims who are portrayed in terms of a series of discrete voices, configured only in terms of subjective disbelief. Goldberg finds that this shifts attention from historical understanding to a more aesthetic, subjective apprehension of the place of victims in the Nazi genocide. He perhaps too optimistically thinks that a fuller turn to cultural history might remedy what he sees as the limitations of Friedländer's account while integrating its impressive achievements.[44]

Wulf Kannsteiner's approach is quite different. His own overall framework is a combination of structuralism, derived from Hayden White, and the empiricism of more conventional history. Explicitly, he tries to read and account for what he sees as the innovative "modernist" writing of Friedländer in terms of the categories developed by White. This ambitious project does not attend to the fact that Friedländer, in his own introduction to *Probing the Limits of Representation: Nazism and the "Final Solution,"* takes a circumspect distance from White, whose work he appreciates but whose neo-Kantian or, for Friedländer, "postmodern" and "extreme[ly[relativistic" combination of determinatively shaping categories (or tropes) and the restriction of truth to empirically based statements referring to isolated, discrete events he finds questionable.[45] In effect, Kannsteiner overrides Friedländer by arguing that the latter has in his magnum opus come around to White's views and found convincing what Friedländer termed White's "compromise position."[46] Thus Kannsteiner argues that Friedländer has a central thesis in terms of redemptive anti-Semitism but overwhelms the thesis with an excess of facts and seeming exceptions to the point of not only destabilizing but even deconstructing, if not undermining, the thesis and its key concept. This is a presumably "ironic" structure in the text that comes along with the use of other tropes that also disorient any causal sequence or mode of temporality. One could well argue instead that Friedländer has a basic, or even central, thesis, at least with respect to perpetrators, that he explicitly and nonironically qualifies by allowing for a multiplicity of contingencies and "voices" that frame the thesis as nontotalizing but nonetheless pertinent. Still, there is at least a tension (or a divided quest)—perhaps functioning as an alienation effect—notably in the second volume, between Friedländer's explicit desire to represent the Holocaust as a "totality" and to provide "an integrative and an integrated history" (xv), on the one hand, and his subsequent statement, after a page break leading to it, that "no single conceptual framework can encompass the diverse and converging strands of such a history" (xvi), related to the role of disruptive effects in the narration.[47] In any event, Kannsteiner finds Friedländer's putative modernism to be a kind of impressionism imbued with perplexity—similar to that some have ascribed to a classic instance of "modernist" literature: Joseph Conrad's *Heart of Darkness*.[48] Indeed, the Holocaust itself seems to emerge as a "heart of darkness" that is disorienting in its excess and, overwhelming all containing categories, may even lead to its apperception as "sublime."

Hence Kannsteiner (like Alon Confino) is inclined to go in the aesthetic direction that Goldberg feared, although for Goldberg melodramatic effects might accord more with the pleasure principle than any "sublime" excess beyond it.[49] Kannsteiner himself believes that the transfer of disbelief to the reader is an ethical rather than aesthetic effect of the text, and he affirms this process in his own voice without elucidating why and how disbelief may be construed as ethical. (Is it that, if one is truly "ethical," one must experience disbelief in the face of certain extreme events even if one knows they did indeed occur and is familiar with numerous accounts of them and of other, at times recent, atrocities? Does "being ethical" in this case require a certain type of repression or disavowal, perhaps even an explicit decision or paradoxical suspension of belief: Yes, I know but still I don't, or I can't, believe?)

The notion that Friedländer's style is impressionistic—albeit impressionistic in a manner largely anchored in the sources—may be suggested by his accumulation of details, anecdotes, and quotations culled from some forty diaries and other written documents left by victim/witnesses such as Victor Klemperer, Adam Czerniaków, and Etty Hillesum.[50] As Goldberg points out, despite the masterful stylistic orchestration, there seems to be no overall narrative framework or even concept for victims. One might add that, in contrast to Friedländer's manifest intent, Hitler emerges as the primary protagonist of the account, receiving a disproportionate number of references.[51] While the narrative stays focused on the history of victims, Friedländer attempts to provide a "thorough" account that synthesizes the results of earlier research. It seems inevitable that the perpetrators, and notably the key perpetrator, would at times come center stage despite the desire to accord the principal place to the voices of victims, especially since Friedländer himself places such great emphasis on anti-Semitic Nazi ideology, whose principal proponent was Hitler, as well as on the *Führer*-Bond, whose object was once more Hitler.[52]

Even though certain historians (Alon Confino, for example) have been inclined to analyze Friedländer's text in largely stylistic or "literary" terms, most would probably not be surprised that Friedländer himself does not pursue what some might see as the "literary" problem of analyzing diaries and testimonies on the levels of genre, rhetoric, and subject-position. One could argue that closer attention to the latter would have produced disjunctive or disruptive effects that might have proved quite unsettling, especially for professional historians. Friedländer briefly notes the differences, especially in politics, style, and religion, between diarists, for example, the anti-Zionist Victor Klemperer, a converted Protestant with "the light ironic touch of his revered Voltaire," who sought assimilation, married a Christian, and survived the war in Dresden, and Chaim Kaplan, a Zionist choosing to remain in the Warsaw ghetto, who had the "emphatic style of biblical Hebrew," received a Talmudic education, and had a "lifelong commitment" to "Hebrew education" (63). But, after this point early in the text, there are quotations and summaries by and large without further commentary or analysis. And despite the chronicle-like simplicity of the narrative and the self-effacement of the narrator, Friedländer's account has, if anything, a greater, more authoritative degree of narrative integration and unification than that of Littell's with his Aue-narrator. While each voice in *Nazi Germany and the Jews* may retain its own unsettling force, to some extent the narrative tends to employ the diaries or testimonies in a similar way. They are treated as expressing "voices" attesting to the experience of victims, a procedure that may have a somewhat homogenizing effect. The assumption seems to be that these voices simply and directly speak for themselves, perhaps even with a quasi-visceral immediacy that pierces through both narrative complacency and the defenses of the reader. However debatable this assumption may be, one may arguably contend that the very idea of an analytic and theoretical, even more so a manifestly multilayered, "experimental" style (especially with respect to the interplay of narration, theoretical reflection, and sustained analysis), is itself discomfiting in relation to a subject that exerts a pressure and even retains a certain solemnity, especially for historians.[53]

Perhaps a less controversial observation is that, despite his central concern and key metaphor being "voice," Friedländer makes no significant use of video archives of oral testimonies where the voices of victims have not only been paramount but where one might indeed hear the grain of their voices, the hesitations in speech, and the excruciating break in discourse when the witness reaches an overwhelming moment in the narration. Despite their limitations, oral testimonies might have enabled a better sense of the actual voices of victims that would have made "voice" more than a standard metaphor in relation to written documents. Although it would have moved beyond the time frame of the "final solution" where Friedländer for the most part stays, a turn to video archives would also have raised the crucial problem of the relation between past and present, including the role of haunting revenants with which the victim has to contend in the arduous, sometimes arrested attempt to become a survivor and social agent.

I have intimated that an elegiac tone and even a labor of mourning play an important role in Friedländer's text, never fully healing wounds, even attempting to disrupt closure, yet providing an account with a performative dimension that addresses readers and implicates them in a disconcerting past. Here one may ask whether this endeavor would have been reinforced by engaging more fully the interaction between past and present and attempting to recreate the lives both of largely assimilated western European Jews, who posed the danger of invisibility or "passing" for the Nazis, and of ostensibly different Ostjuden, living in a vibrant culture of Yiddishkeit that was all but destroyed by the Nazi onslaught.[54] Such an approach might have joined to the written text a CD-ROM of former victims telling their diverse stories, including their ways of living with and trying to work over and possibly through a haunting, often traumatic past.[55] One might add that greater attention to the problem of the relation between the past and its aftermath would at least have served to raise the intricate problem of Arab, more specifically Palestinian, and Israeli relations not only in the period from 1933 to 1945 (which Friedländer discusses) but over time and into the present, including the role of a past that has not yet passed away or been worked through. There is also the complex, contested issue of the relations or even interactions between the Nazi genocide and violence in the colonies, which at times reached genocidal proportions that may make any notion of uniqueness seem Eurocentric—an issue that at least deserves some attention in any contemporary study of the "final solution."[56] To make these observations is not to argue that Friedländer should have written a book he had no intention of writing, but it is to indicate the interest and even the insistence of a path not taken. Still, the very reliance on written documents is a way Friedländer's account remains traditional, and it may abet an avoidance of the difficult theoretical and practical problem of the relation between past and present as well as between event and experience as mediated by memory—a problem in any case not eliminated by a reliance on written diaries.[57] Here one has the issue of the various ways Friedländer's history may remain traditional if not conventional in spite of his attempt to disrupt conventionality through the transmission of "disbelief." Allow me to recapitulate some of these ways: the reliance on written documentation virtually to the exclusion of oral and graphic testimonies; the subdued, if not minimalist yet predominantly synoptic, authoritative style; the narrative that might be seen at times as a chronicle-like, seemingly impressionistic assemblage of incidents and anecdotes that still appear to fit into a larger mosaic set in a more or less standard chronological framework; the focus on the past without explicitly exploring the problem of the relation between past and present; and the reticence about entering into forms of discourse that are more developed, theoretical, or at times speculative, even when they seem called for by certain key concepts. "Disbelief" is not the only such concept. Perhaps the principal one, which is the key interpretive component of the narrative (at least with respect to perpetrators), is "redemptive anti-Semitism," which Friedländer, as I have noted, does relatively little to elaborate. The concept does to some extent inform but is not developed to any significant extent in the chapters other than the one in which it appears (chapter 3 of the first volume). And even with respect to that chapter, one may ask whether the elaboration is sufficient on a theoretical level.

I have indicated that, in an earlier essay, Friedländer discussed Himmler's Posen speech of October 1943 in a manner that provides some insight into why Jews were phantasmally perceived as a threat, thus helping to explicate the notion of "redemptive anti-Semitism" in what I think is its relation to a broader set of factors or forces: transgressive excess; a quest for an absolute that might prove abyssal; possibly sublime elation; the figuration of the leader (or the movement) as a charismatic, quasi-divine savior; the liberation from an oppressive, putatively polluting presence; the purification and regeneration of the community by the "extermination" of alien beings (variably and at times ambiguously seen as biologically inferior, as "pests" or "vermin," as "spiritually" degraded, as powerful world-historical threats, *and* as phobic sources of quasi-ritual contamination with whom sexual relations, for example, were construed as *Rassenschande*—racial disgrace or infamy); as well as the apocalyptic assimilation of *Endlösung* (the "final solution") to *Erlösung* (salvation or redemption).[58] Yet, in the second volume of his narrative, the only reference to Himmler's Posen speech seems dismissive and employs a very discreet tone: the Posen speech is "adorned . . . with some flights of rhetoric" (543). It is interesting to compare this statement with what Friedländer wrote of this speech in *Memory, History, and the Extermination of the Jews of Europe:*

The horror and uncanniness (understood here in the sense of the German word *Unheimlichkeit*) of these lines lies at first glance in what for the reader may appear as a fundamental dissonance between explicit commitment to breaking the most fundamental of human taboos, i.e., wiping from the face of the earth each and every member of a specific human group (eleven million people, according to Heydrich's calculation at the Wannsee Conference) and the declaration that this difficult task was being accomplished satisfactorily, without any moral damage. This sense of inversion of all values is reinforced by the mention, later in the speech, of those rare weaknesses which have to be ruthlessly extirpated, such as stealing cigarettes, watches, and money from the victims.

However, the source of this strangeness is not limited to this dissonance. It is augmented by a further key sentence of that part of the speech: "This [the extermination of the Jews of Europe] is the most glorious page in our history, one not written and which shall never be written." Himmler thereby conveys that he and the whole assembly are well aware of some total transgression which future generations will not understand, even as a necessary means toward a "justifiable" end. (105)[59]

Here, as in my prior quotation from Friedländer's earlier commentary on it, Himmler's Posen speech does not seem to be adequately described as "adorned . . . with some flights of rhetoric." If one may refer to a rhetorical flight, it was not a mere adornment but carried much stressful weight, including an indication of the possible motivation of key perpetrators, upper-level insiders addressed at Posen by a very important insider. In any event, the bolder theoretical initiatives evident especially in the two concluding essays of *Memory, History, and the Extermination of the Jews of Europe* might well be articulated with "redemptive anti-Semitism" and other analyses but play little if any role in *Nazi Germany and the Jews*. On the face of it, Friedländer follows the standard practice of separating the exploratory essays from the narrative of the masterwork. This would seem to relegate the former to the status of "think pieces" that, while perhaps interesting, are not on the level of "serious" history and do not warrant significant commentary in, or integration into, a major historical study such as *Nazi Germany and the Jews*. They are easily put into a separate (and probably not equal) "theory" sphere that does not interact with, or pose significant challenges to, the flow of a narrative, even one that explicitly seeks disjunctive effects. Yet many historians might applaud this practice, whose infringement would be disruptive for disciplinary protocols, counteract effects of "immediacy," and render the work less "readable" or accessible to a popular audience.

Still, toward the very end of the second volume of *Nazi Germany and the Jews*, Friedländer returns to issues bearing on redemptive anti-Semitism.

He asserts that "there is no point in probing once more 'the mind of Adolf Hitler' or the twisted emotional sources of his murderous obsessions" (656). Instead, "the major question that challenges all of us" is "why tens of millions of Germans blindly followed him to the end, why many still believed in him at the end, and not a few, after the end. It is the nature of 'Führer-Bindung,' this 'bond to the Führer,' to use Martin Broszat's expression, that remains historically significant" (656–57). This question certainly is historically significant. But one may enter the caveat that the motivation of principal perpetrators who were crucial in initiating the genocidal process, is, as Friedländer is well aware, also "historically significant." In explicating the bond with the Führer, Friedländer touches on the question of the phantasmal and ideological motivation of at least a segment of the Nazi movement and the German population. While acknowledging Hitler's importance in rebuilding Germany and "above and beyond everything else" in instilling "in the majority of Germans a sense of community and purpose," he nonetheless asserts the crucial "ongoing presence of religious or pseudoreligious incentives within a system otherwise dominated by thoroughly different dynamics . . . some kind of 'sacralized modernism'" (657).[60] And he stresses "once again . . . the phantasmal role played by 'the Jew' in Hitler's Germany and the surrounding world" (658). One may doubt the extension of the explanatory force of redemptive anti-Semitism as a primary motivation, from Hitler and a more or less elite core of Nazis (perhaps as well as a significant number of others) to the majority German population (or "the many who followed him to the end"), as Friedländer seems at times inclined to do.[61] Still, the broader, differential set of problems here would bear on the role of the phantasm in relation to ideology, racism, victimization, and a sacral or at times quasi-sacrificial animus involving purification and regeneration of the Volksgemeinschaft through violence as it applied to Jews and other radically "othered" groups that might at times be swept up into a tangled, destructive dynamic.[62]

I have intimated that Friedländer may well be entitled to a general concept or narrative frame for his account of victims, one that may be obvious but that need not undercut the unsettlement brought about by the account he gives and the voices that arise in it. With respect to victims, the primary concept would not be "redemptive anti-Semitism," although there was a current of thought taken up by some Jews (including Karl Marx) that looked forward to the "emancipation" or redemption of Jews from Judaism into a state of universal humanity or a form of presumed "authenticity."[63] The more pronounced category for Jewish victims during the "years of extermination" might well be "response," specifically, the way that often traumatized, even devastated victims responded to excessive, extremely violent, and seemingly incomprehensible Nazi aggression.

Response included the various modes of survival that could, in these specific circumstances, be seen as acts of resistance. Friedländer may overly stress (as Amos Goldberg intimates in calling for a closer reading of diaries) the near total breakdown of solidarity among oppressed Jews in often impossible situations. Still, as Friedländer himself argues, in such situations, survival itself might be seen as an act of resistance. Friedländer recounts many such acts, including acts that would be termed resistance in any context, such as those of Abba Kovner in Vilna, who famously proclaimed, "We shall not be led like sheep to the slaughter" (326); of the resistance group around the Bielski brothers in western Belorussia (364–65), which against the odds grew to fifteen hundred members; of Mordechai Anielewicz (524) and "Antek" Zuckerman (326); as well as lesser-known figures such as Pawel Frenkel, Leon Rodel, and David Apfelbaum (524) in Warsaw, and others. Yet, as I have indicated, Friedländer notes the bitter irony that "armed Jewish resistance, as important as it was in symbolic terms, did not save lives but accelerated the rhythm of extermination" (556). Indeed, all roads taken or not taken by Jews, once the process of extermination was underway, typically led to their death—what might be seen as a historical but not mythological or quasi-transcendental fatality. In any event, I shall end with another famous case that has at least symbolic value but might not be thought of in this context.

Among the many Jews who felt abandoned in increasingly dire circumstances, Friedländer refers to Walter Benjamin, in a manner that does not privilege him above other victims but, in brief terms, evokes his state of mind and the reasons for his suicide. He quotes Benjamin's letter to Gershom Scholem asserting that "every line that we publish nowadays—as uncertain as the future to which we transmit it may be—is a victory forced upon the powers of darkness." And, in his own voice, Friedländer adds: "At the Spanish border, carrying an unpublished manuscript in a briefcase that was never found, too ill, too exhausted, and mainly too desperate to try and cross the border once again, Benjamin killed himself" (127).

This brief allusion to Walter Benjamin may serve to indicate that, contrary to Jonathan Littell's comment, what happened to victims, including their at times significantly different responses, is not an uninteresting story that poses no challenging problems for understanding. In both its inherent complexity and its fraught aftermath, it remains an important, disconcerting story that poses many exigent problems for historical representation, literary rendition, and critical, theoretical reflection.[64]

✿ Chapter 5

The Literary, the Historical, and the Sacred

The Question of Nazism

In this concluding chapter, my approach is manifestly exploratory. The emphasis falls on the relation between history and critical theory, although literature remains a key concern. I return to issues raised in the preceding chapter and pursue them further, especially with respect to the complicated issue of the motivations of perpetrators of mass murder and genocide.[1] The question of the role of the sacred and the sacrificial—or what recently has been termed the postsecular—is a prominent motif with respect both to Nazism and more generally to processes or phenomena in "modernity" that may go in very different, even divergent directions.

Both literature and history have in the past been elevated to a sublime, if not a sacred, status in the wake of a perceived crisis in religion. A fusion of religion and art, including the literary—or even a religion of art, or at least a displacement of religious motifs onto a conception of art—made an appearance, however diverse and contested, in certain Romantics.[2] It took another form later in the nineteenth century in art for art's sake, an ideal verging on a "religion" of art that attracted Flaubert and Conrad, among others, even prompting (notably in Flaubert) the idea of monk-like brotherhoods withdrawn from the world and dedicated to art.[3] In certain "aesthetes" (at times figured as "decadents"), for example, Walter Pater and Oscar Wilde, and later in politically oriented Surrealists, it found another incarnation in the redemptive idea of art-becoming-life, or (as in the early Nietzsche) in the notion that life was justified only as an aesthetic phenomenon.[4] (The analog in the early Marx was the project of having [German Idealist] philosophy become life, along with a messianic view of the revolution and the romantic ideal of transcending the division of labor so that everyone could approximate a many-sided Renaissance man.)[5] In a different key, history was seen as a manifestation of the ways of God on earth or at least as a bearer of meaning if not progress, expressed most forcefully perhaps in an important dimension of the thought of Hegel, which informed Ranke's metaphysical conceit that his seemingly positivistic research actually traced the movements of the hand of God in history. Of course, various writers and thinkers struggled with the issue of their relation to religion, at times attempting to delineate subtle distinctions between formulations that seem similar (an attempt that comes to a very fine point in Derrida's understanding of the almost indiscernible difference between aspects of his thought and negative theology). Yet certain efforts to oppose art (or science) to religion were insistent, even when a positivist, objectivist, or naturalist affirmation itself seemed to take on prophetic tones or to be made with heated fervor, as, for example, in T. H. Huxley or, in a different key, Zola. Durkheim came to see sociology as being an "objective" reformulation of the problems of religion and value whereby society itself was tantamount to God, a seemingly paradoxical affirmation that nonetheless indicated the way society might indeed be a new center of belief and commitment, and sociology itself a methodology that quasi-theologically located the ultimate source of all meaning and value in the social.[6] For Durkheim a fusion of religion and society was the core of a "primitive nebula" from which all social institutions emanated through processes of differentiation that continued to trail clouds of glory.

Karl Löwith's *Meaning in History* was one of the most concise and influential explorations of the displacements of religion and theology in the historical quest for meaning—what became known, defended, and criticized as the "secularization thesis."[7] Other genres or forms of thought, notably philosophy, have had a complex relation to religion and theology. Culture itself could be taken as a secularized successor to cult and a stand-in for religion— or at least as the font of meaning in life. It is at times unclear whether the radical critique of a vision of art, literature, history, philosophy, or even culture itself as a bearer of meaning is motivated by a nihilistic denial of any source of meaning in "modernity," by an insistence that nothing can or should take the place of religion, by a stress on self-conscious fictions, or by the conviction that different, perhaps sociopolitical ways should be forged to attain viable if not redemptive meaning in life—views that may meet in a tangled convergence related to a longing for new gods as well as to a suspicion or even a firm belief that such a revival is hopeless. In any case, in writers such as Sebald and Coetzee, among numerous others, the relations among literature, history, politics, and the sacred (or the "postsecular") become explicitly problematic and difficult to trace.

Violence, at times bound up with the apocalyptic, arguably quasi-religious desire for a radical break in, or even transcendence of, the "burden" of history has played a key role in sociopolitical practice, ideology, and certain artistic or philosophical movements.[8] And violence is often, if not typically, correlated with terror and traumatization of both self and others.[9] Tendencies gathered under the label of modernism stressed the importance of the new and involved a radical break with the past, even a leap into the unknown. Jean-François Lyotard saw postmodernism itself, not as a break with, but as an intensification of, modernism, and paradoxically this intensification might well include a renewed insistence on the need for a radical, apocalyptic break with the past and a breakthrough to the unprecedented or sublimely unrepresentable.[10] The quasi-religious mission of avant-garde art was to keep faith with the unrepresentable (however traumatizing) in the face of consoling temptations toward representation and figuration. The insistence on keeping faith with the unrepresentable arguably has an affinity with the notions of sublimity, radical transcendence, the totally other, and the Hidden God (or, in more secular terms, the Kantian noumenal sphere or the more decidedly traumatic as well as ecstatic Lacanian real). This may well be the case with respect to thinkers who take their distance from or even eschew the very term "postmodernism," for example, Slavoj Žižek and at times Jacques Derrida, despite Žižek's criticisms of the latter. It is manifestly the case in the work of Lyotard (where the sublime, in its radical transcendence of limits, does violence to the imagination, and consensus or compromise does violence to the "differend" or irreconcilable difference). The political dimensions of such figures remain allusive, or at least unprogrammatic, but the turn to violence is often pronounced, including a notion of violence as somehow intrinsic to language or to the human being.

In earlier figures, artistic, literary, or philosophical innovation of a radical sort was at times linked to political violence. And the much heralded aestheticization of violence could merge with a sacralization or rendering sublime of violence, a merger reinforced by the continued appeal of the French Revolution (including the Reign of Terror for its more "radical" defenders) on the left and of "divine right" or more generally politically theological orientations on the right (notably in the sacrificial, bloody interpretation of history and the Revolution itself in Joseph de Maistre, the value of whose thought was endorsed by Baudelaire). Even Walter Benjamin's "Critique of Violence" (1920–21), despite its extremely allusive or even cryptic argument, denigrated mythical or state violence yet looked to Georges Sorel in valorizing "divine" violence in a manner that indirectly appeared to associate it with the general strike in political and social action.[11] Derrida in his commentary on this essay also seemed to affirm the necessity of a *coup de force* as a prenormative basis of political formations, and he has repeatedly stressed the putative "violence" of language itself, even while—at least in addenda that almost appear as afterthoughts or belated recognitions—critically drawing back from the seemingly obvious, dubiously legitimating implications of Benjamin's argument concerning divine violence, perhaps even with respect to later political movements such as Nazism and fascism that Benjamin (and Derrida) explicitly opposed.[12] Other appeals to violence have been less qualified than Derrida's, including those of Žižek (explored in the epilog to this book).

Common reference points in the recent past, such as André Breton, Georges Bataille, Maurice Blanchot, Martin Heidegger, and Carl Schmitt, were sometimes unguarded about the necessity of violence as well as the correlation of political violence and violence in literature or writing.[13] Heidegger's most extreme arguments in this respect were in his pro-Nazi writings of 1933–4, but the insistence on violence, including the violence of all interpretation, is a leitmotif of his thought.[14] After the failure of his attempts to stabilize and help provide a constitution for the Weimar Republic, Schmitt became a supporter of the Nazis and formulated a "political theology" based on the hyperbolic argument that all the essential concepts of modern political thought are displaced theological concepts. Most important, sovereignty of the nation-state, with its putative monopoly on legitimated uses of violence, derived from the sovereign status of God, with the implication that, like the radically transcendental, willful God of certain variants of Christianity, the secular sovereign was the one who declared both the onset and the termination of states of emergency and of exception that suspended the constitution and the rule of law. It would seem apparent that there are affinities between this view and the Nazi claim that the will of the *Führer* had the force of law and that ordinary laws or conceptions of criminality were suspended in the higher light of the *Führer's* will.[15] Bataille and Blanchot, who themselves saw their thought as closely related, did not take this route, but there were elements in their prewar thinking that appealed to extreme, even terroristic violence, and some of these elements left at least traces in their postwar writings.

Bataille offered a theory of the violent, sacrificial bases of all society and saw modernity as providing countless instances of sacrificial violence, from self-mutilation to capital punishment and political movements. He was initially "fascinated" by fascism with its charismatic leaders, but he drew back in the late 1930s when he saw the way fascism, and especially the Nazi regime, developed. Yet even in his opposition to fascism, he called for violence in the streets on the part of a popular front that invoked what some saw as fascist means, particularly mass violence, presumably to oppose fascism. Breton claimed that this gesture was part and parcel of a *surfascisme*, and he and Bataille exchanged mutually derogatory remarks concerning each other's orientations. Bataille took exception to the infamous assertions in the "Second Manifesto of Surrealism" (1930), but one may ask whether they were really that distant from possible dimensions of the kind of street violence Bataille himself advocated or, more blatantly, from an assertion in the late 1930s of Blanchot. In 1930 Breton wrote, in terms that closely approximated random violence and sublime elation in radical action against a "degenerate" society and culture:

> One can understand why Surrealism was not afraid to make for itself a tenet of total revolt, complete insubordination, of sabotage according to rule, and why it still expects nothing save from violence. The simplest Surrealist act consists of dashing down into the street, pistol in hand, and firing blindly, as fast as you can pull the trigger, into the crowd. Anyone who, at least once in his life, has not dreamed of thus putting an end to the petty system of debasement and cretinization in effect has a well-defined place in that crowd, with his belly at barrel level. The justification of such an act is, to my mind, in no way incompatible with the belief in that gleam of light that Surrealism seeks to detect deep within us.[16]

In the July 7, 1936, issue of *Combat*, Blanchot could write the following with respect to France's Third Republic under Léon Blum:

> It is necessary that there be a revolution because one does not modify a regime that controls everything, that has its roots everywhere. One removes it, one strikes it down. It is necessary that the revolution be violent because one does not tap a people as enervated as our own for the strength and passions appropriate to a regeneration of decency, but through a series of bloody shocks, a storm that will overwhelm—and thus awaken—it. . . . That is why terrorism at present appears to us as a method of public salvation.[17]

Here violence and terrorism are advocated as a kind of traumatizing shock therapy to regenerate and redeem a decadent, enervated people. One should insist that the writings of figures such as Blanchot and Bataille, as well as those of complex, often self-contesting writers such as Heidegger—and even more so an explicitly self-questioning figure such as Derrida—are not to be conflated with the propagandistic, ideologically saturated writings of Nazis or fascists. But there still may be aspects of their writing and thought that call for careful scrutiny. Even after the war, Bataille could write an essay based on John Hersey's study of Hiroshima in which the latter itself seems to become, in Bataille's ecstatic prose, a sublime object. As I observe in *History and Its Limits*, Bataille discusses the bombing of Hiroshima and its aftermath with reference to "a core of darkness [that] remains untouchable" (221), "a boundless suffering that is joy, or a joy that is infinite suffering" (232), and sovereign *dépense* (useless expenditure) beyond agency and politics, apparently (and fatalistically?) conflating natural disasters with events brought about by human agents.[18] And, as noted in the preceding chapter, Blanchot in 1948 published "Literature and the Right to Death," which recalls many of the appeals to violence and terrorism, including "revolutionary" violence and terror, that apparently were not left behind in his prewar enthusiasm for the far right. To use Derrida's expression, there were at least specters of prewar appeals to violence and terror, including their sublime if not sacred qualities, that haunted the postwar work of these two icons of recent theory, whose writing, especially in the case of Blanchot, comes to take on extremely elusive and opaque forms, which one may read in a variety of ways (including in terms of what Nicolas Abraham and Maria Torok saw as the "encrypted" incorporation of phenomena that were not worked through or, in their terminology, critically interiorized).[19]

I have briefly and inadequately been indicating how Nazism and various fascisms had limited resonances in broader cultural currents. Particularly striking are the ways Nazism opened crypts and cut through complexities and difficulties. It not only explicitly rejected possibly recuperable forms of "modernism," construing them as "degenerate art," but, like fascism in general, subordinated culture and its components to politics in a conception of the political that itself might have religious or sacral dimensions.

Most insistently with respect to Nazism, the question has arisen of its role as a civil or political religion, with the leader having for his followers a quasi-divine status. Insofar as this was the case, violence itself might be sacralized both as a manifestation of the will of the leader and as a modality of ritual, even as a quasi-sacrificial process, both in the form of self-sacrifice and of sacrifice of victims whose fate was decreed by the leader. Pronounced in this respect is the prominence of a misguided quest motif that is especially effective in bringing about a confluence of the aesthetic, the political, and the sacred (or sublime), for example, when violence itself becomes a sacralized or sublime object of both ideology and practice promising regeneration or redemption.

It is well known that aesthetics under the Nazis showed a marked preference for realist, monumental, and romantically stylized forms, notably in the celebration of peasant life, family, community, heroism in war, and racial purity. Art exemplifying such an aesthetic was on display in the July 1937 "Great German Art Exhibition" in the House of German Art in Munich. Close spatially, but very distant aesthetically, was the "Exhibition of Degenerate Art" (*Entartete Kunst*) in which the outstanding work of such figures as Marc Chagall, Max Ernst, Wassily Kandinsky, and Paul Klee was put on display as exemplifying the corrupt, degraded taste of modern and especially "Jewish" art, with its preference for abstraction, distorted forms, and Expressionist or Surrealist motifs.[20] Indeed, what the victimized shared—from the disabled or "mentally ill" of the T-4 "euthanasia" program to the Jews and other victims of genocide or extreme abuse—was nonconformity to the "Aryan" ideal.

It would be an understatement to observe that the most significant German literature of the time was not produced by those dedicated to Nazi Germany. Important writers, such as Bertolt Brecht, Else Laske-Schüler, Thomas Mann, and Anna Seghers, were blacklisted or (as in the foregoing cases) in exile, and touted instead was the ideologically conformist work of such forgotten figures as Adolf Bartels and Hans Baumann. Often commented on is the flight of major filmmakers and film stars, including Marlene Dietrich, Paul Henreid, Alexander Korda, Hedy Lamarr, Fritz Lang, Peter Lorre, F. W. Murnau, Max Orphüls, and Billy Wilder, among others.[21] Yet culture under the Nazis was not monolithic or "totalitarian," although there was a regime of often harsh censorship and propagandistic control.[22]

Still insufficiently explored is the extent to which literature and other forms of art produced by Nazis and fascists, despite certain complications, often fused the aesthetic and the religious and engaged in a sacralization or rendering sublime of the political and of violence itself. (Sacralizing processes are often ignored or underemphasized in familiar appeals to the "aestheticization of violence" with which sacralization may be combined.)[23] Nazis and fascists (notably Joseph Goebbels), striving for an immediate or even visceral relation to the public, tended to give priority not to literature but to mass media. And a primary "art form" was the public pageant, notably the rally and the parade that had ritual or sacral dimensions in the glorification of *Führer* and *Volk*. Nazis and fascists were more prone to act or live out their fantasies, fears, and fictions than to write about (or otherwise symbolize) them in controlled, critical, mediated fashion. Goebbels himself published an early novel, *Michael* (1929), a manifestly quest-oriented narrative in which a young Aryan seeks the kind of illumination that Goebbels himself would later find in Nazi politics and the worship of Hitler, who for him, as for many others, was in quest of a redemptive grail. The novel, narrated in diary form, tells of a young soldier who seeks God as well as national rebirth and meets with a sacrificial death. Serving Hitler, Goebbels himself wrote diaries in which his adulatory closeness to the *Führer* and his fanatical dedication to the persecution of Jews are analogous to leitmotifs in a Wagnerian opera. One might even see Goebbels as basking in the light of Hitler as a real-life, triumphant version of his protagonist Michael, with the archangelic figure of Germania now fully transfigured to attain a godlike status, and Goebbels himself turning from writing novels to keeping an almost daily account of his feats in choreographing political propaganda and its dissemination to a mass audience. As minister of propaganda, he of course paid special attention to such media of mass communication as film, radio, and the press.[24]

Hitler's own *Mein Kampf* (1925–6), dictated in prison to Rudolf Hess, maintained the oral tone of the *Führer*'s speeches and had pronounced elements of a propagandistic, romanticized quest myth in its recounting of Hitler's life and ideology as they fused with a need for a political movement that would regenerate and redeem self and society. Art and life merged in a warped *Gesamtkunstwerk* that operatically dramatized the "destined" course of the Nazi party and the German nation, its leader, and its fighting forces, even demanding the elimination of peoples that were perceived as dissonant, contaminating forces—dangers to the lived, at times quasi-religious work of sociopolitical art. At the end of the war, even Hitler's suicide and that of Goebbels and his wife Magda, who also took the lives of their six children (engendered in accordance with the *Führer*'s imperative for large families and all of whose names began with "H"), seemed less pragmatic than dramatic, sacrificial, and apocalyptic in nature—a lived Wagnerian *Götterdämmerung*.[25]

One need not uncritically accept the amalgamating concept of totalitarianism to be able to recognize the tendency of fascist movements and regimes to blur or obliterate distinctions between genres and categories. This blurring included distinctions between various forms of art and between art itself and especially politics and the sacred (or what might belatedly be termed the postsecular). Fascism and Nazism made an amalgam of art, ideology, and propaganda. Insofar as one distinguishes between art and propaganda (or even ideology) and affirms the role of some form of critical distance in art, even while remaining sensitive to the latter's more or less subtle ideological dimensions, one is led to question the very concept of a fascist aesthetic. Instead, certain features

identified as fascist are arguably more general than fascism in any clearly circumscribed sense, gathered up and stitched together from "modern" culture at
large, diffused even in the aftermath of the fall of fascist regimes and Nazism,
and not constitutive of a discrete, much less autonomous, fascist aesthetic.

After a harrowing account of the unfolding of the "final solution"
and just before the concluding section of volume 2 entitled "Shoah," Saul
Friedländer notes that "the Germans wanted to keep a 'record' of it all—'for
the education of future generations,' in Goebbels's words. Film was the medium of choice."[26] Friedländer pays special attention to three films ordered
by Goebbels immediately after the beginning of the war: *Die Rothschilds* (*The
Rothschilds*), *Jud Süss* (*Jew Süss*), and *Der Ewige Jude* (*The Eternal Jew*). The
first two films were relatively successful in the United States, Great Britain,
and several European countries but at first were not shown in Germany (21).
Jud Süss received critical acclaim and was awarded the Golden Lion at the
Venice Film Festival. Michelangelo Antonioni even exclaimed: "We have no
hesitation in saying that if this is propaganda, then we welcome propaganda"
(quoted, 100). (In a footnote Friedländer ironically observes that "Antonioni
remains better known as director of *L'Avventura* and particularly *Blow-Up*"
[689n].) *Jud Süss* was indeed propaganda, but its stereotypical story, centered
around a Jewish financier seducing an innocent Aryan woman who feels
driven to suicide, was (as Antonioni remarked with enthusiastic aestheti-
cism) well crafted and "aesthetically" appealing. *The Eternal Jew* was another
matter. It was too blatant for audiences who felt disgust at its scurrying rats
and the original images of the ritual slaughtering of animals by Polish Jews,
whose laughing faces were contrasted with the pitiful stares of the dying
animals (101). With respect to the attempts of victims to engage in artistic
activities in the most dire circumstances, Friedländer quotes an entry in the
diary of Adam Czerniaków (dated July 8, 1942): "Many people hold a
grudge against us for organizing play activities for the children, for arranging
festive openings of playgrounds, for the music, etc. I am reminded of a film:
a ship is sinking and the captain, to raise the spirits of the passengers, orders
the orchestra to play a jazz piece. I have made up my mind to emulate the
captain" (quoted, 395). Of course Jews were subjected to many restrictions,
including in their artistic endeavors, such as being prohibited from playing
or even listening to what Nazis considered echt German music. They were
also barred from performing for German audiences or attending with them
theater performances or plays, since a Jewish presence would desecrate, soil,
and endanger the "German spirit" (98). One rationale of sewing the Star of
David on the clothing of Jews was to enable others to avoid contamination
through contact with them.

Leni Riefenstahl would be a central and particularly complex figure in any longer study that included Nazi film and documentary. Her "masterpieces," *Triumph of the Will* (1935) and *Olympia* (1938), are disconcertingly successful combinations of artistic excellence, technical prowess, and ideological, even propagandistic effects. In one sense, *Triumph of the Will* was a work of art that addressed and helped to construct a work of art—a film about an aestheticized public ritual and a sacralized polity. Yet, insisting on her own version of art for art's sake, Riefenstahl herself denied the role of other dimensions, including Nazi ideology, in her films, notably in her comments in Ray Müller's 1993 film *The Wonderful, Horrible Life of Leni Riefenstahl*.[27] In it the elderly yet irrepressible and lively Riefenstahl seems to be manifestly in denial, as she insists, despite pointed and sometimes ironic questioning by the filmmaker, on construing her films in narrowly aesthetic, technical, and experimental terms while vociferously denying not only any ideological component but also any personal or social relation to Nazis such as Goebbels (despite entries from his diaries) and even any use of "Gypsies" from a camp in her film *Tiefland* (despite a document reproduced on screen indicating such use). Yet evident at times is her uncritical, affirmative presentation of the regime and its charismatic leader (famously filmed, on his arrival in Nuremberg for the 1934 party rally, from the perspective of a godlike descent from the clouds, then greeted, as Sebald puts it in *Austerlitz*, by "the sea of radiant uplifted faces and the arms outstretched in yearning").[28] Also apparent is her adulation of the monumentalized, chiseled human form, an attitude that, in its specific context, could be extricated from Nazi ideology only by the most surgical aesthetic and technical formalism. The range of effects in her films goes from the beautiful to the sublime, by and large with the careful excision of the ugly and the deformed, except when what Nazis would include in the latter is unavoidable (such as the role of Jesse Owens in the 1936 Olympics). The film on Riefenstahl's "wonderful, horrible life" begins with shots from her early "mountain" films, which first brought the attractive young woman to Hitler's attention, and ends with the octogenarian in the ocean depths scuba diving, including along the way her discovery in her sixties of the Nuba, a Sudanese tribe whose forms would deserve a place in *Olympia* (or in Arno Breker's monumental sculptures) and whose "ideology" (as represented by Riefenstahl) might find at least a cameo spot in *Triumph of the Will*.[29] There are pronounced elements not only of glorification but also of elation in Riefenstahl's films, especially striking in someone who may not have been "interested" in politics however much it manifestly was "interested" in her and her work. With their compelling "uptake," inducing a participatory response in the viewer (although nonparticipatory viewers may well find the endless marching scenes tiresome), her films are at least compatible with more "sublimating" and perhaps even sacralizing dimensions of the Nazi regime.

Yet what are the postsecular or sacralizing tendencies in Nazi ideology and politics that often converged or merged with aesthetic tendencies, not only in the way they were deployed in ostensible works of art but in the glorification of the ideal Aryan and the construction of the Jew as alien, ugly, degenerate, or anti-aesthetic? Here a much debated question is whether fascism or at least Nazism itself can, at least in certain ways, be seen as a civil or secular religion—in one formulation, a political religion, and in another, a postsecular phenomenon.[30] This issue is typically addressed on the basis of the very questionable assumption that we understand quite well and securely know what we mean by religion and secularity along with other concepts often invoked in discussions of them (such as the aesthetic or even the literary, including the "aestheticization of violence"). Of interest here is a late essay by Derrida, a typically intricate, difficult, questioning, and self-questioning essay entitled "Faith and Knowledge: The Two Sources of 'Religion' at the Limits of Reason Alone."[31] I shall put forth a few comments about this essay and perforce simplify and make a selective use of Derrida's analysis without dwelling on aspects of it with which I take issue.[32]

Derrida's writing is itself, for many, performatively "literary," unsettling any boundary between the literary and the philosophical, and it engages, at times in a participatory fashion, the problem of the religious or perhaps the postsecular. What I find pertinent for my purposes is how Derrida worries, works, and unsettles the concepts of religion and secularity, along with related concepts, to indicate how little we can say we know or understand with any degree of confidence, much less certainty (a not unfamiliar strategy in Derrida, which it would be tempting to interpret, at least on one level, as a posttraumatic response to historical phenomena that came to preoccupy him, such as the "final solution" and colonialism). He does not simply introduce a necessary degree of hesitancy and self-critical doubt that may be missing, or at least not taken beyond a certain point, in the work of some if not many historians and social scientists. He may also radically undo the concepts with which he is working. He nonetheless tries, however contestably, to sketch out the meanings given to religion and related phenomena that deserve critical attention. The title of his essay involves a dual reference to works of Kant and Bergson—initiators of two discursive practices or traditions that have interacted in complex ways in French and, more generally, modern thought. And, in discussing the problem of religion, Derrida stresses the importance of the pragmatic question of recent uses and abuses of the term, including how it is invoked in the confused idea of the return of religion (did it ever go away?).

He also raises doubts about a presumably disenchanted or secular modernity as well as the way religion is sometimes linked ideologically to fascism, as in the charged, dubious concept of Islamo-fascism.

Derrida emphasizes the duality—what unsurprisingly emerges in the course of the essay as the multiplicity—of the meanings attributed to religion. Still, he elaborates the idea of two senses or "sources" of religion. One is the sense that relates it to faith—"the *fiduciary* (trustworthiness, fidelity, credit, belief or faith, 'good faith,' implied in the worst 'bad faith.')" (One might think here of various kinds of "pacts" enacted between writers and readers, for example, with respect to history, fiction, and autobiography.)[33] He also treats the relation of faith to the "totally other" (63). Thus, in his first sense or somewhat heterogeneous set of senses of religion, Derrida stresses faith as well as the totally other.

The second set of senses relates religion to the sacred and the holy, between which there are also divergences and tensions. (The German *heilig* is translated as either "holy" or "sacred," whereas the French has two terms: *saint*—as in *le Saint Esprit*—and *sacré*.) I note that the definition or conception of religion in terms of the sacred, rather than, say, a belief in immortality or in God (as well as the totally other), has been very important in a French tradition of thought to which Derrida is to some degree indebted or by which he is himself hailed or interpellated—the Durkheimian tradition, including such important figures as Marcel Mauss, Georges Bataille, Roger Caillois, René Girard, Julia Kristeva in certain ways (at least via Mary Douglas), and many others, including to some extent Henri Bergson. Derrida also indicates the importance of the holy and the problem of the relation between the sacred and the holy. I would simply suggest in passing that the holy is often related to notions of the radical transcendence of divinity (as is the "totally other" and perhaps even faith or at least the "leap of faith"). The sacred relates to more immanent, this-worldly, at times carnivalesque forces such as ritual, including (but not reducible to) sacrifice, which Derrida discusses in many places, including his *Gift of Death*.[34] (Yet it is interesting that one refers to the "holy" rather than the "sacred" fool—as well as the indwelling of the Holy Spirit—but to the "sacred" monster, *le monstre sacré* such as Derrida himself.) The holy as the *heilig* is very important in German thought, including Heidegger's thought, in a sense privileged for Derrida for an interesting reason, because of "its extreme character and of what it tells us, in these times, about a certain 'extremity'" (59), from which Derrida himself is not immune. One may also mention Rudolf Otto, whom Derrida does not discuss.[35]

Derrida sees the holy or *heilig* as related to hailing and the way one is hailed or called by an address to which one must respond. One thinks, say, of Abraham or Moses as well as the hailing of Mary. Derrida refers to a possible division "in the alternative between sacredness without belief (index of this algebra: 'Heidegger') and faith in a holiness without sacredness, in a desacralizing truth, even making of a certain disenchantment the condition of authentic holiness (index: 'Levinas'—notably the author of *From the Sacred to the Holy*)" (64).[36] (With respect to the reference to Levinas and disenchanted holiness, one might add Karl Barth or Rudolf Bultmann—indicating a meeting of a certain Judaism and a certain Protestantism, both of which tend to desacralize or "disenchant" the world through a notion of the radical transcendence of a totally other Hidden God, who may be both the ultimate object of desire and the most extreme, dangerously traumatizing force—arguably similar in certain ways to the "real" in Lacan.) Derrida does not mention what is pertinent to problems I shall discuss shortly: the role of hailing or calling in the fascist salute and forms of address such as Heil Hitler or Sieg Heil. He nonetheless emphasizes how the *heilig* conveys notions of the unscathed, the pure, the undefiled, the uncontaminated, the immune that is safe and sound, in one sense the avoidance or voiding of the traumatizing or anxiety producing, and, in Nazi Germany, the quest to be *Judenfrei*. (In a different yet possibly related sense, could one add the quest for "pure art," which for certain writers, such as T. S. Eliot and Céline, would also strive to be pure of, yet obsessed by, Jews?)

This notion of the unscathed, pure, and uncontaminated has been a crucial object of critical inquiry throughout Derrida's thought. It is related to his deconstruction of binary oppositions through which one attains purity in a concept or a phenomenon by concentrating and projecting onto the other all internal alterity, or difference from oneself, to arrive at the pure, integral, unscathed, presumably self-identical entity or concept. This procedure is crucial both to a logic of pure identity and difference and to a sacrificial scapegoat mechanism.[37] For Derrida such a logic undermines itself by repressing or disavowing internal alterity and hybridity (the female in the male, the animal in the human, the heteronomous in the autonomous, the "East" in the "West," or the Jew in the German, say, as well as the sacred in the holy or the other than aesthetic—the historical, the empirical, the journalistic, the ideological, the religious—in the aesthetic). This process of willy-nilly generating what contests pure identity and pure difference is what he designates by various terms over time, perhaps most famously as *différance*, related to the intertwined processes of temporalization and spacing. And the issue of more or less flexible limits and of the problematic but necessary role of variable, nonabsolute, but at times strong distinctions in the wake of the deconstruction of binary oppositions is crucial in the bearing of deconstruction on historical and political analysis as well as on normative judgment.

I have intimated that Derrida has joined others in referring, perhaps at times in an extreme, questionable fashion, to autoimmunity in the sense of the way a system produces its own antibodies that unsettle its pure identity and, at a certain threshold, its very being or life. I would also note that the process of *différance*, which takes a particular swerve in autoimmunity and which I would relate to internal dialogization, self-questioning, and self-contestation, also helps one to understand Derrida's oft-repeated and rather bewilderingly paradoxical assertion that a condition of possibility is a condition of impossibility. I would gloss this assertion as meaning that something's condition of possibility is the very condition of its impossibility "as such"—as a pure, un-divided, integral, autonomous, "uncontaminated" entity or essence—hence implying the impossibility of the "as such" as such. (Conversely, something's condition of impossibility as such is its very condition of possibility as what it is, with its internal alterity, marking, trace structure, or difference from itself, in a sense its originary hybridity that threatens any simple opposition between a pure, integral inside and an outside.)[38] In his essay on "Faith and Knowledge" Derrida also makes observations indicating that the waters of the two sources of religion are themselves typically mingled in a veiled and even muddied, impure, or secret manner.

Toward the end of the essay, Derrida asserts that "the experience of witnessing situates a convergence of these two sources: the unscathed and the fiduciary" (65)—a thought that resonates with the widespread turn to experience, trauma, witnessing, and testimony in the recent past, including in important writers such as Sebald. Perhaps surprisingly for some readers, Derrida also argues that an elementary testimonial trust precedes all questioning, indeed that the slightest testimony "must still appeal to faith as would a miracle." (This argument might be taken to point to the testimonial, autobiographical, "trusting," and even confessional dimension of all literature or even of all signification. In a sense, one is always giving oneself away.) And he makes the provocative, in certain ways problematic, assertions that the experience of disenchantment itself "is only one modality of this 'miraculous' experience" (64), that disenchantment is "the *very resource of the religious*," and that "the possibility of *radical evil* both destroys and institutes the religious" (65)—views that I think apply more to the "faith" side of the "sources" of religion. In the present context I cannot inquire further into these assertions. I would simply observe (as Derrida intimates) that attempts to separate and oppose the "two sources" or their analogs, however contestable, have occurred and may be conjoined with conflict and even with wars, as in the wars of religion and the Reformation.

Derrida also discusses two putative etymological sources of the term "religion" that in a sense cut across, or form tributaries to, his two main sources.

One is *relegere*, important in the Ciceronian tradition and meaning "harvest" or "gather." The other and perhaps more prevalent is *religare*, "to bind, link, obligate"—related to having scruples that hold one back from doing or even thinking possibly transgressive things. I have intimated that I think that the more prominent concepts, at least in Christian theology, that are related to the two main sources specified by Derrida—to simplify, the sacred-holy-pure and faith-radical alterity—are immanence and transcendence. The relation or nonrelation between immanence and transcendence has, I think, a claim to being the paradigmatic aporia or paradox of Christianity (notably with respect to what, for Kierkegaard, was the "scandal" of the incarnation—a "scandal" that messianism tries to defer: the "scandal" of the transcendent becoming immanent or God becoming man). The transcendence/immanence aporia or paradox (or its displacements and allegories) may even have this paradigmatic status in the so-called Western tradition more generally—something intimated in what was for some time, at least in the English-speaking world, Derrida's signature essay, "Structure, Sign, and Play in the Discourse of the Human Sciences," specifically his analysis of the problem of the center as both inside and outside (immanent and transcendent to) the circle it determines.[39] One may also refer to dimensions of Derrida's early and later thought that are not explicitly brought together and thematized as a problem: the famous assertions that there is no hors-texte ("outside the text")—a notion more on the side of immanence—and that every other is totally other (*tout autre est tout autre*), a generalization of radical transcendence. The transcendence/immanence aporia or paradox is also operative in a displaced manner in theories of meaning as immanent to its vehicles or signs or, on the contrary, arbitrary and in a sense transcendent with respect to them. One might even ask whether "meaning" has become a "god term" in studies of history, culture, and society that see their goal (or even grail-like quest) as the determination or recovery of meaning. (Here one might refer to meaning-cullers, retaining the duality of the term "cull"—to gather and to kill.)

The immanent sacred is related to a multiplicity of phenomena—notably sacraments and rituals, including sacrifice but (*pace* René Girard) not reducible to it. The transcendent sacred (possibly construed as the holy) may be figured as the unrepresentable, the ineffable, the totally other, the Hidden God. It may serve as a bar to mediations, such as sacraments and rituals, including sacrifice. I note in passing and later return to the point that to the extent fascism and especially Nazism arguably have a significant relation to the religious and the sacred, it is, I think, more to a specific form of the immanent sacred, especially when the latter is absolutized and bound up with a quest for redemption and total purity that may generate anxiety about contamination and prompt a turn to rituals, including purifying and sacrificial rituals that get rid of anxiety-producing, typically scapegoated others. From a transcendent perspective, Nazism may be seen as a diabolical, immanent, political religion, as it was by Eric Voegelin and others.[40]

Another distinction, at times taken to binary, oppositional, or separatist extremes, is that between faith and works or actions. Faith (like certain transhistorical, universalizing approaches to theory) is more inclined toward the radically transcendent, and works are more related to the immanent, this-worldly, and mediated. (Yet a this-worldly figure such as Hitler may be the object of a certain kind of faith, for example, faith in his always doing the right thing, however inexplicable it may seem.) The problem of faith and works was of course at issue in the Reformation. I would suggest that there are analogous concepts and concerns in historiography and social science, especially with respect to the relation between ideology or belief, even theory, and practice. Recently in history there have been attempts to stress the importance of practice, often correlated with Bourdieu's notion of habitus as what is embedded, goes without saying, or is simply assumed (in a sense, fully immanent to experience or a way of being). In literary criticism one finds at times an animus against critical theory and an insistence on the appreciation of the literary text in and for itself as the site in which everything of value, including meaning, is and should remain embedded. (A similar animus may also be at play in the revival of "presence" and the immediacy of aesthetic or historical experience, for example, in the recent work of Hans Ulrich Gumbrecht or Eelco Runia.)[41] Bourdieu was himself within the Durkheimian tradition, and for Durkheim sacred practices, including rituals, constituted, at least in traditional societies, a habitus.

Most historians would see fascism and Nazism as somehow combining practice and ideology. Of course much depends on what one means by ideology, whose senses are also multiple, which is not to say that the concepts of practice and habitus are transparent. I shall simply touch on the two extremes, or at least two sources or currents, of ideology that are often opposed or separated from one another. One is the systematically articulated system of concepts or beliefs. You find at least an approximation of this in highly self-conscious intellectuals, say, Kant, Hegel, or Marx. Whether any modern movement or regime has an ideology in this sense is dubious. A regime may have a doctrinal or dogmatic basis, but it may be a stretch to compare this with an articulated system. Very few historians would see Nazism as having a systematic ideology, although many would see it as having a doctrinal or dogmatic basis in racism, especially racially oriented anti-Semitism and the desire for a racially pure, unscathed, *Judenfrei*, utopian *Volksgemeinschaft*—a racial utopia.[42]

The second, and I think more historically pertinent, notion of ideology was formulated by Louis Althusser and taken up by many others. It has curious resonances with aspects of "religion." And it has many different forms and valences, including a quasi-religious, at times pious approach to the literary, especially when the latter is conjoined with an aversion to theory and even to literary critics who may "spoil" an "authentic," immediate appreciation of the text or art work. For Althusser, ideology addresses, hails, or "interpellates" one and calls for a committed response. In more secular terms, it also issues a call or, in colloquial terms, says "hey you." In more "religious," or at least affectively charged and even visceral, terms it may, beseechingly or commandingly, call one's name, for example, Hail Adolf or even Heil Hitler. It is related to subject formation, and it need not appeal to systematic thought. Indeed, a systematic ideology that is explicit and well articulated opens itself to scrutiny and may invite criticism. An ideology (including an ideologically saturated, unself-critical narrative) that hails or interpellates can be more vague, even confused, and linked more compellingly, more bindingly, and more unreflectively to practices, even rituals and more or less structured forms of acting out phantasms.

I have frequently used or referred to a concept that has become prominent recently: the postsecular.[43] As I intimated in the introduction, the postsecular is neither the secular nor the religious or sacred but somehow both—or betwixt and between. It comes into its own in the attempt to re-enchant the world, even to evoke a sense of the uncanny, the epiphanous, the extraordinariness of the ordinary, indeed the miraculous or the endowed with grace, charisma, the gift of grace. The postsecular has very labile, often rather confused relations to the aesthetic, notably including the enshrined "trinity" of the performative, the uncanny, and the sublime. As I also intimated earlier, my own appeal to the concept of the postsecular involves both use and mention, indicating both hesitancy in making certain affirmations and a desire to leave open certain questions I raise.

I would raise again the issue of the possible relations between the sacred and the sublime as seemingly religious and secular (or perhaps postsecular) correlates—the sublime as a displacement or at least analog of the transcendent sacred (or perhaps the holy), indeed what is out of this world (in a phrase often used with reference to works of art). (Beauty is more immanent and mediated—less excessive or extreme. The uncanny disorients beauty but, insofar as it may be seen as a returning repressed, it is closer to the immanent [for Freud, ultimately the mother's genitals or womb]. The return of the sacred in the secular, including the sublime, is a somewhat paradoxical, particularly disorienting mode of the uncanny—as is a sublime elation stimulated by viewing or enacting the abuse or killing of palpably "immanent" sources of putative contamination.) One may also mention what I have termed "traumatropisms"—different attempts to transfigure trauma into the sublime or the sacred, for example, in the sacralization or sublimation of founding traumas such as (in different ways) the Crucifixion, the French Revolution, the Civil War, the Holocaust, and the First World War for Hitler and for others, for example, for Ernst Jünger with respect to the ecstatic *Fronterlebnis*.[44] For Hitler the devastating disappointment of loss of the war was intensified by the evangelical promise of its outbreak. (In Germany, this sense of devastation was of course exacerbated by developments in the interwar period, including runaway inflation followed by the Great Depression.) As Hitler, evoking the advent of the First World War, put it in *Mein Kampf*:

> For me, as for every other German, the most memorable period of my life now began. Face to face with that mighty struggle all the past fell away into oblivion. For me these hours came as a deliverance from the distress that had weighed upon me during the days of my youth. I am not ashamed to acknowledge today that I was carried away by the enthusiasm of the moment and that I sank down upon my knees and thanked Heaven out of the fullness of my heart for the favour of having been permitted to live in such a time.[45]

One obviously has here the language of the conversion experience that turned into extreme disappointment at the war's end, which may well have fostered a quest for another way to be born again or redeemed. I would reiterate that the general question of the labile, often confused relations between the sacred or the religious and the aesthetic are very important in certain currents in modernity, including but in no sense restricted to fascism.

Allowing for the very problematic meaning or meanings of religion, the sacred, and the aesthetic, I cautiously move on to fascism and, in particular, Nazism and ask whether they can be seen in any significant way—not entirely or even essentially—but in any significant way as related to the religious and the sacred, including their contested and often confused relations to the aesthetic.[46] (I shall not go into the more delimited and more readily researchable question of the actual empirical relations between fascist regimes and religious institutions such as the Catholic Church or the related question of clerico-fascism.[47]

These relations are intricate and run from compromise to active collaboration as well as less frequent but important contestation and, at times, opposition.)[48]

I have mentioned the conception of ideology that incorporates displaced religious aspects, notably in its role in forming subjects through hailing, calling, or (in Althusser's term) interpellation—subjects who may well engage in practices bound up with ideological phantasms, beliefs, or convictions. What is, I think, of general significance during the interwar period is the widespread appeal of fascism, including its appeal for intellectuals, and the extremely labile nature of ideologies in terms of shifts in position of individuals across the spectrum and of "borrowings" from ideology to ideology, even when they were militantly opposed to one another—including a tendency to valorize violence in intrinsic or regenerative, even sacrificial, and not only in limited strategic terms. As intimated earlier, in the sacrificially oriented Georges Bataille, this led for awhile to a defense of what was termed *surfascisme*, or taking from fascism its methods presumably in order to oppose fascism—a kind of homeopathic strategy that could well lead to overdosing on the antidote, especially when that antidote involved the typically escalating appeal to violence.

A further problem, however, is the relation between fascism and Nazism. This question involves the broader issue of totalitarianism, which has been used, with certain qualifications, to include fascism, Nazism, and Soviet Communism. The concept had a pronounced ideological role in the Cold War, almost analogous to that of terrorism and the "war on terror" today. (One might almost say, paraphrasing Freud, that where ideologically totalitarianism once was, there terrorism has come to be, with certain states both attacking or disavowing terrorism and more or less covertly employing terroristic techniques to combat it.) This ideological role jeopardized the more analytic uses of the concept of totalitarianism. And the question with respect to the latter is whether the concept, even as an analytic model or ideal type that one acknowledges was never fully realized in empirical reality, obscures too many differences. Mussolini and certain of his ideologues did affirm a totalitarian state as a goal. And the concept of totality was prevalent. Stanley Payne and others see political religion (PR) in partial contrast to civil religion (CR) as centered on the state and totalitarian in incentive.[49] But whether totalitarianism is a way to highlight the similarities between Nazism and fascism or fascisms is questionable. Arendt herself, with whom Payne agrees in his book of 1995 (p. 206), argued that the concept of totalitarianism did not apply to Italian fascism and perhaps not even to Nazism, although it might have, had the Nazis won the war. So that leaves the Soviet Union and the problem of the Cold War. Perhaps most important, reliance on the concept of totalitarianism may well obscure the specificity of genocide.

Even without invoking the problematic concept of totalitarianism, one may note that there were certain "totalizing" incentives (for example, in the collapse or undoing of certain distinctions) as well as overlaps and actual alliances between Nazis and fascists. Interestingly, both claimed to be spiritual—more spiritual than materialistic Marxism and materialistic capitalism. Both appealed to violence in furthering supposedly spiritual ends and valorized violence in ways that might even be seen as conjointly aestheticizing *and* sacralizing, notably as regenerative if not redemptive, elevating, exhilarating, and perhaps even sublime. And both were expansionist, with the Nazis seeking *Lebensraum* and colonies in eastern Europe. It has even been argued that the Nazi quest for *Lebensraum* had a causal role or at least was a very significant factor in the Holocaust. Once they invaded the east, the Nazis had to deal with an enormous number of Jews—notably in Russia, Poland, and Hungary. And they had to clear space for ethnic Germans. So the Holocaust could be seen as caused or at least strongly influenced by problems in population control. This view fits in with what is probably the major tendency in the historiographical literature—that stressing bureaucratic processes, conflict over turf, industrialized mass murder, the machinery of destruction, and more recently, at least in certain quarters, biopower. I think this approach points to one important and related set of factors. (Quite important as well is the often affirmed Nazi variant of social Darwinism that called for the extinction of "lower" races.) But I do not think these factors are sufficient to explain the genocide. And it is noteworthy that killing actions began before Nazis controlled large land masses and peoples, and genocidal practices were part and parcel of the conquest of those areas. Dan Michman has even argued that the development of ghettos was not instrumentally rational in motivation but stemmed from deeply internalized fear and repulsion in encountering "radically other" *Ostjuden*.[50]

Some historians have insistently argued that what differentiated Nazism from other fascisms was as important, if not more important, than what they shared, especially the Nazi role in the "final solution" or the genocidal treatment of Jews as well as the widespread, violent abuse of other victims and victim groups. Genocide has generally not been seen as a defining dimension of fascism. Saul Friedländer in his own way plausibly makes this argument.[51] But Friedländer, like many historians, recognizes that other nationalities and countries were active collaborators in the genocide, at times even outdoing Nazis or going beyond what was required or even requested of them. The SS were reportedly sometimes taken aback by the excesses of their Ukrainian and certain other Baltic "helpers."[52] It is well known, after Robert Paxton's research, that Vichy France deported children to the camps when such action was not required by the Nazis.[53] Jan T. Gross has told the story of how Poles abused and massacred Jewish neighbors and took over their property without being coerced by Nazis during the pogrom of July 10, 1941, at Jedwabne.[54] He has also recounted how, even after 90 percent of Poland's three-and-a-half million Jews had been "eliminated" during the Nazi occupation, the deadliest pogrom of twentieth-century Europe took place in the Polish town of Kielce on July 4, 1946, a year after the war ended, as Poles once again killed Jews. For Gross, quite significant in motivating the pogrom was the fear that Jews would reclaim expropriated property, a fear that may have been reinforced by a sense of guilt or unease about what certain Poles had earlier done to Jews and might do again.[55] For Gross the long-standing accusation of Jewish involvement in ritual murder remained prevalent in Polish society or at least was invoked on numerous occasions.[56] And Polish Gentiles, recognized as "righteous" at Yad Vashem, were afraid to reveal that, at the risk of their own lives, they had helped Jews during the war, because of the expected hostile reaction of their own anti-Semitic neighbors.[57]

Another important point that has recently become more prominent is that the Holocaust seems less unprecedented (or "unique") if not seen in a purely Eurocentric context but related to practices and policies with respect to people of color in the colonies. In addition to the well-documented 1904 genocide by German occupying forces against the Herero in German West Africa (Namibia) along with the arguably genocidal slaughter of the Nama, one may note that the French in Africa, the Belgians in the Congo, and the white South Africans were at times quite extreme in their violence against indigenous "enemies."[58] A strong case has been made for the recognition of genocidal action against the Armenians under the Ottoman Empire during and just after the First World War. There has also been heated debate about the occurrence of a genocide against native peoples in the Western Hemisphere. The practices of Australia with respect to aborigines were assimilative and often quite violent, including killings in the colonial period and, in the twentieth century, the forcible removal of some twenty to fifty thousand children of mixed parentage from aboriginal families and their placement in institutions or in white foster homes.[59] All of these important cases and controversies would require extensive discussion sensitive to issues of time, place, and context, for example, with respect to comparisons or analogies with the Holocaust or Nazi genocide against Jews (including comparisons or analogies concerning the treatment of animals in factory farming and experimentation, as in Charles Patterson's *Eternal Treblinka* [the title comes from a phrase of Isaac Bashevis Singer, himself a Holocaust survivor and a Nobel laureate, who wrote that for animals "life is an eternal Treblinka"] or, in a more nuanced manner than in Patterson, in Boria Sax's *Animals in the Third Reich*).[60] One issue is whether and to what extent other forms of collective violence involved a sense of contamination and a desire for purification or cleansing, perhaps including eradication or denial of the animal in the human (especially one's own group) along with the projective designation of other groups as subhuman animals.

While not pretending to resolve the complex issues I have mentioned, what I would like to suggest is that the Nazi genocide is not reducible to, but may have involved, "religious," purifying, regenerative, apocalyptic, redemptive dimensions—one might conceivably call them postsecular—that were in some confused and confusing way at times connected with numerous other factors, including aesthetic concerns, perhaps even a negative yet possibly exhilarating aesthetic of the sublime (with a role for the beautiful as well, which the "ugly," anti-aesthetic—even "pest"- or "weed"-like—Jews impaired or destroyed). I think these dimensions are especially applicable to the actions and motivations of certain elite Nazis and perhaps a significant number of others as well, including Hitler and Himmler, who were bound together by a strongly cathected nexus, with Hitler becoming for Himmler (and others, especially among elite Nazis such as Goebbels) a kind of anxiety-inducing, indeed traumatizing, godlike figure who issued sacred orders. Obedience to Hitler's sacred orders, based on a faith, a fidelity, and a trust, uncontested by criticism, indeed allied with fanaticism, and allowing for no critical distance in relation to the will of the *Führer*, was proclaimed as a Nazi, and especially an SS, cardinal virtue. In the words of Hermann Göring, "there is something mystical, unsayable, almost incomprehensible about this man . . . we love Adolf Hitler, because we believe, with a faith that is deep and unshakable, that he was sent to us by God to save Germany." In the analysis of Joachim Remak: "For reason, [National Socialism] substituted faith—faith in 'the movement', faith, to an even greater extent, in Hitler."[61] The object of faith (*Glaube*) was more the movement (*die Bewegung*) and, of course, Hitler, than the party or the state, although there might be a metaphoric identification between Hitler, the party, and the nation or the *Volk* (as in Rudolf Hess's speech filmed in Riefenstahl's *Triumph of the Will*).

In a recent essay defending the use of the notion of political religion in a sacralized politics, Klaus Vondung has even asserted (with some exaggeration concerning the range of its explanatory force): "I understand the apocalyptic view of Hitler and other Nazis as the most poignant manifestation of the National Socialist political religion and, above all, as the only plausible explanation for the holocaust—if indeed an explanation in the sense of exposing motives and policy is possible at all." He continues:

[Hitler] viewed world history as being determined by the struggle between two universal forces, whose irreconcilability he chiefly expressed in the dualistic symbolism of "light-darkness." Subsequently, he believed the decisive battle to be close at hand, which would bring victory over the "deadly enemy of all light." This "power of evil" manifested itself for him in the Jews, the "evil enemy of mankind," onto whom he transferred the responsibility for all material deficits of the world, as well as other imaginary dangers and threats. Hitler viewed the well-being of the entire world as being dependent on Germany's victory in the final apocalyptic struggle.[62]

Vondung also notes that "the attitude of *Glaube* (belief, faith, sometimes even with the meaning of 'creed') played a very important role in [Hitler's] thought and vocabulary. . . . Within this *Glaube*, in this case to be translated as 'creed,' blood did assume a spiritual, if not holy, quality even in Hitler's thought." Vondung adds that for Alfred Rosenberg, "notions of race and blood primarily have a spiritual or cultural meaning," and Rosenberg "proclaims a 'religion of the blood' (*Religion des Blutes*)" (112).

The broader suggestion I would make is that, to the extent they were operative, Nazism's "postsecular" dimensions do not represent some regression to barbarism, much less "brutishness," but instead make up an intricate dimension of "modernity"—what might in its most perplexing form be termed a constitutive outside: what is inside modernity as its uncanny repressed or disavowed other.[63] This "extimate" other (to use Lacan's term) may emerge, possibly with a virulence related to its repressed or disavowed status, but at times it also comes to be articulated in a more or less explicit way. One place this articulation arguably occurs is, I think, in Himmler's October 1943 Posen speech (or speeches), which I have discussed in other places and to which I shall allude later. (My own repeated yet varied references to it are overdetermined: the speech has a hauntingly possessive quality that may induce in the commentator a suspension between acting out and working through—as in Freud's famous fort-da "game" in *Beyond the Pleasure Principle* (1920) or, with respect to Himmler's Posen speech itself, in Syberberg's *Hitler,* as well as in Derrida's understanding of speculation as analogous to a fort-da process[64]; the speech is a rare instance of a key perpetrator reflecting on motivations—and in the presence of other elite perpetrators; thus far the speech has received insufficient recognition and analysis—or even rather dismissive if not "banalizing" treatment—by both historians and others, including critical theorists.)[65] One might even speculate that the seemingly uncanny return of ritual murder charges against Jews in late nineteenth- and early twentieth-century Europe itself resulted from a projection of phobic, ritualistic attitudes toward them.[66] What I am pointing to in particular is a symbolically, even quasi-ritually "purifying" and not simply hygienic response to Jews and possibly other victims, who were projective objects of anxiety, allowing Nazis (and not only Nazis) to deny sources of disquiet in themselves by construing alienated others as causes of pollution or contamination, as well as ugliness, in the *Volksgemeinschaft*. These phobic, toxic, contaminating presences had to be gotten rid of (*entfernen*) in order for the sacred community to achieve quasi-ritual purity, integrity, and regeneration—a new beauty and even sublimity, indeed redemption or salvation in a racial utopia (*Endlösung* as *Auslösung* and *Erlösung*—"final solution" as release and redemption or salvation). The sense of regeneration or being born again, and possibly redeemed, was fueled in ecstatic collective rituals, celebrations, rallies, parades, and related events that were not simply aesthetic or dramatic performances, although they were that as well.

Extremely important, and not incompatible with more "religious" conviction, is the sense that a sacred duty was being fulfilled in eliminating Jews, which might have to be taken on faith and undertaken with something like purity of intention. As Himmler puts it at Posen: "A number of SS men have offended against this order [to take nothing of goods confiscated from Jews for oneself]. There are not many [Himmler and others were apprehensive that such "corruption" was in fact prevalent in the SS], and they will be dead men—*without mercy* [*Gnadenlos!*—the one time Himmler emphatically raises his voice during the speech]. We have the moral right, we had the duty to our people to do it, to kill this people who want to kill us. But we do not have the right to enrich ourselves with even one fur, one Mark, with one cigarette, with one watch, with anything." Himmler continues: "We have carried out this most difficult task for the love of our people. And we have taken on no defect [or damage] within us, in our soul, in our character [*keinen Schaden in unserem Innern, in unserer Seele, in unserem Charakter daran genommen*]."[67] Apparently, Nazis were for Himmler absolved of all criminality and guilt.

What were the source and the nature of the elation or excitement that seems evident in such scenes?[68] Was it uncanny, sublime, aestheticizing, carnivalesque, sadistic, vengeful, an accompaniment to fanatical self-righteousness or to "brutality" (an anthropocentric misnomer that explains little), or some confused amalgam of ideological commitments, tangled emotions, and phantasms?[69] And how does one parse Himmler's words to high-ranking SS insiders at Posen, with his references to the shudder caused by the Night of the Long Knives (*es hat jeden geschauert*), the experience shared by those who have been through it (*durchgestanden*) and know what it means to see "a hundred corpses lie side by side, or five hundred, or a thousand"? Indeed what does one make of this strangely disconcerting appeal to the formative power and authority of experience? How does one understand his formula for becoming hard and avoiding traumatic breakdown by enduring the aporia or combining in oneself the antinomies of decency or uprightness (*anständig geblieben zu sein*) and sticking out scenes of mass murder? Why do such events constitute, for Himmler, "an unwritten, never-to-be-written page of glory" in German history? And why does the speech include apocalyptic apprehensions and then a prayer-like invocation that enjoins his listeners to "direct [their] thoughts to the Führer, our Führer, Adolf Hitler, who will create the Germanic Reich and will lead us into the Germanic future"? And then a dedication: "To our Führer Adolf Hitler: Sieg Heil! Sieg Heil! Sieg Heil!" Can an acceptable response to these questions be reduced to the contention that Nazis were simply hardened "brutes" or criminals, ignoring the process by which they became hard and baldly asserting that any notion of a role for the negative sublime in their orientation or outlook is simply beside the point? Without pretending that definitive answers are available, I raise these questions because I think the propensity to reduce the Nazis to hardened criminals and dismiss any notion of a negative sublime or even of the quasi-religious as operative in Nazis and, in particular, in Himmler's Posen speech(es) of October 1943 is at play in certain recent analyses.[70] And how does one understand the relations among the literary, the political, and the quasi-ritual in the work of Louis-Ferdinand Céline, perhaps the most innovative modern writer who affirmed an affiliation with rabid, visceral anti-Semitism and Nazi ideology? Are there gaps between these dimensions of his work, even a caesura between his novels and his ideological pamphlets, or is there a close interaction between them?[71]

Before concluding, I would like to be as explicit as possible about the nature of my argument. I am not offering an overall inclusive and exhaustive account of the motivation of the vast majority of Germans under the Nazi regime, even those who devotedly followed the leader. Nor am I denying the significance of other forces and factors. I am trying to explore what I think are aspects of the perpetration of genocide and perhaps of extreme collective violence in cases other than the Shoah—aspects that still call for further research and conceptualization. I am also raising the question of the manner and extent to which a sacralizing or regenerative understanding of violence and a desire for purification from supposedly contaminating forces play a complex role in "modern" culture in general and in literature or art in particular. The task for empirical research would be to see whether and to what extent archival and testimonial sources substantiate or run counter to the notions of sublime elation, regeneration through violence, and a quasi-ritual animus related to feelings of contamination or pollution by the other, notably (but perhaps not only) the Jew, whose elimination was deemed necessary for liberation or even for a redemption of the *Volksgemeinschaft*. And a challenge to literature and art, as well as their analysis, would be to examine closely the ways these phenomena and related processes have been, or could conceivably be, rendered in a manner that is not simply a participatory enactment. I think these processes are rather clear in Hitler and Goebbels as well as in dimensions of others, including Himmler at least in terms of his bond with, or even adulation of, Hitler. I also think they may apply to certain elated participants in killing actions, perhaps less so in the more routinized activities in the camps.[72] And while the Jews had a specific salience for certain key Nazis, including Hitler, Himmler, Goebbels, and Eichmann, the "redemptive" dynamic, involving purification and regeneration through violence and victimization, might possibly apply to other groups as well, thus placing the concept of "redemptive anti-Semitism" in a somewhat larger context and opening it to careful, critical, comparative study.

Formulated in somewhat different terms, I have been trying to investigate the nature of the claim that might be made for "redemptive anti-Semitism," set in a larger framework of racism, victimization, and quasi-sacrificial purification and regeneration through violence, thereby exploring in certain ways the term that is central to Saul Friedländer's *Nazi Germany and the Jews* but, as I have argued, that may not have been sufficiently elaborated on a conceptual or theoretical level in that very important work.[73] Here a crucial problem is to investigate the relations between "ritual" or quasi-religious considerations and other forces or factors active both in the Nazi genocide and in other social or cultural phenomena (including works of art) by pointing out and critically analyzing them, while resisting the tendency to elide or even repeat the equivocations and confusions of Nazi discourse and practice themselves.

Acknowledging complications in any specific empirical analysis, I would nonetheless like to conclude with the question of the extent to which post-secular sacralizing forces are quite important in history, even in what we term "modernity," especially in the form of scapegoating and purifying, victimizing practices, along with their relation to "aesthetic" factors such as circumscribed exclusionary conceptions of beauty (or "what fits"), a penchant for purity or "cleansing" that has at times ritualistic overtones, and a desire for sublime exaltation as well as carnivalesque glee, notably through scenes of excess and intrinsically valorized regenerative violence.[74] A crucial issue is how to assess the role and to elaborate a critical account of a victimizing, purifying frame of reference in ways that further at least three things:

1. An informed, critical, *nonsacrificial* understanding of problems on the levels of foreign policy, economic exploitation, and social structure, including gaps in wealth and income both across and within societies. To state explicitly what should be obvious: I do not endorse the quasi-sacrificialism, with its relation to transgressive (yet possibly legitimated) excess, regenerative violence, and desires for purification, that I think has been significant in modernity. Instead, I think it should be subjected to deconstruction and sustained critique, thereby facilitating its working through toward a basically different mode of relating to others. And I would be quite happy if it could be convincingly shown that it has in fact not been important and forceful.

2. An attempt to critically disengage scapegoating and victimization, as well as any notion of originary, regenerative, or divine violence, from the sacred and to raise the question of what in the sacred (or the postsecular) is defensible or of value, or at least what might be of value in a significantly transformed institutional context.[75] A related effort is to elaborate distinctions among very divergent modalities of the sublime. To highlight this point, one might juxtapose statements from Himmler's Posen speech (notably, "many of you know what it means to see a hundred corpses lie side by side or five hundred or a thousand") with the famous lines beginning William Blake's "Auguries of Innocence": "To see a World in a Grain of Sand / And a Heaven in a Wild Flower / Hold Infinity in the palm of your hand / And Eternity in an hour." One might see these passages as similar in certain ways.[76] But the uncanny or shocking juxtaposition that in one respect seems to mark the closest proximity in more decisive ways conceals abyssal differences. Montage here may be misleading and function to obfuscate the importance of the difference between a discriminatory call or appeal to kill a scapegoated group of humans while sentimentalizing other animals (which you find in Himmler, especially by supplementing the Posen speech with sections of his conversations with his masseur, Felix Kersten) and Blake's affirmation, both sublime and disarmingly ethical, that anything like genuine love for humans implies the nonabusive embrace of the claims of all animals.[77]

3. A renewal of the problem of the relations between history and literature in an explicitly nonreductive manner, including with respect to the role of the sacred or the postsecular and to various theories that are focused on that role. Nazis certainly opposed certain forms of literature and art while defending others. But they were not concerned with the specificity or distinctiveness of the "literary" or of the artistic

in general. Rather, their concern was the subordinate function of literature and art as ideological supports of the regime, its ideology, and its leader. Such a function is a primary target of theoretical inquiry with a critical relation to its object, disclosing and counteracting its role in culture and society. Yet a critical theory is not like the stereotype of a "covering law." At best it devotes attention and provides insight with respect to more or less significant dimensions of a problem without totally accounting for it. And even if one cannot provide a conclusive definition of the literary, one can nonetheless insist on respecting its relative specificity and the distinctiveness of certain texts in which literary dimensions play a particularly prominent role. To do so implies a valorization of these dimensions, for their very specificity may be denied or obliterated, as they were in historically particular ways under the Nazis and may be in other cultural currents or movements. Even if one questions the conferral of an absolute, indeed sacral privilege upon literature and finds the concept of the purely literary or the literary "as such" to be incoherent, one may still maintain that literature has often been a special site for certain imaginative, provocative, critical, and self-critical explorations in recent history.

On a broader level, the basic issue is how to relate the psychic, the social, the political, and the broadly cultural (including the literary as well as the ideological) in critically analyzing and generating counterforces to symptoms and causes of basic problems. Violence along with trauma is one of these problems, which achieves an extremely destructive manifestation in genocide. A related problem is actual and desirable interactions between excess and limits in various areas of activity, along with the possibilities and limitations of the turn to the postsecular, with its displaced relations to religion. Here consolation, including the consolations of religion, philosophy, or literature, is not the issue. Consolation remains psychic and intra-individual, as does a turn away from politics and social involvement. The issue is rather how best to inquire into and to further more desirable relations and interactions among individuals and groups that are not constricted by unexamined egocentric and anthropocentric assumptions.

Epilogue

Recent Figurations of Trauma and Violence:
Tarrying with Žižek

Slavoj Žižek has arguably been the most in-
fluential as well as the most controversial theorist of the recent past, beginning at least in 1989 with Verso's publication of his first well-known book
The Sublime Object of Ideology, which was followed by a profusion of publications that have continued unabated to the present. His work is avidly read
by a significant group not restricted to scholars, and the rate at which Žižek
publishes requires sincere devotion or at least voracious curiosity on the part
of his readers. Žižek has indeed become a cultural phenomenon. Even his
wedding some years ago to a young Argentine supermodel was followed in
the local press with the type of attention usually devoted to a film or rock
star. And Žižek's live performances may vie with those of famous entertain-
ers. Indeed, one of the appeals of his writings as well as his live performances
is his ability to shock. But under the ostentatious display and the shock effect is also a level of seriousness, including advocacy of violence and a rather
disabused if not cynical view of any nonviolent mode of social change in a
world in which he believes all protest as well as all worthwhile intellectual
activity is immediately co-opted and recycled as self-advertising pulp fiction by the powers that be. In this analysis, I take Žižek seriously and often
at his word, even while recognizing the role of the parodic and self-parodic
in his oral and occasionally in his written "performances." A moot issue is
the extent to which Žižek transferentially repeats the appeals to violence in

movements such as fascism that he explicitly criticizes, opening himself (as he realizes) to the charge of being a "left fascist." Whatever one may make of this charge, Žižek's sympathy for violence on the left is explicit and at times insistent.

Violence typically traumatizes, unless there is some "mechanism" whereby one is hardened to the experience or able to transfigure it into the sacred or the sublime. Here a crucial issue is whether one is indeed traumatized by an experience that is typically traumatizing for the perpetrator as well as the victim. The "trick" of something like Nazi ideology or even of militaristic ideology in general is that it may harden the self through a kind of preemptive or homeopathic numbness that (if it works) averts overt traumatization or at least breakdown of the perpetrator.

In inquiring into trauma, violence, and their transfigurations, one may distinguish between the historical and the transhistorical as well as question the tendency to collapse the historical into the transhistorical, if not the transcendental, rather than to explore critically their complex articulations. (The problem posed here is that of relations among the historical, the transhistorical, and the transcendental.) At times an ideology, fetishistic narrative, or even a seemingly critical theory can perform the transfiguration of trauma as well as convert the historical into the transhistorical or even the transcendental. This may of course happen in state-sponsored violence, such as war for God and country, or in less pronounced but pervasive police or paramilitary activity, whose importance and whose excesses must be kept in mind, as well as in nongovernmental movements or ideological currents. I shall focus on rather subtle and problematic figurations of trauma, but the more blatant and directly destructive forms should remain a constant concern while not leading to unmediated associations or unwarranted amalgamations.

This approximation of trauma and the sublime, as well as *jouissance* and elation or ecstasy, is often pronounced in certain Lacanian approaches in which trauma is related to, or identified with, the transhistorical "real," and all historical or empirical instances of trauma, whether collective or individual, are derived from, or taken as illustrative of, the transhistorical if not the transcendental. The traumatic transhistorical "real" is understood in terms of the void, gap, or split in the anxiety-ridden, divided, or necessarily alienated self that is never identical to, or at one and at home with, itself. Instead of working out a problematic articulation of the historical and what is postulated as transhistorical, the historical here tends to be subordinated to the transhistorical. This is one reason why the interest of at least certain Lacanians in history seems to be primarily, if not exclusively, for illustrative purposes, even when it comes to historical processes as imposing as colonialism, slavery, and genocide. Thus a Lacanian account will often have a frame narrative featuring the real and its accompaniments (such as the symbolic and the imaginary), with any historical material constituting an inserted narrative or subplot.

One may, in a qualified, explicitly speculative manner, acknowledge, at least within important dimensions of the so-called Western tradition, the pertinence of something like a transhistorical trauma, or gap, split, void, or absence that has been figured over time in various ways, including the fall and original sin (or *felix culpa*), the passage from nature to culture (with the possibly valorized yet traumatizing "fall" from instinct), Oedipalization with the break from the pre-Oedipal relation to the mother, the entry into language or signification (often seen as traumatic or forced), and the "nihilating" relation of the for-itself to the in-itself. I would add that such an acknowledgement might, as I would recommend, raise as an explicit problem and not prematurely foreclose the question of the relation between the quasi-transcendental, which is universal, and the transhistorical, which may be a function of given traditions. In any event, one may view critically certain understandings of, or implications drawn from, a notion of transhistorical or even quasi-transcendental trauma and its various figurations and offshoots. One dubious understanding is that which simply subordinates the historical to the transhistorical, if not the transcendental, an understanding that is as dubious as its opposite, which is more prevalent among historians and sociologists, to wit, the "historicist" derivation of all anxiety and disorientation from particular historical events or situations.

One could discuss many important thinkers and writers in terms of variations on the foregoing constellation of views, not all of whom are distinctively Lacanian.[1] As I have indicated, one may arguably find this constellation at times in W. G. Sebald, including his notion of a natural history of destruction which, in its own way, subsumes the historical into a transhistorical, melancholic, impossibly mournful story of endless catastrophe and points to the ruin as the man-made locus of the subsidence of history into nature and its cycles. And a key reference point is, of course, Walter Benjamin not only on the ruin but on inconsolable melancholy and the Angel of History as a traumatized, benumbed, quasi-oneiric witness to mounting catastrophic ruins—a witness who looks and remembers but cannot act.[2]

One of the most thought-provoking theorists, notably with respect to the issue of melancholia, resistance to working through, and the affirmation of momentary miraculous epiphanies, is Eric L. Santner who has joined many others in signaling the importance of Sebald and has even become in his recent work very close intellectually to Žižek, as is evident in a kind of postsecular manifesto, "Miracles Happen: Benjamin, Rosenzweig, Freud, and the Matter of the Neighbor," his contribution to the collective volume published with Žižek and Kenneth Reinhard, *The Neighbor: Three Inquiries in Political Theology*.[3] Žižek's own contribution is entitled "Neighbors and Other Monsters: A Plea for Ethical Violence."[4] Other performances, as well as the films that frame them, would be worth discussing, including Astra Taylor's *Žižek!* (with the exclamation point perhaps inviting a reading of the title as a command—a command to come out and "Žižek") and *NSK Predictions of Fire*, in which Žižek, seen as sitting on high, offers an emphatic defense of the performances of the Slovenian Leibach group. These performances seem to involve equivocal mimicry of fascist procedures (heavy-metal occultism, ominous monologic voices, the boy drummer from Leni Riefenstahl's *Triumph of the Will*). Žižek nonetheless sees them in no uncertain terms as homeopathically baring the device of practices "we" must confront. Santner's own broader project, notably in *On Creaturely Life: Rilke/Benjamin/Sebald*, is to triangulate the orientations of Agamben, Badiou, and Žižek. Here I shall simply reiterate Santner's importance and say a few things about Žižek as well as merely allude in passing to Agamben and Badiou. The rather rapid rise to prominence, indeed the almost overnight discovery and ascent to superstardom, of Žižek, along with the rediscovery and newly accorded status of Agamben and Badiou, are themselves intellectual and cultural phenomena that deserve extended critical reflection.

My focus on problematic aspects of Žižek's approach is not meant to deny its significance. I have suggested that a crucial dimension, if not the main thrust of his approach, is to put himself forward as a carnivalesque proponent of hyperbole, a kind of court jester of modernity, whose insistent provocations undercut any attempt at systematic analysis and critique. One may acknowledge this point but see it as applying mostly to his in-person performances and less frequently to his writing, where there is often a recycling of old jokes used instrumentally to make a philosophical or political point. In any case, the carnivalesque side of Žižekian self-presentation might contest but would not simply eliminate his more "serious" arguments, including what he is quite willing to call his dogmatic Lacanianism. On another level, Žižek's performative "hysteria" may well exert a contagious power of fascination that elicits mimetic effects and functions to override a critical response to what he asserts.

I would note an interesting complication: Žižek's Lacanianism is often combined with a Marxism or post-Marxism in a manner that may not be fully integrated but at times indicates convergences. At least on a historical level, Marxism is often invoked as an ultimate explanatory theory such that capitalism becomes the fundamental cause of various problems, at times in a convincing and at other times in an overly reductive manner. He is forceful in bringing out what he terms "the fundamental systemic violence of capital" and the way it may be concealed by a focus on "directly visible 'subjective' violence . . . performed by a clearly identifiable agent" (such as a terrorist) as well as on humanitarian efforts that address symptoms rather than causes of human and ecological disaster.[5] But he short-circuits the relation between the transhistorical and the historical in asserting that the Lacanian "real is the inexorable 'abstract,' spectral logic of capital that determines what goes on in social reality"—a spectral logic brought to an extreme point in the 2008 financial crisis and its very real, continuing effects in society.[6]

The collapse of the transhistorical into the historical—the "real" into capitalism or, elsewhere, into concentration camps[7]—is one indication that Žižek can go in questionable directions. On a more specifically historical level, he downplays the importance of racism in the Nazi genocide in a way that one would be surprised at present to find even in old-guard Marxists. He asserts that Hitler's "targeting of the Jews was ultimately an act of displacement in which he avoided the real enemy—the core of capitalist social relations themselves" so that "the capitalist order could survive."[8] Žižek also uncritically accepts Giorgio Agamben's pointed but one-dimensional understanding of the Jew in the Nazi genocide simply as an instance of *homo sacer*, existing only as abject bare life, and thus not being perceived by Nazis as a contaminating, conspiratorial presence whose elimination would have ritual, redemptive, or quasi-sacrificial effects. (Thus, there is for Žižek no redemptive anti-Semitism, in Saul Friedländer's term, or the idea that crucial if not central to Nazism was the quest for a racial utopia.)[9] Žižek even insists: "One should therefore not be afraid to assert the formal parallel between the state annihilation of *Homini sacer*, for example, the Nazi killing of the Jews, and the revolutionary terror, where one can also kill without committing a crime and without sacrifice—the difference resides in the fact that the Nazi killing remains a means of state power." The differential criterion is in this context rather weak: revolutionary terror may have a quasi-sacrificial, ritual dimension (with opponents or critics treated as scapegoats and seen as traitorous sources of contamination) and can serve emerging state power. Moreover, the Nazi genocide, while not simply another pogrom, was not only a means of state power but had the support and active participation of significant numbers of both Germans and other national or ethnic groups. More shockingly, Žižek's analysis approximates the Nazi genocide to Benjamin's cryptic "divine violence," which Žižek accepts uncritically and with the utmost seriousness on his own behalf. He sees putatively divine violence as a "sign without meaning" or a (subjectively) miraculous Event, in Badiou's term, which he nonetheless interprets as in "the domain of sovereignty" and as having objects (presumably including the Jews in the Nazi genocide) that are "fully and completely guilty" (he may mean, one hopes, perceived as guilty) and "annihilated without being made a sacrifice."[10]

On the level of practice, however, Žižek has recently turned to a Bartleby-the-scrivener type of opting out or perhaps dropping out of a socioeconomic system that he finds so out of kilter that nonintervention may be the most advisable, indeed somehow the most "violent" response. Hence he affirms in no uncertain terms: "'Do you mean we should just do *nothing*? Just sit and wait?' One should gather the courage to answer: YES, precisely that."[11] This do-nothing *attentisme*, perhaps construable as a waiting for the apocalypse, is nonetheless for Žižek a component of what he terms his "endorsement of emancipatory violence" (206) that I shall address more fully later on.

In Žižek, the aporetic sensibility or the taste for paradox is pronounced. When he prefaces an assertion with "one should not be afraid" or "one should have the courage," one should indeed brace oneself for a comment that is shocking, dubious, and typically paradoxical. Two of his oft-repeated formulations are that (in the terms of Wagner's *Parsifal*) "the wound is healed only by the spear that smote you" and (echoing Derrida) the condition of possibility is the condition of impossibility.[12] I think one may gloss these assertions in a way that mitigates without eliminating paradox. The first is an appeal to the homeopathic logic of the antidote. But the problem is the dosage applied. I think the tendency in Žižek is to overdose on the antidote by going to the extreme limit almost every time. Yet the spear can heal the wound only if it is used in a certain way to cauterize or suture—not fatally burn or further wound its object. And, as I noted in the previous chapter, the condition of possibility is the condition of impossibility in that it is the condition of impossibility with respect to the "as such" (something Žižek at times forgets). To say that there is no such thing as the "as such" as such would be another way of saying that an essential condition of total purity or integrity is impossible, and it would thus serve to undermine both a logic of the absolute and a denial of one's own vulnerability as well as to counteract a sacrificial scapegoat mechanism whereby what causes anxiety in the self is projected onto a clear and distinct other. It would still leave open the problem of distinguishing between more or less accentuated differences, say, between victims and perpetrators or between forms of violence and nonviolence.

Žižek at times seems to go in the direction of my glosses. But his aporetic formulations may also become sensationalistic and reinforce a logic of the absolute, the extreme, and sacrifice or invite overdosing on the antidote.

This occurs when paradox itself is set in a frame wherein there is a sublime sacrificial gesture: one takes an oppressive regime's ideology more seriously than does the regime itself, thus presumably pushing it to an implosive or explosive limit. Or one gives all or goes to the extreme limit with no expectation of return, yet, like Abraham with the knife poised over Isaac's neck, one receives everything back through a transcendent act of grace. As Žižek puts the point in one of many such paradoxical formulations (all of whose terms in this case appear in italics): *"The intervention of Grace is not something distinct from the preceding loss, but is this very loss, the same act of self-renunciation, conceived from a different perspective."*[13] Hence, for example, the sacrifice intended by Abraham is his salvation or the death of Christ is his resurrection. (The ram that is the actual object of displacement and in fact sacrificed in the Akeda does not elicit Žižek's concern, as it has not been of concern to many other commentators—unlike Christ's excruciating passion and death that precede his resurrection.) Here, in Hegelian fashion, the concept for Žižek does much transformative work. Yet the position of absolute idealism is ultimately questioned through an appeal to Lacan (typically the trump card in Žižek). In presumed contradistinction to the view of "deconstructionists," the radically performative act of grace or creation ex nihilo is not pure because there is the nondiscursive "substance" or "real kernel" of enjoyment (202). "Enjoyment" is of course an inadequate translation of *jouissance*, which refers to deeply equivocal, sublime, indeed monstrous excess beyond the pleasure principle in the direction of the death drive. Still, Žižek insists that he, like Lacan and, in his view, Derrida as well, "remains thoroughly a 'transcendental' philosopher."[14] I think this means not only that he shares with Kant a focus on conditions of possibility but also that his insistence on the aporia or double bind and the priority he gives to often compulsively repeated, self-consuming formal analysis entails a diminished attention to the intricacies of historically specific problems and to real historical possibilities within the context of those problems, in contrast to the combination of endgame scenarios and violent leaps into the void or the beyond. Indeed (as in Agamben and perhaps Badiou) the emphasis on transcendental conditions of possibility links up with the impossible dream of radical transcendence of hitherto-known history into what must remain a blank utopia or empty form, increasingly conjoined in Žižek with an insistence on decisive violence.

For Žižek, as for some others, violence is transcendentally intrinsic to language itself, and (as if there were only two extreme alternatives) he even sees unsurpassable alienation as the lesser evil compared with that which it both counters and complements: the horrible, excessive closeness that, for him, engenders social violence. "What if," he asks rhetorically, "humans exceed animals in their capacity for violence precisely because they *speak*? As Hegel was already well aware, there is something violent in the very symbolism of a thing, which equals its mortification."[15] In brief the word or sign, however it is used, must necessarily sacrifice its object. (I find this prevalent transcendental view to be questionable. For example, there are specific situations in which not using language or not naming is linked with violence that may be sacrificial, say, with respect to animals that are to be killed, including the unnamed dog at the end of Coetzee's *Disgrace*.)[16] Žižek dismisses the notion of limits to excessive desire as premodern and proclaims: "Modernity is . . . defined by the coordinates of the Kantian philosophical revolution, in which the *absolute excess is that of the law itself*." Indeed, "it is language itself which pushes our desire beyond proper limits, transforming it into a 'desire that contains the infinite,' elevating it into an absolute striving that cannot ever be satisfied."[17] This stereotypically postromantic view is part and parcel of what might be termed a transcendentally legitimated, fatalistic modernism whereby excess *must* overwhelm all limits—a conception through which Žižek's own thought may be complicit with the infinitely expansive, excessive logic of unregulated capitalism that he seems to criticize. A question here is whether a mutually critical provocation of history and theory requires a different orientation and mode of thought in which any transcendence or break, however traumatic and resistant to historicist reduction, is situationally inflected as well as related, however problematically, to immanent critique.

A further issue is whether an inquiry into presuppositions or presumably transhistorical forces should make room for skepticism concerning a transcendental postulation concerning absolute conditions of possibility (including modernity's "law" of absolute excess) or creations ex nihilo (related to the "real" or Events of grace).

Žižek tries to take his rethinking of Lacan in political directions that are self-proclaimed to be "radical," often with a "more-radical-than thou" inflection with respect to the question of who is or is not really going all the way. Radicality seems to be conflated with extremism or excess, at least in the sense of systematically taking things to an implosive or explosive limit that confronts one with the "real" and involves some form of revolutionary violence. Indeed, for Žižek the very essence of the human is a monstrous, inhuman excess that marks the incursion of the real and has a "radical" political outlet, including the enactment or perhaps acting out of symptoms that one not only enjoys but are somehow converted "dialectically" into a transformative cure—the spear that heals the wound it causes. Traversing the fantasy is constitutive of this process and even seems to be the foundational political Act (capital A), which might be related to the Lacanian ethical imperative not to give up on one's desire (*ne cédez pas sur son désir*). The Act, similar to the Event in Badiou, is a fundamentally revolutionary initiative that places in radical question existing political assumptions and limits. In so doing, it presumably "touches the real" in disclosing what a sociopolitical regime has concealed, repressed, or disavowed—what it cannot publicly avow without risking delegitimation and disorder. (In *The Ticklish Subject*, Žižek appears to see such an Act in a Harper Valley PTA–type reading of the more intransigent, nonapologetic dimensions of the teacher Mary Kay Letourneau, who is even presented as a modern Antigone in her sexual relation [or nonrelation] with her then pubescent student paramour.)[18] In the Act, one discloses a regime's dirty little secret, which manifests itself in multiple symptomatic formations and forces it into the open. Ideology that encrypts or encodes the secret is not false consciousness but a constitutively necessary formation for both psyche and polity. Traversing the fantasy is thus not transcending fantasy, but it does require a passage from what Žižek terms imaginary identification based on resemblances (for example, the presumed resemblance of the neighbor, but not the non-neighbor, to oneself) to a paradoxical recognition of that which eludes resemblance and appropriation—the residual stain and the hole in the Other or in Being that bars any self-identity, community, or totality. Traversing the fantasy opens onto the monstrosity of others as well as the lack in the Other. It wards off any final solution, although how it would relate to more provisional or negotiated resolutions or viable political institutions remains an open question—a question whose openness is for Žižek constitutive of democracy. It also indicates how one cannot determine what the Other desires or find a foundational answer in the Other, for the Other is itself punctured or "voided," indicating an empty source of desire in the Other that we cannot fulfill. From this perspective, one might argue paradoxically that God died although he never existed. His nonexistence as a hole in being nonetheless elicits excessive desire, must persist as a constitutive lack in the human being, and cannot be recognized or worked through both as potentially traumatizing and, more affirmatively, as an enabling absence that invites improvisation and possibly constructive action.

In any comparative study, the specific nature of state violence as well as the channels available for effective protest and change in the direction of more viable institutions would be a crucial question. The level of generality of Žižek discourse on violence and related issues (desire, alterity, radical negativity, democracy, and so forth) does not enable one to raise this question in a sustained, differential manner. For him all hitherto existing and current regimes have their dirty secrets that a radical politics must disclose, and this disclosure has to be in some sense violent, at least insofar as it confronts one with the traumatic real—a confrontation that in its strangely disconcerting enormity seems to be uncanny, sublime, and monstrous. In various places Žižek argues, in the manner of Walter Benjamin in "The Critique of Violence," that the Act itself effectively repeats the endlessly repeated act that founds all political regimes as such, namely, the excessive gesture or *coup de force* that is in some sense violent and beyond or beneath the law.[19] (I note not only the limited resonance with Derrida but also the "as such" that transcendentalizes or essentializes the violent gesture.) Hence the Act might be seen as a founding trauma or even a miraculous *acte gratuit* that destroys what exists and yet somehow may give rise (if you believe and are really lucky) to an unpredictable, radically transfigured state of affairs or manner of being. This, for Žižek, is the opaque and narrow gate, the seemingly apocalyptic, perhaps manic gesture or Big Bang, through which the fantasy may be traversed, cynicism (even melancholia) transcended, and the possibility of radical politics renewed in the bleak, ruined landscapes of the contemporary world. In his recent work, for example, his 2005 "Neighbors and Other Monsters: A Plea for Ethical Violence," this gate opens onto neighborly love wherein one reaches out to the other, who may well be monstrous, indeed who must be a bearer of the essentially monstrous, inhuman excess that, transhistorically and even universally if not transcendentally, is taken by Žižek to differentiate the human as such from other animals. (Apparently, when it comes to the difference between the human and the animal, there is an "as such" as such.) At times the turn to the sublime implies a transcendence of the empirical for, as Žižek puts it in a reference to Kant on the French Revolution: "The reality of what went on in Paris belongs to the temporal dimension of empirical history; the sublime image that generated enthusiasm belongs to eternity. . . . *Mutatis mutandis*, the same applies for the Western admirers of the Soviet Union."[20]

Appealing to the unlikely revolutionary trinity of Kant, Che Guevara, and Christ, Žižek even asserts:

In their love/hatred, revolutionaries are pushed beyond the limitations of empirical "human nature," so that their violence is literally *angelic*. Therein resides the core of *revolutionary justice*, this much misused term: harshness of the measures taken, sustained by love. Does this not recall Christ's scandalous words from Luke ("if anyone comes to me and does not hate his father and his mother, his wife and children, his brothers and sisters—yes even his own life—he cannot be my disciple" [Luke 14:26], which point in exactly the same direction as another famous quote from Che? "You may have to be tough, but do not lose your tenderness. You may have to cut the flowers, but it will not stop the Spring." This Christian stance is the opposite of the Oriental attitude of nonviolence, which—as we know from the long history of Buddhist rulers and warriors—can legitimize the worst violence. It is not that the revolutionary violence "really" aims at establishing a nonviolent harmony; on the contrary, the authentic revolutionary liberation is much more directly identified with violence—it is violence as such [another "as such"] (the violent gesture of discarding, of establishing a difference, of drawing a line of separation) which liberates. Freedom is not a blissfully neutral state of harmony and balance, but the violent act which disturbs this balance. (186)

Angelic or divine violence and blissfully neutral harmony would hardly seem to be inclusive and exhaustive alternatives. Yet here we have Žižek's own periodic gesture of shooting discursively from the hip in a "sublime" Act (?) of "tough love" that shocks and numbs, if not dumbfounds, the reader. It seems questionable whether this entire orientation has room for a notion of working through as immanent critique involving the type of transformative political action that engages and changes specific political institutions and practices—the type of working through that I find affirmed, for example, in Theodor Adorno's essay, "What Is Meant by Working Through the Past?" ("Was bedeutet: Aufarbeitung der Vergangenheit?").[21] In glossing divine violence, Žižek at one point even goes so far as to approximate it to acting out:

Divine violence is precisely not a direct intervention of an omnipotent God to punish humankind for its excesses, a kind of preview or foretaste of the Last Judgment: the ultimate distinction between divine violence and the impotent/violent *passage à l'acte* of us, humans, is that, far from expressing divine omnipotence, divine violence is *a sign of God's (the big Other's) own impotence*. All that changes between divine violence and a blind *passage à l'acte* is the *site* of impotence.[22]

In his 2007 introduction to a collection of writings by Robespierre on virtue and terror, Žižek decisively cuts through what in some of his other work might be seen as hesitation or a lack of clarity about the nature of the violence he advocates. With the sovereign peremptoriness of Humpty Dumpty replying to Alice about the meaning of glory, Žižek offers a knockdown definition of what he thinks Walter Benjamin meant by the notion of divine violence. He does so in paraphrasing Engels on the dictatorship of the proletariat as exemplified in the Paris Commune (despite the commonplace historical fact that the latter was hardly a dictatorship of the proletariat):

"Well and good, gentlemen and theorists, do you want to know what this divine violence looks like? Look at the revolutionary Terror of 1792–94. That was the Divine Violence" [now in capital letters— DLC]. (And the series goes on: the Red Terror of 1919 . . .) That is to say, one should fearlessly identify divine violence with a positively existing historical phenomenon, thus avoiding all obscurantist mystification. When those outside the structured social field strike "blindly," demanding *and* enacting immediate justice/vengeance, this is "divine violence"—recall, a decade or so ago, the panic in Rio de Janeiro when crowds descended from the *favelas* into the rich part of the city and started looting and burning supermarkets—*this* was "divine violence" . . . Like the biblical locusts, the divine punishment for men's sinful ways, it strikes out of nowhere, a means without end[. . . .] The Benjaminian "divine violence" should be thus conceived as divine in the precise sense of the old Latin motto *vox populi, vox dei*: not in the perverse sense of "we are doing it as mere instruments of the People's Will," but as the heroic assumption of the solitude of a sovereign decision. It is a decision (to kill, to risk or lose one's own life) made in absolute solitude, not covered by the big Other.[23]

Žižek goes on to insist that he is indeed speaking about divine violence and not violence "deprived of the 'divine' dimension and thus reduced to a strategic intervention serving precise and limited goals" (xi). Thus he assumes the voice of a political prophet who enunciates what is divine, envisioning violence as an intrinsic, nonstrategic force of liberation or even regeneration. He believes he is in accord with Alain Badiou, whom he quotes on Saint-Just, virtue, and terror; and he invokes terms and concepts familiar from the work of Agamben and Carl Schmitt as well as Georges Sorel (although in Sorel the Terror of the French Revolution is criticized as "bourgeois"). I simply note that in the process, he does not articulate the relations between the transhistorical and the historical. He transfigures the transhistorical into the transcendental and the divine, and he has it come crashing down into history with the Pauline, if not apocalyptic, force of a bolt from the blue. And not one but a seemingly endless series of traumatizing, terroristic historical events appear to acquire foundational status.

It is noteworthy that Žižek explicitly wants to oppose fascism, even if the cogency of his understanding of how best to do it is doubtful and raises questions about the blurred borders between leftist and rightist orientations that construe "radicalism" in a certain extremist way. Indeed he valorizes violence as intrinsically emancipatory or regenerative, and insists, in flamboyant

rhetoric, on continually going to the limit and beyond.[24] In a different register, I would also allude to a Western tradition that may have a differential
bearing on the thought of Žižek among others, including Lacan—the radical sectarian strain in Christianity, evident in Paul, Augustine, Pascal, and
Kierkegaard, a strain that held prophetic Judaism in high regard and achieved
institutional form in the Protestant Reformation, notably in Calvinism and
related sects (including Catholic "Augustinian" Jansenism in France). This
strain of Christianity stresses anxiety as the dominant affect in the human
being who is internally split and whose essential existential relation or nonrelation is the terminally melancholic impossible vis-à-vis with the enigmatic,
inscrutable, nonsymbolizable Hidden God. This big Other, the ultimate real,
is radically transcendent, in a sense a constitutive lack that does not effectively
provide cover or shelter, which may be impotent but is nonetheless utterly
traumatizing—a foreclosed lost object of endless, unsatisfiable desire whose
infinite love for the believer works at best in mysterious and at times seemingly sadistic ways that one could hardly call compassionate. (The sublime
and anguished plight of Abraham in the face of a divine sacrificial supraethical command, having aspects of the psychosis-inducing double bind, might
be taken as paradigmatic here [love your son but, if you love me, kill your
son].) In light of one's relation to this "Real," history is relatively trivial and
merely illustrative of transhistorical truths or dilemmas. In *The Ticklish Subject*, Žižek is especially insistent that, for Lacan, God was always already dead
and that, for any beyond to be possible, one must pass through the void or
the death drive as a disgustingly monstrous residue, the lowest of the low—a
point he sees Badiou as not fully realizing and that helps to account for the
appeal of the abject figure of the *Muselmann* in Žižek. In case his point
escapes the reader, he finds the source of modern subjectivity not in the
humanists but in "Luther's famous statement that man is the excrement that
fell out of God's anus."[25] From this perspective, politics, insofar as it is not
merely a series of *divertissements* (in Pascal's term), is "a way of putting to use
the terrific force of Negativity in order to restructure our social affairs" such
that "in a Truth-Event the void of the death drive, of radical negativity, a
gap that momentarily suspends the Order of Being, continues to resonate."[26]

Toward the end of his introduction to Robespierre's texts, Žižek turns in
an institutional direction without abandoning certain questionable aspects of
his approach. He asserts:

> The true task does not lie in momentary democratic explosions which
> undermine the established "police" order, but in the dimension desig-
> nated by Badiou as that of the "fidelity" to the Event: how to translate/

inscribe the democratic explosion into the positive "police" order, how to impose on social reality a *new* lasting order. *This* is the properly "terrorist" dimension of every authentic democratic explosion: the brutal imposition of a new order. And this is why, while everybody loves democratic rebellions, the spectacular/carnivalesque explosions of the popular will, anxiety arises when this will wants to persist, to institutionalize itself—and the more "authentic" the rebellion is, the more "terrorist" is this institutionalization. It is at this level that one should search for the decisive moment of a revolutionary process: say, in the case of the October Revolution, not the explosion of 1917–18, not even the civil war that followed, but the intense experimentations of the early 1920s, the (desperate, often ridiculous) attempts to invent new rituals of daily life: with what to replace the pre-revolutionary procedures of marriage and funerals? How to organize the most common interaction in a factory, in an apartment block? It is at this level of what, as opposed to the "abstract terror" of the "big" political revolution, one is tempted to call the "concrete terror" of imposing a new order onto daily life, that the Jacobins and both the Soviet revolution and the Chinese revolution ultimately failed—not for the lack of attempts in this direction, for sure. (xxxv–xxxvi)

It is noteworthy that "terrorist" goes into problematizing quotation marks in this statement, but "brutal" does not. One may question the idea of imposing as a "concrete terror" a new institutional order that remains a police order (in effect, a reign of terror). And one may raise doubts about aspects of the four principles of Badiou's elaboration of the Event or what Žižek affirms as "the eternal Idea of the politics of revolutionary justice": to wit, voluntarism, terror ("a ruthless will to crush the enemy of the people"), egalitarian justice ("its immediate brutal imposition"), and trust in the people. Even if one accepts, as I would, certain explications of these principles, such as the idea that "one should impose the same world-wide norms of per capita energy consumption, carbon dioxide emissions, etc." (xxxvi), "punishment of all who violate the imposed protective measures" (which does not require the prefatory "ruthless" that Žižek rather predictably inserts), and "the wager that the large majority of the people support these severe measures" (xxxvii), one might still argue against the all-or-nothing dismissal of any pragmatic mediation of demands, the hyperbolic heads-must-roll rhetoric that directly slides into practice, the rejection of any tolerance for the mitigating role of "metarules of how to apply . . . explicit norms" (xviii) with some degree of practical judgment and habitual know-how, and the penchant for an unmediated, paradoxical Kantian–cum–decisionist combination of strict universal norms or laws and contingent, normless, leap-like, abyssal, presumably heroic decisions. With respect to voluntarism, Žižek, in his commentary on Badiou's approach to Saint Paul, puts forth "radical" rhetorical questions that conjoin creation ex nihilo, decisionism, and dogmatism:

> Perhaps the lesson of all this is more radical than it appears: what if what Badiou calls the Truth-Event is at its most radical a purely formal act of decision, not only not based on an actual truth, but ultimately *indifferent* to the precise status (actual or fictitious) of the Truth-Event it refers to? What if we are dealing here with an inherent key component of the Truth-Event—what if the true fidelity to the Event is 'dogmatic' in the precise sense of unconditional Faith, of an attitude which does not ask for good reasons and which, for that very reason, cannot be refuted by any 'argumentation'?[27]

What one apparently has here is the decisive leap of faith that is formalistically devoid of content and entails dogmatism. And high theory (or theoreticism) meets ultraformalism. One might also question the implicit anthropocentrism and abruptly arrested universality that subtends the affirmation of "principled equality of all men *qua* speaking beings" (xxix). But the turn to institutional issues and the call for a renewal of practices, including certain rituals, represent a noteworthy gesture that unexpectedly brings Žižek into a possible dialogue (or maybe duel) with Durkheim, for whom the basic problem of France after the Revolution was the institutional realization of its values or ideals. The mention of Durkheim at least indicates how a more specific analysis and critique of social processes and practices, informed by a more acute historical orientation than that found in Durkheim, may be more cogent in working through problems than Žižek's influential and often unmediated collage of Lacanian theory, as he understands it, and rapid-fire forays into history or contemporary events.

I have intimated that one psychoanalytic concept that has little place in Žižek is that of working through. Without offering it as a panacea, I would suggest that it is important to understand working through as a both a narrative and other-than-narrative psychosocial and political practice of articulation. Working through should not be understood, as it often is, in stereotypical ways as purely psychological and as the simple alternative to, or binary opposite of, compulsive repetition, acting out, or even impossible mourning. Nor should it be equated with closure, therapeutic cure, healing all wounds, and dialectical transcendence of a traumatic past or problem. Rather, with crucial differences depending on subject-positions, it offers the possibility of enacting variations in repetition that may be significant (at times decisive) enough to bring about effective change, including transformations that, in context, may well be disruptive or even traumatic but are not simply Pauline bolts from the blue, formalistic decisionist events, or transcendent acts of divine violence.

I conclude by noting that some of Žižek's most persuasive arguments in his book *Violence* do not appeal to the notion of divine violence or its analogs but to processes I would suggest are attempts to work through problems. This is particularly the case in his discussion of the Israeli-Palestinian conflict. Here he asserts that "a true political act . . . renders the unthinkable thinkable" (126). This occurred for him when Yitzhak Rabin "recognized the PLO as the legitimate representative of the Palestinians and thus the only true partner in negotiations" (125), thus reversing the official Israeli stand of no negotiations with what was taken to be a terrorist organization. He also argues that Palestinians should give up "the claim that the liberation of their territory from Israeli occupation will give an impetus to the democratization of the Arab world" and recognize that "one should *start* by openly confronting corrupted clerical and military regimes from Syria and Saudi Arabia which use the Israeli occupation to legitimize themselves." One should also affirm that "the basic meaning of *jihad* in Islam is not war against the external enemy, but the effort of inner purification. The struggle is against one's own moral failure and weakness" (126). He then asks a question and gives a somewhat surprising answer:

> So to the big question: what would be the truly radical ethico-political act today in the Middle East? For both Israelis and Arabs, it would consist in the gesture of renouncing (political) control of Jerusalem, that is, of endorsing the transformation of the Old Town of Jerusalem into an extra-state place of religious worship controlled (temporarily) by some neutral international force. . . . Each of the two sides would have to realize that this renunciation of the ethnically "pure" nation-state is a liberation for themselves, not simply a sacrifice to be made for the other [. . .]
>
> What the Jews and the Palestinians share is the fact that a diasporic existence is part of their lives, part of their very identity. What if they were to come together on *this* ground: not on the ground of occupying, possessing, or dividing the same territory, but of both [both peoples] keeping their shared territory as a refuge for those condemned to wander? What if Jerusalem became not their place, but a place for those with no place? This shared solidarity is the only ground for a true reconciliation: the realization that in fighting the other, one fights what is most vulnerable in one's own life. (127–28)

Things have, of course, changed significantly in the short time since the writing of the book Žižek published in 2008, and the views he expresses will not solve all problems. But they are, I think, a more fruitful beginning than the call for divine violence. Indeed, if taken seriously, they might be seen as a promising merger of pragmatism and utopianism. I would simply add that one of the supreme paradoxical twists of the argument in *Violence* is that, in light of a forceful apology for "good old atheism" and an ironic reference to "the 'postsecular' return of the religious" (133), there is a sense in which divine violence becomes tantamount to atheistic violence for which one accepts full responsibility. Of course, how one understands and enacts or counteracts such violence still remains an issue.

🕊 Notes

Introduction

1. In somewhat different ways, I explore this interest in *History and Its Limits: Human, Animal, Violence* (Ithaca: Cornell University Press, 2009). See also Michael S. Roth, *Memory, Trauma, and History: Essays on Living with the Past* (New York: Columbia University Press, 2012).

2. See, for example, Slavoj Žižek, "Neighbors and Other Monsters: A Plea for Ethical Violence," in *The Neighbor: Three Inquiries in Political Theology*, ed. Slavoj Žižek, Eric L. Santner, and Kenneth Reinhard (Chicago: University of Chicago Press, 2005) and Slavoj Žižek, *Violence* (New York: Picador, 2008).

3. See, for example, Philip Bond, ed., *Post-Secular Philosophy: Between Philosophy and Theology* (London: Routledge, 1998) and Ananda Abeysekara, *The Politics of Postsecular Religion: Mourning Secular Futures* (New York: Columbia University Press, 2008).

4. See, for example, M. H. Abrams, *Natural Supernaturalism: Tradition and Revolution in Romantic Literature* (New York: W. W. Norton, 1971).

5. See Hans Blumenberg, *The Legitimacy of the Modern Age*, trans. Robert M. Wallace (1966; Cambridge: MIT Press, 1983). (Note that an earlier date before the facts of publication indicates when the book was first published.) Jürgen Habermas has discussed the "postsecular society" in terms that still assume the status of the secular and the religious as distinct or even separate spheres or realms. See his "Notes on a Postsecular Society," available online at http://www.signandsight.com/features/1714.html (accessed May 8, 2012). The essay first appeared in *Blätter für deutsche und internationale Politik* (April 2008) and was initially written for a lecture that Habermas gave on March 15, 2007, at the Nexus Institute of the University of Tilberg, Netherlands.

6. For a brief discussion of the role displacement plays in Max Weber's *Protestant Ethic and the Spirit of Capitalism*, see my *History and Its Limits*, 24–25n.

7. See my discussion of Foucault in *History and Reading: Tocqueville, Foucault, French Studies* (Toronto: University of Toronto Press, 2000), chap. 3. The English translation of Foucault's own abridgement of the 1961 French edition is entitled *Madness and Civilization: A History of Insanity in the Age of Reason*, trans. Richard Howard (New York: Random House, 1965). The full translation of the 1972 edition is published as *History of Madness*, ed. Jean Khalfa, trans. Jonathan Murphy and Jean Khalfa (London: Routledge, 2006).

8. See Mona Ozouf, *La fête révolutionnaire 1789–1799* (Paris: Gallimard, 1976).

9. The poem ends with the famous lines: "Thanks to the human heart by which we live, / Thanks to its tenderness, its joys, and fears, / To me the meanest flower that blows can give / Thoughts that do often lie too deep for tears." Like many of

Wordsworth's poems, it enacts a struggle with a sense of loss approaching desperation toward a renewed affirmation of life and joy, at times striking a seemingly redemptive note. Such at least was the way he has been read by many, including John Stuart Mill. With specific reference to "the famous Ode, falsely called Platonic," he describes, in his *Autobiography* (1873; New York: Library of the Liberal Arts, 1954) his recovery from a breakdown in 1826 at the age of twenty: "[Wordsworth] too had similar experience to mine . . . he also had felt that the first freshness of youthful enjoyment of life was not lasting: but . . . he had sought for compensation, and found it, in the way in which he was now teaching me to find it. The result was that I gradually, but completely, emerged from my habitual depression, and was never again subject to it" (96). In fact, on the occasion of the death of his father, accompanied by the realization that his friends were scandalized by his relation with Harriet Taylor (despite its "Platonic" nature), Mill had a second, more severe breakdown in 1835, which is not mentioned in the *Autobiography;* it left him with a variety of ailments such as head and stomach pains as well as very noticeable muscular twitches in the face. See, for example, the discussions in Gertrude Himmelfarb, *Victorian Minds: A Study of Intellectuals in Crisis and Ideologies in Transition* (New York: Knopf, 1968) and Bruce Mazlish, *James and John Stuart Mill: Father and Son in the Nineteenth Century* (New York: Basic Books, 1975).

10. See Giorgio Agamben, *Remnants of Auschwitz*, trans. Daniel Heller-Roazen (New York: Zone Books, 1999). See also my discussion of Agamben in *History in Transit: Experience, Identity, Critical Theory* (Ithaca: Cornell University Press, 2004), chap. 4, esp. 157–62. Here is one use of the term by Sebald in response to a question at an interview (by Joseph Cuomo on March 13, 2001) at Queens College in New York: "One didn't really talk about the Holocaust, as it is called, in the 1960s in schools [in Germany], nor did your parents ever mention it, God forbid, and they didn't talk about it amongst themselves either. So this was a huge taboo zone." Lynne Sharon Schwartz, ed., *The Emergence of Memory: Conversations with W.G. Sebald* (New York: Seven Stories Press, 2007). Sebald goes on to note that, when he started at the University of Fribourg in 1964–5, these issues became public, notably because of the Auschwitz trial in Frankfurt and the Eichmann trial in Jerusalem in 1961. Yet he adds: "I couldn't really imagine it at all; it was some form of abstraction; there were large numbers and you didn't know who these people really were" (105).

11. I have discussed these issues in earlier publications. See, in particular, *Representing the Holocaust: History, Theory, Trauma* (Ithaca: Cornell University Press, 1996), esp. chap. 2.

12. See, for example, Jürgen Habermas's *Philosophical Discourse of Modernity,* trans. Frederick Lawrence (1985; Cambridge: MIT Press), 161–210. Benjamin Ivry writes in "Sovereign or Beast? Jacques Derrida and His Place in Modern Philosophy," *Jewish Daily Forward*, December 10, 2010, available online at http://forward.com/articles/133536/sovereign-or-beast/ (accessed May 13, 2012): "Ruth Barcan Marcus of Yale University was among the eminent thinkers (alongside Willard Quine, René Thom and John Searle) who scorned Derrida for 'translating into the academic sphere tricks and gimmicks similar to those of the Dadaists or of the concrete poets,' as claimed in a co-signed letter protesting a 1992 Cambridge University honorary doctorate awarded to Derrida."

13. See also the analyses and appreciations of Derrida in *Derrida's Legacies: Literature and Philosophy,* ed. Simon Glendinning and Robert Eaglestone (New York: Routledge, 2008).

14. Jean-Paul Sartre, *L'idiot de la famille,* 3 vols. (Paris: Gallimard, 1971–72). I discuss Sartre's approach extensively in *"Madame Bovary" on Trial* (Ithaca: Cornell University Press, 1978).

15. My own basic understanding of "theory" is in terms of a necessarily limited, historically tested, but at times explicitly speculative way of heightening attentiveness, criticism, and self-criticism, especially with respect to what is often overlooked, such as framing devices and implicit, if not repressed or disavowed, assumptions and implications.

16. An extreme form of transhistorical thought that denigrates the significance of history may be found in work of Arthur Schopenhauer. On the latter issue, as well as on various approaches to the philosophy of history, see the 2012 Cornell doctoral dissertation of Tarandeep Kang, "The Place of India in Enlightenment and Post-Enlightenment Philosophies of History."

17. On transhistorical tendencies in Agamben, see my *History in Transit,* esp. chap. 4, and *History and Its Limits,* esp. chap. 6. These books also include discussions of Žižek. In chapter 3 of the present book, I argue that Sebald should not be seen solely in terms of melancholia or a transhistorical fatalism. In general, the narrowly historicist and the insistently transhistorical or ultraformalistic are limit cases that do not define in an inclusive manner the work of all historians, social scientists, novelists, or theorists, even those I discuss critically (notably in the first chapter) for at times going in one or the other direction. Over the last generation (and with significant variations) the so-called new historicism and forms of cultural studies as well as of intellectual and cultural history have moved in directions that counteract going to these extremes.

18. See, for example, Derrida's "The Force of Law: The 'Mystical' Foundation of Authority," *Cardozo Law Review* (1980): 920–1045. See also my *History and Its Limits,* chap. 4. On Derrida and religion, see John D. Caputo, *The Prayers and Tears of Jacques Derrida: Religion without Religion* (Bloomington: Indiana University Press, 1997) and John D. Caputo and Gianni Vattimo, *After the Death of God,* ed. Jeffrey W. Robbins, afterword Gabriel Vahanian (New York: Columbia University Press, 2007). For an attempt to read Derrida as a "radical atheist," which still remains within the orbit of the postsecular and its debates, see Martin Hägglund, *Radical Atheism: Derrida and the Time of Life* (Stanford: Stanford University Press, 2008). Derrida is also a key reference point in Abeysekara's *Politics of Postsecular Religion.*

19. The response to Derrida in historiography has been largely negative, but for an analysis both of resistances and of Derrida's sometimes subterranean role, see Ethan Kleinberg, "Haunting History: Deconstruction and the Spirit of Revision," *History and Theory* 46 (2007): 113–43. One prominent historian who has made explicit use of deconstruction along with other modes of critical theory (such as Foucauldian genealogy and gender studies) is Joan Scott. See, for example, her "History-Writing as Critique," in *Manifestos for History,* ed. Keith Jenkins, Sue Morgan, and Alun Munslow (New York: Routledge, 2007), 19–38.

20. Derek Attridge, *J.M. Coetzee and the Ethics of Reading* (Chicago: University of Chicago Press, 2004). I briefly discuss this important book in chapter 3.

21. See Jacques Derrida and Gianni Vattimo, eds., *Religion* (1996; Stanford: Stanford University Press, 1998), 1–78.

22. Paul Eisenstein, *Traumatic Encounters: Holocaust Representation and the Hegelian Subject* (Albany: State University Press of New York, 2003). For a forceful argument that Žižek is essentially a theologian and should explicitly come out as such, see Marcus Pound, *Žižek: A (Very) Critical Introduction,* afterword Slavoj Žižek (Grand Rapids, MI: William B. Eerdmans, 2008). It should be noted that Pound is not critical of theology or of its role in Žižek but of Žižek's inexplicitness with respect to it as well as of certain turns in his thought. In his "afterword," Žižek does not really engage Pound's argument but instead elaborates his own perspective.

23. Paris: Gallimard, 2006. Translated as *The Kindly Ones,* trans. Charlotte Mandel (New York: Harper, 2009).

24. For a discussion of the postsecular in literature, see John A. McClure, *Partial Faiths: Postsecular Fiction in the Age of Pynchon and Morrison* (Athens: University of Georgia Press, 2007). The back cover has endorsements from theorists with a marked interest in the postsecular: Harold Bloom, William E. Connolly, and Amy Hungerford. McClure discusses, in addition to the authors mentioned in his title, Don DeLillo, N. Scott Momaday, Leslie Marmon Silko, Louise Erdrich, and Michael Ondaatje. He argues that the authors he treats and the theorists to whom he alludes (including Jacques Derrida, Richard Rorty, Charles Taylor, and Gianni Vattimo) "do not provide, or even aspire to provide, any full 'mapping' of the reenchanted cosmos." Nor do they "promise anything like full redemption" but instead are "selectively dedicated to progressive ideals of social transformation and well-being" (ix). McClure's own sense of the latter remains both general and generous, taking especially the form of an affirmation of "open dwelling," eschewing fundamentalist exclusions, and inviting both sustained critique and self-questioning humor. He sees such "dwelling" as possible both in organized religions and in more improvisational practices.

25. See the excellent collection of Bataille's writings, *Visions of Excess, Selected Writings 1927–1939*, ed. and intro. Allan Stoekl, trans. Allan Stoekl with Carl R. Lovitt and Donald M. Leslie Jr. (Minneapolis: University of Minnesota Press, 1994).

26. See Girard's *Things Hidden since the Foundation of the World*, trans. Stephen Bann and Michael Metteer, research undertaken in collaboration with Jean-Michel Oughourlian and Guy Lefort (1978; Stanford: Stanford University Press, 1987).

27. Here it is important to avoid the use of euphemisms, for example, "culling," which, with respect to animals, is often more accurately termed "mass killing." It is the latter that must be justified or at least argued to be necessary if one supports certain procedures. Also open to question is a lethal construct in which a deer becomes a weed or a threatening kind of oversized vermin (typically, a big rat). The use of deadly euphemisms with respect to humans took a well-known form in the Nazi regime but is far from restricted to it. One notorious example is the use of the term "collateral damage" for the results of bombing in areas with well-known concentrated civilian populations and which may even become a strategy of intimidation and terror.

1. The Mutual Interrogation of History and Literature

1. William H. Sewell, *Logics of History: Social Theory and Social Transformation* (Chicago: University of Chicago Press, 2005).

2. Gabrielle Spiegel, ed., *Practicing History: New Directions in Historical Writing after the Linguistic Turn* (New York: Routledge, 2005).

3. See, for example, Shoshana Felman, *Writing and Madness: Literature/Philosophy/Psychoanalysis* (Stanford: Stanford University Press, 2003). An important exponent of the "unreadability" of (genuine) literature was Paul de Man. See, for example, his *Allegories of Reading: Figural Language in Rousseau, Nietzsche, Rilke, and Proust* (New Haven: Yale University Press, 1982). In one variant of trauma theory, the analog of unreadability is the unrepresentability of trauma. See, for example, the much-cited work of Shoshana Felman and Dori Laub, *Testimony: The Crisis of Witnessing in Literature, Psychoanalysis, and History* (New York: Routledge, 1992).

4. Displacement as used in this study may be argued to involve distorted similarities and similar distortions rather than identities or pure differences. One may find this notion or its analogs (prominently including repetition with alteration or change, at times traumatic change) in such figures as Benjamin, Freud, and Derrida.

5. Leo Bersani, *From Balzac to Beckett* (New York: Oxford University Press, 1970), 144. I explore and qualify this view of Flaubert in *"Madame Bovary" on Trial* (Ithaca: Cornell University Press, 1982).

6. Along with some others, Hayden White would not fall under this generalization. White even proposed that one read historiography (or the writing of history) as essentially a poetic (or literary) form, thus opening it to formal, particularly figurative or "tropic," analyses. See his classic *Metahistory: The Historical Imagination in Nineteenth-Century Europe* (Baltimore: Johns Hopkins University Press, 1973).

7. Georg Lukács, *Theory of the Novel: A Historico-Philosophical Essay on the Form of Epic Literature*, trans. Anna Bostock (1920; Cambridge: MIT Press, 1971). See also *Soul and Form*, trans. Anna Bostock (1910; Cambridge: MIT Press, 1974); *History and Class Consciousness: Studies in Marxist Dialectics*, trans. Rodney Livingstone (1923; Cambridge: MIT Press, 1971); *The Historical Novel*, trans. Hannah and Stanley Mitchell, intro. Fredric Jameson (1937; Lincoln: University of Nebraska Press, 1983); and *Studies in European Realism*, intro. Alfred Kazin (1948; New York: Universal Library, 1964). Perhaps the most important recent legatee of Lukács is Fredric Jameson, whose encompassing project can be read as an attempt to rewrite Lukács in more sophisticated terms, notably with respect to problems posed by "postmodernism." See, for example, *Marxism and Form: Twentieth-Century Dialectical Theories of Literature* (Princeton: Princeton University Press, 1971), esp. chap. 3 ("The Case for Georg Lukács"); *The Political Unconscious: Narrative as a Socially Symbolic Act* (Ithaca: Cornell University Press, 1981); and *Postmodernism or, The Cultural Logic of Late Capitalism* (Durham: Duke University Press, 1991). Especially with respect to Jameson's *Political Unconscious*, see my *Rethinking Intellectual History: Texts, Contexts, Language* (Ithaca: Cornell University Press, 1983), chap. 7.

8. Olivier Le Cour Grandmaison, *Coloniser, Exterminer: Sur la guerre et l'État colonial* (Paris: Fayard, 2005).

9. In his nonetheless important and influential *Orientalism* (New York: Random House, 1978), Edward Said offers what are by and large symptomatic readings of literary as well as other texts with respect to "Orientalist" colonial discourse. See also the anniversary edition of 1994 in which Said, in an afterword, reflects on his book and its reception.

10. Sven Lindqvist, *"Exterminate All the Brutes": One Man's Odyssey into the Heart of Darkness and the Origins of European Genocide* (1992; New York: The New Press, 1996).

11. Pierre Bourdieu, *The Rules of Art: Genesis and Structure of the Literary Field*, trans. Susan Emanuel (1992; Stanford: Stanford University Press, 1995).

12. For a reading of the novel along these lines that predates Bourdieu's *Rules of Art*, see my *History, Politics, and the Novel* (Ithaca: Cornell University Press, 1987), chap. 4. The chapter is appropriately entitled "Collapsing Spheres in Flaubert's *Sentimental Education*." It was printed as "L'effondrement des sphères dans *l'Education sentimentale* de Flaubert" in *Annales ESC* (mai–juin 1987): 611–29. Emblematic of this collapsing of spheres is the way Jacques Arnoux takes objects back and forth between his home, the *foyer* of the idealized Mme Arnoux (herself an analog of quasi-religious yet deceptive "pure" art) and the apartment of the prostitute Rosanette. Also emblematic is his commercialized production of "glitzy" religious artifacts, a process itself conveying the recurrent "modern" if not modernist apprehension that objects of devotion are being transfigured into kitsch (or what the Flaubert-narrator terms *"le sublime à bon marché"*—the sublime at bargain-basement prices).

13. In different ways, the writing of Samuel Beckett, Maurice Blanchot, and Alain Robbe-Grillet exemplify this process of self-erasure. Paradoxically, the appeal to the mirror as the paradigm of realistic representation may repress the way the mirror splits or doubles what it represents, indicating the fantasy status of an evocation of "lost" unity, plenitude, or full presence of being (self, community, or representation and reality). See, for example, the Lacanian analysis in Mladen Dolar, "At First Sight," in *Gaze and Voice as Love Objects*, ed. Renata Salecl and Slavoj Žižek (Durham: Duke University Press, 1996), esp. 138. See also the discussion of Dolar and doubling in Eric L. Santner, *On Creaturely Life: Rilke/Benjamin/Sebald* (Chicago: University of Chicago Press, 2006), 192–93.

14. See *Specters of Marx: The State of the Debt, the Work of Mourning, and the New International*, trans. Peggy Kamuf (1993; New York: Routledge, 1994). Blanchot and Mallarmé were among Derrida's most significant reference points, as they were for Paul de Man.

15. Theodor W. Adorno's sense of the "autonomy" of art is closer to this paradoxical view than to a technical formalism, which helps to account for his admiration for Beckett and his animus against Lukács and Sartre.

16. For a discussion of these novelists, see my *History, Politics, and the Novel*.

17. See, for example, Paul Eisenstein, *Traumatic Encounters: Holocaust Representation and the Hegelian Subject* (Albany: State University of New York Press, 2003), which I discuss later in this chapter.

18. From *Concluding Unscientific Postscript*. Quoted in Howard V. Hong and Edna H. Hong, "Historical Introduction," *Kierkegaard's Writings VII* (Princeton: Princeton University Press, 1983), x.

19. Alexander Dru, ed., *The Soul of Kierkegaard: Selections from his Journals*, intro. Alexander Dru (Mineola, NY: Dover, 2003), 232. (The quote dates from 1854.)

20. Howard V. Hong and Edna H. Hong, eds., *Søren Kierkegaard's Journals and Papers*, trans. Howard V. Hong and Edna H. Hong (Bloomington: Indiana University Press, 1970), 384.

21. Despite its ambitiousness, Jonathan Littell's *Les Bienveillantes* (Paris: Gallimard, 2006, translated by Charlotte Mandel as *The Kindly Ones,* [New York: Harper, 2009]) does not, in my judgment, successfully negotiate this problem.

22. I think this conflation of everyday ethics and the sublime (or the sacred) threatens to occur when one understands justice in terms of excess, generosity, or even grace, an issue to which I return, especially in chapter 3.

23. Sebald, *On the Natural History of Destruction*, trans. Anthea Bell (1999; New York: Modern Library, 2004), 44–45.

24. For an elaboration of certain points I touch on, see my "History and the Devil in Mann's *Doctor Faustus*," chapter 6 in *History, Politics, and the Novel.* See also the partially overlapping discussion of Eisenstein's book in my *History and Its Limits: Human, Animal, Violence* (Ithaca: Cornell University Press, 2009), 30–31n.

25. Jonathan Culler's *The Literary in Theory* (Stanford: Stanford University Press, 2007) is an extremely sophisticated articulation of a formalist approach that moves both toward an opening to other fields or disciplines and in the direction of a certain closure, at least when it comes to the relation between history and literature. Culler defines the literary in terms not restricted to literature, although the latter foregrounds the literary in a particularly accentuated manner. He writes: "Literature . . . has become less a distinct object, fixed in a canon, than a property of discourse of diverse sorts, whose literariness—its narrative, rhetorical, performative qualities—can be studied by what were hitherto methods of literary analysis. And the values that are often taken for granted in literary reading of nonliterary materials are frequently literary values: concreteness, vividness, immediacy, paradoxical complexities." Culler sees theory as having an expansiveness paralleling that of the literary: "Theory is no longer something distinct and alien that some scholars promote or practice and others combat: it is everywhere, but, no longer seen as new and distinctive, it can be denounced as dead or passé" (18). Theory here is like God, who is everywhere and nowhere and who for some, if not many, has died. And "the literary in theory" seems tantamount to literary theory. When Culler turns to history, it is conjoined or conflated with Saussure's notion of the diachronic and focused on specifically literary history, notably in terms of the processes of "the dialectic of defamiliarization and automatization" and "the historicity of semiotic systems": "Formalism posits a study of literature that focuses on an underlying system always in evolution, since the mechanism of evolution is the functioning of literary works themselves" (10). I think Culler has identified important problems, but there is a larger issue with respect to the question of history and literature, that is, how those problems are or are not articulated with historical processes and events that are not "literary" in any restricted sense. Culler seems to remain within the division of labor or the tendency toward the (relative) autonomization of spheres in modernity. Not only is this positioning problematic from the viewpoint of critical theory but various areas of literature follow the tendency toward autonomization to different degrees,

and in none of them does it have uncontested authority. As Bakhtin (who is not one of Culler's significant reference points) stressed time and again, the novel has been one of the more open and responsive literary genres. And major historical events or processes have impinged on literary texts and genres (including poetry) in ways ranging from avoidance or disavowal to sustained engagement and complex inscription. So too have various discourses treating historical events or processes, and it is commonplace to observe that various modes of signification interact with other modes via the signifying process, which itself need not be divorced in any absolute way from "experience" or even from the more or less immediate (at times traumatic) impact of events. (This is not, however, to imply that a discourse, including historiography, may cogently claim to represent, express, or evoke that immediacy other than in ways "mediated" by stylistic and rhetorical devices.) Poetry has been more formalized than the novel and thus more marked by a diachrony (or "history") internal to the genre. But even poetry has been affected by extrageneric forces in both symptomatic and critical ways, including massive historical events and processes such as the First World War, the Nazi genocide, racism, and colonialism. How can one decide, for example, whether the Shoah was more important for the poetry of Paul Celan or Nelly Sachs than was literary practice with respect to a poetics of generic forms? Would it even make sense to try? And Yeats was not the only writer for whom the ghost of Roger Casement (along with many other ghosts) was beating at the door. The problem is how to inquire into the interaction between historical processes and formal changes in literature—an issue both subject to essentially contestable formulations and requiring informed speculation (which Culler defends).

26. See Michael Rothberg, *Traumatic Realism: The Demands of Holocaust Representation* (Minneapolis: University of Minnesota Press, 2000) as well as my own recent work, including *Representing the Holocaust: History, Theory, Trauma* (Ithaca: Cornell University Press, 1994), *History and Memory after Auschwitz* (Ithaca: Cornell University Press, 1999), *Writing History, Writing Trauma* (Baltimore: Johns Hopkins University Press, 2001), *History in Transit: Experience, Identity, Critical Theory* (Ithaca: Cornell University Press, 2004), and *History and Its Limits*.

27. Françoise Davoine and Jean-Max Gaudillière, *History beyond Trauma: Whereof One Cannot Speak, Thereof One Cannot Stay Silent*, trans. Susan Fairfield (New York: Other Press, 2004), 121. One of the most important historical studies treating the testimony of victims is Saul Friedländer's *Nazi Germany and the Jews*, vol. 1, *The Years of Persecution, 1933–1939* (New York: HaperCollins, 1997) and *Nazi Germany and the Jews*, vol. 2, *The Years of Extermination, 1939–1945* (New York: HarperCollins, 2007).

28. In chapter 4 this is a question I investigate in a different key by discussing together Jonathan Littell's novel *The Kindly Ones* and Saul Friedländer's two-volume history, *Nazi Germany and the Jews*.

29. For responses to Hayden White's important work in this respect, see Brian Fay, Philip Pomper, and Richard T. Vann, eds., *History and Theory: Contemporary Readings,* (Malden, MA: Blackwell, 1998). See also Robert J. Berkhofer, *Beyond the Great Story: History as Text and Discourse* (Cambridge: Harvard University Press, 1997).

30. Foucault observed: "Everything is present, you see, at least as a virtual object, inside a given culture. Or everything that has already featured once. The problem of

objects that have never featured in the culture is another matter. But it is part of the function of memory and culture to be able to reactualize any objects whatever that have already featured. Repetition is always possible; repetition with application, transformation. God knows in 1945 Nietzsche appeared to be completely disqualified. . . . It is clear, even if one admits that Marx will disappear for now, that he will reappear one day." *Politics Philosophy Culture: Interviews and Other Writings, 1977–1984*, trans. Alan Sheridan and others, ed. and intro. Lawrence D. Kritzman (1988; New York: Routledge, 1990), 45. See also, in the same book, "The Functions of Literature," where Foucault remarks: "In order to know what literature is, I would not want to study its internal structures. I would rather grasp the movement, the little process, by which a type of non-literary discourse, neglected, forgotten as soon as it was made, enters the literary field" (311). In his own distinctive manner, and with changes over time, Foucault was clearly concerned about the relations between history, literature, and theory. See my discussion of Foucault in *History and Reading: Tocqueville, Foucault, French Studies* (Toronto: University of Toronto Press, 2000).

2. The Quest! The Quest! *Conrad and Flaubert*

1. For a discussion of Conrad and Flaubert in terms quite different from my own, see Mark Conroy, *Modernism and Authority: Strategies of Legitimation in Flaubert and Conrad* (Baltimore: Johns Hopkins University Press, 1995). I refer throughout to the most recent Norton Critical Editions: *Heart of Darkness*, ed. Paul B. Armstrong, 4th ed. (New York: W. W. Norton, 2006) and *Madame Bovary*, ed. Margaret Cohen, 2nd ed. (New York: W. W. Norton, 2005). Unless otherwise indicated, page numbers of references are included parenthetically in the text.

2. For a recent critical, illuminating account of the vicissitudes of the "trauma paradigm," see Roger Luckhurst, *The Trauma Question* (London: Routledge, 2008). For Bessell van der Kolk's theory of the eidetic or imagistic engraving of trauma, see p. 108. See also the discussion in my *Writing History, Writing Trauma* (Baltimore: Johns Hopkins University Press, 2001).

3. See "An Image of Africa: Racism in Conrad's *Heart of Darkness*," in *Heart of Darkness*, 336–49. Achebe makes many thought-provoking observations about the text, and his response to it, even in its strongly negative dimensions, had a valuable formative role in his own approach to writing literature. Without fully appreciating how the text figures that "other world" and its "darkness" as very much within the European "world" that colonizes it, he asserts: "*Heart of Darkness* projects the image of Africa as 'the other world,' the antithesis of Europe and therefore of civilization, a place where man's vaunted intelligence and refinement are finally mocked by triumphant bestiality," with "the River Congo" as "the very antithesis of the Thames" (338).

4. Of Marlow, Conrad asserts in his preface to *Youth* (originally published in 1902): "Of all my people he's the one that has never been a vexation to my spirit. A most discreet, understanding man." Included in *Heart of Darkness*, 289.

5. See Alan Simmons, "Conrad, [Roger] Casement, and the Congo Atrocities," in *Heart of Darkness*, 181–92, esp. 186–88. Simmons observes: "A complicated and evasive semiotics acts here as a kind of resistance to the act which will trouble the

European sense of self as civilized" (188). Simmons, however, sees a "parody of the Eucharist in the references to cannibalism" (187). He also quotes Sven Lindqvist as asserting, in *Exterminate All the Brutes* [London: Granta, 1997], that Marlow "has no need to count up the crimes Kurtz committed. He has no need to describe them. He has no need to produce evidence. For no-one doubted it" (quoted, 190). King Leopold II used "uncivilized" acts among Africans as an excuse for Belgian colonialism that was supposed to civilize the "natives" but in fact was engaged in the very practices projected onto them. See Leopold's disingenuous comments on "the sacred mission of civilization" contained in *Heart of Darkness*, 119–20. Roger Casement, in his "Congo Report" of 1904, a considerable portion of which appears in *Heart of Darkness* (131–60), notes that cutting off genitals and extremities was a punitive practice of whites to prove that they had not wasted ammunition but had killed or punished their targets, especially African men. See, for example, 140 and 155.

6. Even the valorization of the elusive, the confusing, or the indefinite might be read in one sense as the defensive transvaluation of experiencing, beholding, even learning about or suspecting traumatizing processes such as mutilation and torture. On these issues, see my *History and Its Limits: Human, Animal, Violence* (Ithaca: Cornell University Press, 2009), esp. chaps. 3 and 4.

7. See Ford Madox Ford, "A Personal Remembrance" and Ian Watt, "Impressionism and Symbolism in *Heart of Darkness*" in *Heart of Darkness*, 316–22 and 349–64.

8. On this issue, see the informative comments of Alan Simmons, who writes: "I feel that the contribution of 'Heart of Darkness' to the reform movement may lie, ultimately, in helping to create the context and the conditions for believing the tales of atrocity coming out of the Congo precisely because the scale of the 'Horror' to which it alludes cannot be adequately conveyed through facts anyway" (189). Adam Hochschild goes further, yet adds a qualification in asserting: "*Heart of Darkness* is one of the most scathing indictments of imperialism in all literature, but its author, curiously, thought himself an ardent imperialist where England was concerned." See "Meeting Mr. Kurtz," in *Heart of Darkness*, 171–81 at 177.

9. Olivier Le Cour Grandmaison, *Coloniser, Exterminer: Sur la guerre et l'État colonial* (Paris: Fayard, 2005), 167; my translation.

10. As Hunt Hawkins observes: "This friendship, started so well in 1890, was to end unhappily twenty-six years later during World War I when Casement, who had arranged German support for the Easter Uprising in his native Ireland, was caught and condemned to hang as a traitor. The patriotic Conrad turned completely against his former friend, refusing to sign a petition to Prime Minister Asquith begging clemency." "Joseph Conrad, Roger Casement, and the Congo Reform Movement," *Journal of Modern Literature* 9 (1981–82): 65–80 at 68.

11. Yet, like Marlow himself, Conrad was fascinated by cartography without recognizing the role of its mapping and boundary-setting procedures as instruments of empire and colonization. See "Geography and Some Explorers," in *Heart of Darkness*, 273–78.

12. Compare J. Hillis Miller, "Should We Read 'Heart of Darkness'?" in *Heart of Darkness*, 463–73. Posing a sharp opposition between literary and other readings, as well as between the allegorical (or antimimetic) and the mimetic as opposed kinds

of writing, Miller concludes that we have an ethical obligation to read the text for ourselves, indeed to "bear witness" to a reading (463) that is allegorical and takes the text "as literature rather than as, say, historical account or as autobiography" (465). Such reading for him leads to the notion that "whatever the frame narrator or Marlow says is ironized or suspended, presented implicitly in parabasis," that "literature is the elaborate tissue of figures and other rhetorical devices," and that the text is an abyssal figure of figuration or a necessarily failed apocalypse "having to do with death, judgment, and other last things" that are not revealed to the reader. For Miller Marlow's narrative in particular is steeped in irony throughout, and the type of irony is "infinite absolute negativity" or "permanent parabasis," in the phrase of Friedrich Schlegel (taken up by Paul de Man). The structure of the text becomes apocalyptic or messianic, one of "endlessly deferred promise" whereby "the presence within the novella of this inaccessible secret, a secret that nevertheless incites to narration, is what makes it appropriate to speak of 'Heart of Darkness' as literature" (472). Even the intricate "misty halos" or "moonshine" (5) passage is read as if it were tantamount to Paul's passage about now seeing through a glass darkly but then (in the always-to-come messianic future) face to face. Thus what begins as a plea for the distinctively if not purely literary reading becomes a definition of the literary in quasi-religious or postsecular terms. The reader is to bear witness to a reading that necessarily turns to testifying to the "heart of darkness" as a negatively theological "it." Hence: "If 'it' is wholly other it is wholly other, and nothing more can be said of it except by signs that confess in their preferring to their inadequacy. Each veil lifts to reveal another veil behind. . . . The presence within the novella of this inaccessible secret, a secret that nevertheless incites to narration, is what makes it appropriate to speak of "Heart of Darkness" as literature" (472)—literature, one is tempted to add, as veiled religion or theology. My own discussion of the quest-like dimension of the text recognizes its self-parodic dimensions and is oriented toward the mutual interrogation of history and literature; it also proposes responsibility for a reading that has ethicopolitical dimensions but situates the latter in the context of a critically dialogic relation between past and present, while questioning a quasi-transcendental orientation with a turn to the messianic and the religious.

13. Here, too, one may belatedly see an instance of the notion that traumatic experience is unspeakable, even for the perpetrator who may undergo a form of traumatization that need not imply a conflation of perpetrator and victim.

14. Sven Lindqvist, *"Exterminate All the Brutes": One Man's Odyssey into the Heart of Darkness and the Origins of European Genocide* (1992; New York: The New Press, 1996). There is an interesting slip when Lindqvist refers to Lothar von Trotta, the general who gave the genocidal order against the Herero in 1904, as Adolf von Trotta (149). One also finds the reference to Adolf von Trotta in Hunt Hawkins's contribution, *"Heart of Darkness and Racism,"* to *Heart of Darkness*, 375. One of the problems in Lindqvist's nonetheless thought-provoking mixed-generic book is the attribution of too much causal weight to the quest for *Lebensraum* in the Nazi genocide and even in European colonial expansion (159).

15. See *Madame Bovary*, 38n.

16. For an extensive discussion of the self-parodic and at times funny dimensions of Sartre's *La nausée* (*Nausea*), see my *Preface to Sartre* (Ithaca: Cornell University Press,

1978), chap. 3. There, I refer to the aborted apocalypse whereby "the technique of the text in deconstructing the traditional narrative is to set up a beginning that brings with it an expectation of a certain ending, which the text itself frustrates" (114). This repeatedly employed technique applies to the famous scene near the end where Antoine seems to have an epiphanous or even redemptive moment in listening to the song "Some of These Days," which he believes was written by a Jewish composer and sung by a "Negress," whereas (as Sartre may have known) the opposite was the case—the singer being Sophie Tucker, the last of the white red-hot mamas, and the writer, Shelton Brooks, an African American (115).

17. In Sebald's work the narrator himself becomes a listener whose mind wanders.

18. Sebald employs a complex form of free indirect style to render (often in the first person) not lived but overheard speech (or hear-say of sorts). (The term for *style indirect libre* in German is *Erlebte Rede*.)

19. One may note that the scene near the end (242–44) where Emma makes the rounds to ask for money and is observed at a distance by two busybodies (Mme Tuvache and Mme Caron) is a repetition or even parody of the scandalous cab (or *fiacre*) scene (193) where Emma and Léon in a closed cab are unnamed figures who copulate as their vehicle hurtles aimlessly through the streets of Rouen, conducted by the demoralized cabman and viewed time and again by the bewildered passers-by.

20. In his "Why Emma Had to Be Killed," *Critical Inquiry* 34 (2008): 433–48, Jacques Rancière rejects both purely intratextual and social readings to address the way a fiction addresses a historical situation in terms of "the invention of the fiction itself" (434). He argues that the real question is not why Emma committed suicide in novelistic or broadly social terms but why Flaubert as writer "killed" her for historically specific artistic reasons. Emma had to be done away with because she aestheticized life by trying through desire and goal-oriented behavior to tie together the singular microevents (Gilles Deleuze's "haecceities") that for Flaubert the artist were the true object of impersonally "narrated" art. Hence, for Rancière there is a great divide between both Emma and Flaubert and two regimes of universal equivalence in modernity—the old regime of characters, epitomized by Emma, who seek to "plot" and enjoy microevents and the new regime of the Flaubertian artist who seeks only pure art by recounting the microevents in their very purity devoid of mystifying desires or projects. This reading, however ingenious and appealing, conflates a narrow construction of Emma's *vécu* with writing a conventional, insufficiently experimental novel (a charge frequently leveled at Emma herself in apparent oblivion of the manner in which her compulsively repetitive, even suicidal life evacuates any plotting or aestheticization). It does not account either for Emma's proximity to Flaubert the artist in seeking an impossible, nihilating transcendence of the ordinary (especially its microevents, such as the daily ordeal of sitting at the dinner table with Charles) or for the way impersonal narration is at most one perspective in a mobile constellation involving the shape-shifting narrator's variable proximity and distance in relation to characters and other narrated objects (with Emma as the most intensely "cathected" recipient of his ambivalence). Free indirect style is a notorious absence in Rancière's analysis, as is the problem of narrative shifts or mutations in general. In a sense, Rancière provides a more sophisticated, philosophical version of Erich

Auerbach's analysis of Flaubert's elimination of a hierarchy of subject matters through the leveling "serious" representation of everyday life, including its random or accidental moments. See *Mimesis: The Representation of Reality in Western Literature*, trans. Willard R. Trask (1946; Princeton: Princeton University Press, 1974), 482–91. See also Auerbach's "On the Serious Imitation of the Everyday," in the Norton Critical Edition of *Madame Bovary*, 423–49). In certain ways, Rancière is also close to readings of Flaubert as an "impressionist" who both levels subjects and affirms absolute style.

21. For a more extensive elaboration of this procedure, see my *"Madame Bovary" on Trial* (Ithaca: Cornell University Press, 1982).

22. One curious feature of the Norton Critical Edition *Madame Bovary* is that, in the text of the novel, *souillures* is translated as "degradation" (179) while in the translation of the trial it is (mis)translated as "blemishes" (326). Although the first translation is better, neither conveys the quasi-ritual sense of pollution or impurity.

3. Coetzee, Sebald, and the Narrative of Trauma

1. Françoise Davoine and Jean-Max Gaudillière, *History beyond Trauma: Whereof One Cannot Speak, Thereof One Cannot Stay Silent*, trans. Susan Fairfield (New York: Other Press, 2004). The title plays a telling variation on the famous last line, Proposition 7, of Wittgenstein's 1921 *Tractatus Logico-Philosophicus*: "Whereof one cannot speak, thereof one must be silent" ("Wovon man nicht sprechen kann, darüber muss man schweigen"). (This is the resoundingly apodictic, poetic yet literal translation by C. K. Ogden with the assistance of F. K. Ramsey (London: Routledge and Kegan Paul, 1922). A more recent, prosaic translation is: "What we cannot speak about we must pass over in silence." *Tractatus Logico-Philosophicus*, trans. D. F. Pears and B. F. McGuinness (London: Routledge and Kegan Paul, 1961), 74. Both translations include the introduction by Bertrand Russell. See also my "Reading Exemplars: *Wittgenstein's Vienna* and Wittgenstein's *Tractatus*," chap. 3 in *Rethinking Intellectual History: Texts, Contexts, Language* (Ithaca: Cornell University Press, 1983).

2. Sebald may perhaps be seen as representing one crucial melancholic mutation in the lineage of Flaubert, in terms of experimentation in the combination of formal innovation with documentation that is at times carried to the disorienting point of a mania paralleling or even enacting what is seen as the maniacally catastrophic course of endless historical and environmental destruction. One can well imagine *The Rings of Saturn* [*Die Ringe des Saturn*], trans. Michael Hulse (1995; New York: New Directions, 1998) as written by a contemporary, even more disillusioned Flaubert. (Sebald carefully supervised the excellent translations of his works by Anthea Bell and Michael Hulse [as well as Michael Hamburger], which I follow.) It would also be interesting to compare and, in good part, contrast *Madame Bovary* (1856) with Coetzee's *Elizabeth Costello* (2003; New York: Penguin Books, 2004). Emma's repetitive quest for a figure approximating her imaginary ideal lover finds little echo in Elizabeth Costello, who pursues a militantly activist albeit self-critical and at times wearying path as a writer and an advocate of the claims of other animals. Coetzee engages in his own variant of a negotiation of relations between formal experimentation and (a largely allusive rather than documentary) realism—a modulated quest often seeming

to be closer to the orientation of son John in *Elizabeth Costello* as well as to aspects of David Lurie in *Disgrace* (New York: Penguin Books, 1999). Indeed, as Emma Bovary threatens to exceed Flaubert's narrative control, so both Elizabeth Costello and Lucy may be more than the Coetzee-narrator (or related characters such as son John and father David) can handle.

3. Here significant yet different reference points are Sven Lindqvist, *"Exterminate All the Brutes": One Man's Odyssey into the Heart of Darkness and the Origins of European Genocide,* trans. Joan Tate (1992; New York: The Free Press, 1994); Olivier Le Cour Grandmaison, *Coloniser, Exterminer: Sur la guerre et l'État colonial* (Paris: Fayard, 2005); and Isabel V. Hull, *Absolute Destruction: Military Culture and the Practices of War in Imperial Germany* (Ithaca: Cornell University Press, 2005).

4. Costello makes two misleading statements concerning the Nazi genocide. She confuses Treblinka with Auschwitz (Birkenau) when she asserts that "at Treblinka alone more than a million and a half, perhaps as many as three million" people were put to death (*Elizabeth Costello,* 63). She also repeats twice (66, 115) the prevalent, bitterly ironic, contested idea that Nazis engaged in the practice of turning into soap the fat of Jews (who were perceived as filthy and contaminating), a process that (in the judgment of many historians and commentators) may have occurred on a limited, uncoordinated, perhaps experimental scale not promoted to industrial status. These historians and commentators include Yehuda Bauer, Yisrael Guttman, Walter Laqueur, Deborah Lipstadt, and Gita Sereny, as well as those working at Yad Vashem. Sereny, for example, writes: "The universally accepted story that the corpses [of those killed in the Warsaw ghetto] were used to make soap and fertilizer is finally refuted by the generally very reliable Ludwigsburg Central Authority for Investigation into Nazi Crimes. The Authority has found after considerable research that only one experiment was made, with 'a few corpses from a concentration camp. When it proved impractical the idea was apparently abandoned.'" *Into that Darkness* (1974; New York: Random House, 1983), 141n. The rumor about turning Jews into soap was circulated during the war itself and subsequently became grist for the mills of Holocaust negationists. Saul Friedländer in *Nazi Germany and the Jews 1939–1945,* vol. 1, *The Years of Extermination* (New York: HarperCollins, 2007) reports that Himmler was indignant at what he saw as the calumnious accusation that murdered corpses were being used for "the manufacture of soap and artificial fertilizer" and wanted a guarantee that everywhere the corpses were either burned or buried and that "nowhere can something else happen with the bodies" (463).

5. The problem of oppressive uses of language as well as their relation to practices such as torture is evident in one of Coetzee's earliest novels, *Waiting for the Barbarians* (1980; London: Penguin Books, 1982).

6. One may note the importance, as Sebald does, of his older contemporary Thomas Bernhard (1931–89), who was at least as critical of Austria as Sebald was of Germany. Sebald acknowledges him as a "constant presence at my side" and sees him as bringing to "postwar fiction in the German language . . . a new radicality," notably including "a kind of periscopic form of narrative" wherein "he only tells you in his books what he heard from others." *The Emergence of Memory: Conversations with W. G. Sebald,* ed. Lynne Sharon Schwartz (New York: Seven Stories Press, 2007), 82–83. I would also mention the seventeenth-century English writer Thomas Browne

(author of "Urn Burial") whose "labyrinthine sentences . . . resemble processions or a funeral cortège in their sheer ceremonial lavishness." One might see Bernhard and Sebald as sharing what the latter attributes to Browne: the belief that "all knowledge is enveloped in darkness" and that "what we perceive are no more than isolated lights in the abyss of ignorance, in the shadow-filled edifice of the world" (*Rings of Saturn*, 19).

7. Sebald, *Vertigo* [*Schwindel. Gefühle.*], trans. Michael Hulse (1990; New York: New Directions, 1996). "*Schwindel*" in German also means "swindle" or "lie." The fact that it is followed by "*Gefühle*"—feelings or sensations—is interesting, especially since the feelings in Sebald sometimes approach posttraumatic numbness that seems "*gefühlos.*"

8. Sebald, *The Emigrants* [*Die Ausgewanderten*], trans. Michael Hulse (1992; New York: New Directions, 1996) begins with a photo of a cemetery and then turns without transition to a description of an old, overgrown country house in which Sebald (or the Sebald-narrator) and his partner Clara rent an apartment. (Sebald's wife was named Ute.) The book ends with a precise description of three women in the Lódz ghetto working at a loom (analogized to the Parcae or Fates) but upsets expectations by providing no accompanying photograph. (One may compare this ending with the imageless description of David Moffie at the beginning of the second volume of Saul Friedländer's *Nazi Germany and the Jews*, which I discuss in chapter 4.) The self-implicating Sebald-narrator, who we are told stands in the very spot where the photographer stood to take the photograph, wonders what were the names of the women who, one assumes, were Jewish and did not survive the genocide. *The Emigrants* might be read as a rejoinder to Edgar Reitz's epical made-for-television series *Heimat* (1984) in that Sebald focuses not on the *Alltagsgeschichte* of "ordinary" provincial Germans (in whose "life-world" the fate of Jews seemed to have a marginal or marginalized status) but on the desperate "afterlife" of traumatized emigrants, notably postwar Jews (Dr. Henry Selwyn, originally from Lithuania, and the anguished painter Max Ferber) and a part-Jew (Paul Bereyter, Sebald's own elementary school teacher) as well as Sebald's great-uncle, given the fictional name Ambros Adelwarth. These figures, like the Sebald-narrator, are subject to intrusive memories of the past. In answer to the question of why he gathered the stories together, Sebald responds: "They are all stories about suicide or, to be more precise, suicides at an advanced age, which is relatively rare but quite frequent as a symptom of what we know as the survivor syndrome" (*Emergence of Memory*, 38). Selwyn shoots himself in the jaw. Bereyter places himself under a train. Adelwarth commits himself to an insane asylum in Ithaca, New York, and voluntarily undergoes electroshock treatment. He suffers "progressive paralysis of the joints and limbs, probably caused by the shock therapy" (11). Adelwarth served as a butler and the companion/steward of Cosmo Solomon, the unstable scion of a wealthy Jewish family, whom he took to the asylum in Ithaca, where Cosmo "faded away" (98). The latter's decline into mental instability is related in the text to the disorienting effects of the First World War (95) and to those of a mesmerizing, unnamed German film, Fritz Lang's *Dr. Mabuse, the Gambler* (1922). According to another of the Sebald-narrator's relatives (Uncle Kasimir), Adelwarth, with respect to the relationship with Cosmo Solomon and other men, is "of the other persuasion" (88), but the text provides no conclusive answer

to the question of Adelwarth's homosexuality. I would note that in another feature that may be connected to Ithaca, New York, the text is punctuated by appearances of "the man with the butterfly net" (an apparent allusion to that *homo ludens* of allusion, Vladimir Nabokov, who taught at Cornell University in the 1950s), a man Ferber depicts in what he "considered one of his most unsatisfactory works, because in his view it conveyed not even the remotest impression of the strangeness of the apparition it referred to" (174). Ferber's ascetic, painstakingly scrupulous, indeed ruinous process in painting obviously resembles what the Sebald-narrator describes as his own participation in "the questionable process of writing" (230). Ferber enters a hospital with pulmonary emphysema perhaps caused or at least aggravated by his endlessly reworked, often erased or even destroyed charcoal sketches along with the disintegrating debris of effaced paintings that cover him and his surroundings with ash-like dust and leave "ghostly presences on the harried paper" (162). Another fascinating feature of the account of Ferber is the long excursus the Sebald-narrator inserts after receiving from Ferber the memoir of the latter's mother Luisa née Lanzberg. (The names "Ferber" and "Lanzberg" are not real, but Sebald did receive the memoir from one of the two figures on whom Ferber is based—his émigré landlord in Manchester and a well-known contemporary painter who did not want his name used. See *Emergence of Memory*, 73–74 and 104.) The memoir is written from 1939 to 1941 when Luisa was sent from Munich to Riga in one of the first deportation trains and then killed (178). But it counters expectations by telling of her early life at the turn of the century, and in a kind of *imitatio* the narrator traces her words and then travels to follow her life trajectory. Narrating in a shifting first-person, he seems to offer her perspective on the existence of Jews, including their religious practices. She lives first in a small village (Steinach), spending what she experienced as a happy childhood, followed by her alienation as a young woman living in an expensive villa in a larger town (Kissingen), in the period before Jews, who made up a third of the population of the region, were expropriated and killed under the Nazis (193–218). Her ecstatic relation with a young musician and her subsequent rapport with a revenant of sorts, a wounded, blind soldier, end with the deaths of the young men and her own collapse into delirium, from which she recovers to enter into an arranged marriage with Paul Ferber's father Fritz who bears the same name as the prematurely dead musician.

9. Schwartz, *Emergence of Memory*, 73.

10. Sebald, *Rings of Saturn*, 54.

11. Sebald, *Austerlitz*, trans. Anthea Bell (2001; New York: Modern Library, 2004). In *Austerlitz,* the unnamed spectral, seemingly Sebald-like narrator has the closest proximity to Austerlitz, whom he accidentally meets a number of times over the years, to whom he attentively listens, and whose story he empathically recounts. That story is punctuated by Austerlitz's posttraumatic "discovery" of his Jewish background and the fate of his parents at the hands of the Nazis. For an ambitious critical survey of the field of trauma studies that often converges with views expressed in some of my works, see Roger Luckhurst, *The Trauma Question* (London: Routledge, 2008). The book provides a genealogy of the term and a broad-based analysis of the role of trauma in fiction, memoirs, photography, and film. In his analysis of Sebald, which focuses on *Austerlitz* (111–16), Luckhurst may, however, be too summary in his judgment that Sebald "seems interested only in the

psychology of melancholic entrapment" (111) and ultimately seems to become a "traumatophile" (116). I agree with Luckhurst that, among the many discussions of Sebald, especially thought provoking are those of Andreas Huyssen in *Present Pasts: Urban Palimpsests and the Politics of Memory* (Stanford: Stanford University Press, 2003) and Anne Whitehead in *Trauma Fiction* (Edinburgh: Edinburgh University Press, 2004).

12. Sebald at times refers to his interest in metaphysical questions and presents asking them as something that differentiates his work from the historian's (*Emergence of Memory*, 135). I think one pertinent sense of the metaphysical here is what might be termed the "metaliteral"—that which cannot be empirically verified but still supplements empirical happenings in a curious, uncanny, perhaps wondrous way.

13. Coetzee, *The Lives of Animals* (Princeton: Princeton University Press, 1999); *Disgrace*.

14. Santner, *On Creaturely Life: Rilke/Benjamin/Sebald* (Chicago: University of Chicago Press, 2006).

15. Reporting on his interview with Sebald, included in Schwartz, ed., *The Emergence of Memory*, Arthur Lubov writes: "He insisted, persuasively, that he was not interested in Judaism or in the Jewish people for their own sake. 'I have an interest in them not for any philo-Semitic reasons,' he told me, 'but because they are part of a social history that was obliterated in Germany and I wanted to know what happened.' He felt a rapport with displaced people in general, and in particular, with outcast writers" (167). Sebald may here be downplaying the intensity of his "interest" in, or at times identification with, Jewish figures, but, if so, this would still not imply his adherence to a specifically German-Jewish tradition of writing and thought. With reference to the "postsecular" more generally, it is noteworthy that, in this interview, he is reported as saying he does not consider himself a writer and as referring to his work as "obsessive" and "devotional" (169).

16. It would be interesting to compare and contrast the different insistences and inflections in the thought of Sebald and Jane Bennett, notably in her *Enchantment of Modern Life: Attachments, Crossings, and Ethics* (Princeton: Princeton University Press, 2001).

17. Schwartz, *Emergence of Memory*, 88.

18. Introduction to Coetzee's collected essays by Derek Attridge (New York: Penguin Books, 2007).

19. For an extensive formal analysis of Sebald's style, see Richard T. Gray's "Narrative Segues: Performing Narrative Contingency: *The Rings of Saturn*," *Germanic Review* (Winter 2009): 26–58. Gray stresses Sebald's improvisational "art of transition," which he compares to Lévi-Strauss's notion of *bricolage*, Michel de Certeau's "subversive" practices of everyday life, and even Konrad Lorenz's concept of the "fulguration," which is analogized, via juxtaposition or parataxis, to the short circuit whereby "two otherwise independent systems are brought into proximity with one another" (51). Segues are for Gray "creative linkages that stitch together . . . diverse fragments into a coherent textual whole" (26). Gray mentions melancholia in a few places but only en passant (45, 48, 54), and he does not try to articulate its relation to the formal problems in narration that he insightfully analyzes. In his passing references to melancholia, he notes the Sebald-narrator's own referral of his rather

manic ambulatory travels to the (quoting Sebald) "hope of dispelling the emptiness that takes hold of me whenever I have completed a long stint of work" as well as to the "paralyzing horror" that results in "a physical paralysis that requires medical attention and confines [Sebald] for a period of time to a hospital bed" (45). Gray also refers to "a pessimistic rumination by the narrator on the 'process of consuming and being consumed' and the 'shadow of annihilation' that haunt all things and inhabit all human history" (48). But Gray's insistently formal analysis somewhat anticlimactically concludes with the assertion that the history of Western civilization that emerges from Sebald's "paratactic reordering and creative re-membering of [Western history's] remnants and fragments is explicitly a critical history, one that bears little resemblance to the passive resignation of the chronic melancholic, for which Sebald is commonly (mis)taken" (54). I would suggest that the complex problem would rather seem to be whether and to what extent Sebald's narrative practice is both critical and symptomatic of the process of decline and entropy that he analyzes and often enacts and how Sebald conjoins a melancholic perspective, including reversals and dismemberments of a progressive narrative, with a paratactic style in which there is (as Gray acknowledges) a tense interaction between fragmentation and some semblance of coherence. Gray does not discuss the epiphanous interludes that disrupt the seemingly prevalent melancholic mood of the narrator.

20. In a manner perhaps indicative of Sebald's own unease if not his deterritorialized subject-position regarding the German language, the Sebald-narrator at the Somerleyton estate ("a maze . . . where I became so completely lost that I could not find the way out again" [38]) has the gardener he encounters say in the first-person that it was in the early fifties, in Lüneburg with the army of occupation, that "I even learnt German, after a fashion, so that I could read what the Germans themselves had said about the bombings and their lives in the ruined cities" (39). Sebald's concern with the bombings of German cities is discussed a few years later in his *On the Natural History of Destruction*, trans. Anthea Bell (1999; New York: Modern Library, 2004).

21. The Sebald-narrator briefly discusses the interest of a colleague who found Flaubert to be "the finest of writers" and took "an intense personal interest in the scruples which dogged Flaubert's writing, that fear of the false which, she said, sometimes kept him confined to his couch for weeks or months on end in the dread that he would never be able to write another word without compromising himself in the most grievous of ways." She "maintained that the source of Flaubert's scruples was to be found in the relentless spread of stupidity which he had observed everywhere, and which he believed had already invaded his own head" (7). In "The Alps in the Sea," included in *Campo Santo*, trans. Anthea Bell (2003; New York: Modern Library, 2005), Sebald recounts how he was "disturbed and fascinated" (42) in reading Flaubert's version of the legend of Saint Julien in which the saint as a well-behaved boy explodes into a mass killer of hosts of animals of all kinds, only to be numbed by the extent of his slaughter and pursued by the ghosts of the dead, ending his torment and his life "spending the night breast to breast and mouth to mouth with that most repellent of all human beings," an ulcerated leper. (*La légende de Saint-Julien l'hospitalier* of 1871 was inspired by a stained glass window in Rouen Cathedral, hence anticipating the "ekphrastic" manner of composition of much of Sebald's work.) Sebald concludes: "Not once as I read could I take my eyes off this utterly

perverse tale of the despicable nature of human violence, a story that probes horror further with every line. Only the act of grace when the saint is transfigured on the last page let me look up again" (44). This interlude strangely resembles a later one in "Dream Textures" (included in *Campo Santo*) concerning Nabokov, who claims that his favorite means of transport in Switzerland was a cable railway where he remained perched in a chairlift observing his shadow from above—"a ghostly butterfly net in its ghostly hand" (149). Sebald does not comment on the violent aspect of Nabokov's famous hobby, but he ends his account by presenting the chairlift passage with its "image of ascension into heaven" as connected by "its final touch of humor" to what he sees as the "finest" passage Nabokov ever wrote, located at the end of the first chapter of the autobiographical *Speak Memory*. It concerns the "figure of his father," thrown into the air in celebration by peasants on his estate in Russia and becoming what Nabokov writes of as "a marvelous case of levitation." Indeed the levitating, seemingly transfigured father becomes the upward-bound counterimage to a corpse, "like one of those paradisiac personages who comfortably soar, with such a wealth of folds in their garments, on the vaulted ceiling of a church while below, one by one, the wax tapers in mortal hands light up to make a swarm of minute flames in the mist of incense, and the priest chants of eternal repose, and funeral lilies conceal the fact of whoever lies there, among the swimming lights, in the open coffin" (quoted 149). Later in *Campo Santo* Sebald comments (with a typical self-referential turn) on Flaubert's "terrifying story" with respect to Bruce Chatwin, whose works are marked by a "promiscuity, which breaks the mold of the modernist concept, as a late flowering of those early traveler's tales, going back to Marco Polo, where reality is constantly entering the realm of the metaphysical and miraculous, and the way through the world is taken from the first with an eye fixed on the writer's own end" (174).

22. Santner, in *On Creaturely Life*, treats Casement, Adelwarth, and Grünewald along with other characters and incidents in an extensive discussion of gender and sexuality in Sebald's texts (167–96). Offering engaging analysis and speculation, informed by references to Freud, Lacan, Foucault, Žižek, and others, Santner weaves together a series of more or less direct homosexual as well as at times particularly disconcerting heterosexual allusions in Sebald. These include a "primal scene" from *The Rings of Saturn* where the dizzy, panicked narrator sees a copulating couple on the beach with "a man stretched full length over another body of which nothing was visible but the legs, spread and angled." The woman is mentioned only after the fact, and the couple itself is described as "misshapen, like some great mollusk washed ashore . . . to all appearances a single being, a many-limbed, two-headed monster that had drifted in from far out at sea, the last of a prodigious species, its life ebbing from it with each breath expired through its nostrils" (*Rings of Saturn* 68, quoted 185). Santner concludes that "Sebald's singular topic [for Santner 'the natural history of modern life'] is always already a history of sexuality" (196).

23. Sebald, *On the Natural History of Destruction*, trans. Anthea Bell (1999; New York: Random House, 2003). The German title is *Luftkrieg und Literatur*.

24. In a postscript to the first two parts of the text, which were first given as Zürich lectures, Sebald segues in a different direction when he asserts: "The majority of Germans today know, or at least it is to be hoped, that we actually provoked the

annihilation of the cities in which we once lived" (*On the Natural History of Destruction*, 103). In one of the strongest critiques of Sebald's work, Ruth Franklin finds in it the aestheticization of history, the elision of the causes of phenomena, the confusion of human action with natural processes, and (in *On the Natural History of Destruction*) the conflation of German suffering with that of Jews in a way that creates the "suspicion" of "moral equivalency." See her "Rings of Smoke," first published in *The New Republic,* September 23, 2002, and included in *The Emergence of Memory,* 119–42. There are indeed in Sebald elements of fatalism (or its correlative, the role of chance and coincidence) as well as a tendency to collapse human action and natural processes. Yet, on the level of what Franklin sees as causes, Sebald obviously believed that the nature and extent of the bombing of German cities at the end of the war was in excess of what was necessary to defeat the Nazis. One may also recall that, primarily for military and strategic reasons, the Allies refused to bomb the railway lines to concentration camps despite appeals on behalf of victims that they do so. And, as Franklin intimates (138), it is difficult to accuse of "moral equivalency" (an incoherent term in any case) someone who addressed the atrocities or the aftermath of the Nazi genocide at times in allusive, conflicted, or confused ways (as in *On the Natural History of Destruction*) but often in an explicit, extensive, and even obsessive fashion. In commenting on the final image of the Parcae or Fates in *The Emigrants,* Franklin, a child of Holocaust victims and survivors, observes that one young woman in the photograph "could have been my own grandmother, who was blonde and whose family owned a textile factory in Lodz." In a manner that creates the impression of an underestimation of blankness as an aesthetic strategy or even of a movement toward sacralization and taboo (reminiscent of the approach of Claude Lanzmann), she accuses Sebald of substituting "an artistic image for a blank space" where "the blankness is, however, closer to the truth" (142). Her analysis ends with a curious comment that may seem to repeat the kind of amalgamating use of language she finds dubious in Sebald: "The art he created is of near miraculous beauty, but it is as fragile, and as ephemeral, as a pearl of smoke" (145).

25. Sebald, *After Nature* [*Nach der Natur: Ein Elementargedicht*], trans. Michael Hamburger (1988; New York: Random House, 2002).

26. *The Origin of German Tragic Drama,* trans. John Osborne, intro. George Steiner (1928; London: Verso, 1977). Benjamin writes: "Melancholy betrays the world for the sake of knowledge. But in its tenacious self-absorption it embraces dead objects in its contemplation, in order to redeem them" (157).

27. I especially have in mind Santner's "Epilogue" where he turns to a notion of the miracle, notably "acts of neighbor-love—small miracles, as it were, performed *one by one*" (206–7), epitomized in passages he quotes from Franz Rosenzweig's book completed in 1919, *Star of Redemption.* In this light he concludes with a reference to "the quietly *miraculous* stride of Sebald's narratives" (207). He also looks to the Lacanian "feminine" logic of the not-all that supplements without overcoming the sovereign/creature dyad in holding out the promise of a different mode of encounter with singularities—neighbors—not ruled by that dyad. Santner maintains that his view has ethical and political as well as aesthetic implications, and he tries to render his argument "concrete" through a careful exegesis of Rilke's "The Archaic Torso of Apollo," with its famous concluding line: "Du mußt dein Leben ändern"

("You must change your life"). It might be as unfair to ask Santner, as it would be to ask Rilke, what the "practical" implications of his view might be beyond "loving" one's neighbor.

28. It is easy to lose one's way in *Austerlitz*, which is written without paragraph breaks. A long sentence of some seven-to-eight pages (236–44) on the concentration camp at Terezin (or Theresienstadt) where Austerlitz tries to find traces of his mother Agáta is punctuated seven times by "said Austerlitz" and once by "continued Austerlitz." It begins with the statement, "It seems unpardonable to me today that I had blocked off the investigation of my distant past for so many years" and, paralleling the released rush of suppressed or repressed memories, continues with a seemingly endless flow of information and reflection about the camp, derived in good part from the eight-hundred-page 1947 study by H. G. Adler, to which the text refers.

29. Included in *Campo Santo*, 97–124. In "An Attempt at Restitution," also included in *Campo Santo* (197–205), Sebald provides this fascinating insight into his "method of procedure": "[In May 1976 Jan Peter] Tripp gave me a present of one of his engravings, showing the mentally ill judge Daniel Paul Schreber with a spider in his skull—what can there be more terrible than the ideas always scurrying around our minds?—and much of what I have written later derives from this engraving, even in my method of procedure: in adhering to an exact historical perspective, in patiently engraving and linking together apparently disparate things in the manner of a still life" (200). Yet one would have to qualify the reference to a still life by pointing out the role of repetition with its relation to belated temporality, trauma, and its aftermath that is so pronounced in Sebald's treatment of time and narrative. (Or, as he puts it in an interview, "when the narrative is finished, its beginnings show up in a new light . . . I mean, after the tock becomes tick again" [*Emergence of Memory*, 104].)

30. On Améry and Hildesheimer, see Melanie Steiner Sherwood's 2011 Cornell dissertation "Jean Améry and Wolfgang Hildesheimer: Ressentiments, Melancholia, and the West German Public Sphere in the 1960s and 1970s." Steiner Sherwood not only offers a close reading of Hildesheimer's works with special attention to their direct or indirect allusions to the Shoah. She also provides a provocative analysis of Améry's defense of *ressentiment*, which he opposed to Nietzsche's understanding of it as a reactive affect close to revenge. Instead, Améry construed *ressentiment* as a moral sentiment and a demand for justice and recognition that might help to enable both Jews and Germans in the postwar context to work through a devastating past. Sebald's own interest in Breendonk fortress, discussed extensively in *Austerlitz*, was prompted by the excruciating torture to which the SS subjected Améry, "hoisted aloft by his hands, tied behind his back, so that with a crack and a splintering sound which, as he says, [he] had not yet forgotten when he came to write his account, his arms dislocated from the sockets in his shoulder joints, and he was left dangling as they were wrenched up behind him and twisted together above his head" (*Austerlitz*, 26).

31. I would note that Sebald's realization of the limitations of melancholy and his defense of mourning for victims are historiographical, ethical, and political—a defense that is critical-theoretical and neither redemptive nor primarily psychological. I would make the same point about my own defense, which would include, with

respect to mourning, the laughter of the wake (a possible prototype for gallows humor). I would add that, unlike melancholia, mourning is not primarily an affect or mood.

32. In the German context, Sebald's orientation may seem untimely, more reminiscent of important currents in the 1960s, '70s, and '80s, culminating in certain respects in the heated *Historikerstreit* of 1986. These currents resisted the "normalization" of the Nazi past and the neoconservative forces with which "normalization" was often allied. Instead, they emphasized the way the Nazi genocide had to remain an open wound or, if it allowed for any significant "healing," mourning, or working through, the process had to resist closure and to eventuate at most in scars that were not only visible but insistently pronounced and even disfiguring. In important ways, views expressed by Jürgen Habermas epitomized this orientation, and the latter may also be detected in Saul Friedländer's two-volume *Nazi Germany and the Jews.* See the pertinent sections of Habermas's *The New Conservatism: Cultural Criticism and the Historians' Debate,* ed. and trans. Shierry Weber Nicholsen, intro. Richard Wolin (Cambridge: MIT Press, 1989) as well as the extensive discussion of related issues in Franz Hofer's 2012 Cornell dissertation, "Memorial Sites and the Affective Dynamics of Historical Experience in Berlin and Tokyo," especially the heated debates throughout the 1970s, '80s, and into the '90s concerning the construction of the "Topography of Terror" on the "rediscovered" Gestapo-Gelände in Berlin that had been abandoned, left in rubble, and largely ignored since the end of the Second World War. In the more recent past, different problems have arisen, notably with respect to the German context, that have arguably changed certain terms of debate. While extreme neoconservatism and even neofascism are not simply things of the past, the post-*Historikerstreit* generation has seen the prevalence of both commemoration and memory work, even leading to debatable concerns about a "surfeit of memory" and a transnational trauma or victim culture. See, for example, Charles Maier, "A Surfeit of Memory?: Reflections on History, Memory, and Denial," *History and Memory* 5 (1993): 136–51; John Mowitt, "Trauma Envy," *Cultural Critique* 46 (2000): 272–97; and especially Didier Fassin and Richard Rechtman, *The Empire of Trauma: An Inquiry into the Condition of Victimhood* (2007; Princeton: Princeton University Press, 2009) where the prevalence of expertise is debatably seen to preempt if not exclude the role of empathy. A resultant problem is how to approach or "represent" the Nazi past in a manner that continues to raise questions for, while not overwhelming or imputing guilt to, a generation born much later, which, however well informed, may be either confused by, or feel distanced (if not detached) from, a past that nonetheless refuses to pass away. To the extent the foregoing brief analysis is pertinent, it might be taken to indicate one possible set of reference points for the elaboration of Sebald's own concerns. One could, for example, point to the aesthetic of sobriety and even the insistence on documentation that Sebald shares with advocates of the memory site as a place of informed, critical reflection, embodied in the "Topography of Terror," especially members of his generation such as the historians Reinhard Rürup and Dieter Hoffmann-Axthelm, the latter a very early advocate of drawing attention and critical awareness to the Gestapo-Gelände in Berlin. (I would also note that Hoffmann-Axthelm, as an architectural historian, interestingly shares the profession of Jacques Austerlitz.) But my analysis might also indicate how a writer

may indeed be untimely and not resonate directly with prominent contemporaneous tendencies even within intellectual or literary elites but in certain ways remain close to the concerns of older generations, including figures such as Alexander Kluge (born 1932) and Peter Weiss (born 1916). In another sense, however, Sebald's orientation bespeaks the role of a repetitive temporality wherein what was once prominent may nonetheless return with modifications, be linked to heightened sensitivities about still active possibilities (such as neofascism and victimization), and have a power of address or interpellation when formulated in ways that convey an ability to disturb and provoke. Even when one is inclined to take issue with one or another aspect of Sebald's literary or intellectual practice (to earlier caveats, I would add his inattentiveness to prejudicial treatment of Islamic and, in particular, Turkish "*Gastarbeiter*" in Germany), I think one might still be affected by this ability. And one may justifiably stress the crucial point that Sebald's skillful and effective deployment of stylistic devices such as repetition, parataxis, segues, and careful framing enable him to trace and render other than narrowly "rational" processes that escape the confines of a restricted documentary reserve.

33. In an essay ("An Attempt at Restitution") included in *Campo Santo*, Sebald provides, with reference to "the memory of those to whom the greatest injustice has been done," this understanding of the specificity of literature: "There are many forms of writing; only in literature, however, can there be an attempt at restitution over and above the mere recital of facts, and over and above scholarship" (205). Sebald uses the word "restitution" in the original German version: "Es gibt viele Formen des Schreibens; einzig aber in der literarischen geht es, über die Wissenschaft hinaus, um einem Versuch der Restitution." "Ein Versuch der Restitution," in *Campo Santo* (2003; Frankfurt am Main: Fischer Taschenbuch Verlag, 2006), 248. Of course much depends on how expansive one's notion of literature (or the literary) is, how it relates to a form such as the essay in which Sebald excels, and what its status is with respect to the insistently hybridized forms Sebald explores. (Sebald refers to his own writing simply as "a form of prose fiction" [*Emergence of Memory*, 37].) It is significant that Sebald refers not to redemption but to restitution, although what he includes in restitution remains open (the value and status victims were denied in persecution? restoration of property or at least monetary compensation, however inadequate to the offenses suffered? some form of acknowledgement or affirmation, including mourning and memory work?).

34. See, especially, David Atwell, ed., *Doubling the Point: Essays and Interviews* (Cambridge: Harvard University Press, 1992).

35. Coetzee, *Slow Man* (New York: Penguin Books, 2005).

36. See, for example, A. Dirk Moses, ed., *Genocide and Settler Society: Frontier Violence and Stolen Children in Australian History* (New York: Berghahn Books, 2005).

37. See Santner, *On Creaturely Life*, 44–45n.

38. See my discussion of Smuts's claim in *History and Its Limits: Human, Animal, Violence* (Ithaca: Cornell University Press, 2009), 179–80. In *The Lives of Animals,* Costello asserts: "Anyone who says that life matters less to animals than it does to us has not held in his hands an animal fighting for its life" (65). The Singer-persona makes arguments that seem to go in the direction Costello criticizes. See also Costello's extensive discussion of what she sees as the empirical analog of Kafka's

Red Peter in the apes who were objects of experiments by Wolfgang Köhler, especially the ape Sultan (27–30).

39. Derek Attridge, *J.M. Coetzee and the Ethics of Reading* (Chicago: University of Chicago Press, 2004). I treat Attridge selectively. There is much of great interest in his work on Coetzee, including the questions he poses in interviews included in *Doubling the Point*.

40. One may compare Attridge's approach to J. Hillis Miller's in "Should We Read 'Heart of Darkness'," included in the Norton Critical Edition of *Heart of Darkness*, ed. Paul B. Armstrong, 4th ed. (New York: W. W. Norton, 2006), 463–74.

41. The problem of containing Costello is foregrounded in Coetzee's *Slow Man* where she barges into things unbidden and even unwanted, giving rise to numerous uncomfortable and comic situations. Her overtures are finally rejected by Paul, the "slow man" amputee protagonist and perhaps by the "slow man's" sympathetic narrator.

42. For excellent recent historical approaches to sexuality and gender, see Judith Surkis, *Sexing the Citizen: Morality and Masculinity in France, 1870–1920* (Ithaca: Cornell University Press, 2006) and Tracie Matysik, *Reforming the Moral Subject: Ethics and Sexuality in Central Europe, 1890–1930* (Ithaca: Cornell University Press, 2008). See also the insightful essay-review of these two books by Sandrine Sanos, "The Subject and the Work of Difference: Gender, Sexuality, and Intellectual History," *Modern Intellectual History* 8, no. 1 (2011): 213–25 and the article by Camille Robcis, "French Sexual Politics from Human Rights to the Anthropological Function of the Law," *French Studies* 33 (Winter 2010): 129–56.

43. Coetzee, "The Novel Today," *Upstream* 6 (1988): 2–5.

44. See, for example, Attridge, *J.M. Coetzee and the Ethics of Reading*, 14n.

45. Here one might allude to Michel Focuault's radically disorienting reference to the fantastic list of animals in Borges's description of a certain Chinese encyclopedia, the *Celestial Emporium of Benevolent Knowledge*. Foucault writes: "This book first arose out of a passage in [Jorge Luis] Borges, out of the laughter that shattered, as I read the passage, all the familiar landmarks of my thought—*our* thought that bears the stamp of our age and our geography—breaking up all the ordered surfaces and all the planes with which we are accustomed to tame the wild profusion of existing things, and continuing long afterwards to disturb and threaten with collapse our age-old distinction between the Same and the Other. This passage quotes a 'certain Chinese encyclopaedia' in which it is written that 'animals are divided into: (a) belonging to the Emperor, (b) embalmed, (c) tame, (d) suckling pigs, (e) sirens, (f) fabulous, (g) stray dogs, (h) included in the present classification, (i) frenzied, (j) innumerable, (k) drawn with a very fine camelhair brush, (l) *et cetera*, (m) having just broken the water pitcher, (n) that from a long way off look like flies'. In the wonderment of this taxonomy, the thing we apprehend in one great leap, the thing that, by means of the fable, is demonstrated as the exotic charm of another system of thought, is the limitation of our own, the stark impossibility of thinking *that*." *The Order of Things* (1966; New York: Pantheon, 1970), xv.

46. One apparent difference between Costello and Coetzee is her professed view of Kafka: "She is no devotee of Kafka. Most of the time she cannot read him without impatience" (209).

47. See, for example, Lila Abu-Lughod, *Veiled Sentiments: Honor and Piety in a Bedouin Society* (Berkeley: University of California Press, 1986) and Saba Mahmood, *Politics of Piety* (Princeton: Princeton University Press, 2005) (on women in Egypt), as well as Lila Abu Lughod, "La femme 'musulmane': Le pouvoir des images et le danger de pitié," *Revue Internationale des Livres & des Idées* 6 (juillet–août 2008): 29–33. For a comparable argument concerning the empowering nature of asceticism in medieval women saints in Europe, see Carolyn Walker Bynum, *Holy Fast and Holy Feast: The Religious Significance of Food to Medieval Women* (Berkeley: University of California Press, 1987).

48. Paul West, *The Very Rich Hours of Count von Stauffenberg* (Woodstock, NY: Overlook Press, 1980).

49. I am following the account of West in "The Elegant Variation (A Literary Weblog)," available online at http://marksarvas.blogs.com/elegvar/2004/01/paul_west_respo.html (accessed on April 16, 2011), including its quotation of West from *The Ithaca News*. West has resided in the Ithaca area and since 1970 has been married to the noted writer Diane Ackerman.

50. On Lanzmann, see my *History and Memory after Auschwitz* (Ithaca: Cornell University Press, 1998), chap. 4.

51. One may note that in passing Costello affirms that "she believes most unquestionably in the ram," (211) alluding, however, not to Genesis 22 but to a sacrificial episode in *The Odyssey.* Attesting once more to the role of internal dialogization and self-contestation in the novel, she describes her role as a writer in a manner for which she earlier criticized Paul West: "I am open to all voices, not just the voices of the murdered and violated. . . . If it is their murderers and violators who choose to summon me instead, to use me and speak through me, I will not close my ears to them. I will not judge them" (205). Belatedly, she realizes she would have done better to address the judges in words that in effect disconcertingly echo those of Anne Frank—quite eerie words once you recognize the allusion: "I believe in the irrepressible human spirit . . . I believe that all humankind is one" (207).

52. The first three issues have been broadly discussed, including in my *History and Its Limits*, chap. 5. On the issue of the capture, commerce in, and largely exploitative use of wild and especially "exotic" animals, see the meticulously documented study by Eric Baratay and Elisabeth Hardouin-Fugier, *Zoo: A History of Zoological Gardens in the West* (1998; Hong Kong: Reaktion Books, 2002), one of whose major themes is the role of the anthropocentric (if not quasi-transcendent), typically violent, and often devastating domination of other animals in the creation of zoos and related institutions (such as menageries) as well as the way the zoo was an aspect of the colonial enterprise in which the conquest of colonized peoples and of animal species (which were often compared) ran along parallel tracks. For a more analytic study, presenting the historical background for contemporary "vexing" issues and focusing on "zoos without the iron bars," featuring artificially "natural" (or even seemingly better-than-natural) habitats, which followed the innovations of Carl Hagenbeck in Germany, see Nigel Rothfels, *Savages and Beasts: The Birth of the Modern Zoo* (Baltimore: Johns Hopkins University Press, 2002). Rothfels argues that these innovations became a model for many later zoos down to the present day, often utilizing colonial acquisitions and misleadingly influencing popular representations of

"exotic" cultures and wildlife, while remaining sources of disquiet for onlookers in quest of a reciprocal yet disconcerting look from the observed and silenced captive animals. (These captives earlier included "native" human specimens who lost their appeal once they began to talk back.) Rothfels states that "the story of Red Peter in Kafka's 'A Report to an Academy' is central to this book" (189). He further observes that "although the story was centrally about problems in human society, it was also about the problems faced by an ape obtained by one of Hagenbeck's catchers and brought to live among civilized humans" (190). Indeed, Red Peter faced abusive treatment both in his capture, where he was shot twice and transported in a cage resembling a torture chamber, and in his training and life as a performing monkey traumatized into becoming almost human. The latter was the only alternative he had to more manifest captivity (in his case a cage rather than an artificially nature-like environment in which iron bars were replaced by less ostensible forms of confinement such as moats that were less offensive for sensitive viewers.) For a discussion of the pertinence of Kafka's "Report to an Academy" for Rothfels, see esp. chap. 2 of his book.

53. See Kierkegaard, *Fear and Trembling*, ed. and trans. with intro. and notes, Howard V. Hong and Edna H. Hong (1843; Princeton: Princeton University Press, 1983).

54. One might read the following passage alongside William Blake, especially his "Auguries of Innocence" that is, among other things, a defense or apology for animals and begins with the well-known words: "To see the World in a Grain of Sand / And a Heaven in a Wild Flower / Hold Infinity in the palm of your hand / And Eternity in an hour / A Robin Red breast in a Cage / Puts all Heaven in a Rage." *Blake's Poetry and Designs*, selected and ed. Mary Lynn Johnson and John E. Grant (1979; New York: W. W. Norton, 2008), 403.

55. For an apocalyptic, at times ecstatic, but scientifically informed understanding of "the singularity," see Vernor Vinge's online essay at http://mindstalk.net/vinge/vinge-sing.html (accessed April 17, 2011). Vinge is a futurologist and member of the Department of Mathematical Sciences at San Diego State University.

56. Attridge at first provides an allegorical reading of *Disgrace* with respect to "the times" both in South Africa and globally, in which he furnishes many suggestive details, including some privy to South Africans, such as the fact or contention that Melanie's *Kaap's* accent in a play, along with other details about her, such as her high cheekbones and perhaps her family name Isaacs, increases the possibility that she is "couloured." I think that it remains unclear whether Melanie—or Melánie as Lurie renders the "dark one's" name exotic—is a person of color, Jewish, or possibly both. As I later note, one significant aspect of the family name Isaacs is that it may evoke the Akeda or story of Abraham and Isaac, a sacrificial and arguably abusive scene between father and child. Attridge nonetheless goes on to criticize allegorical or historically allusive reading and returns to the theme of the centrality of the literary. It is the latter that accounts for the "serious, committed, and responsible engagement of the novel" with its times (177). The manner in which he arrives at this conclusion is oblique and debatable: the role of music in Lurie's turn to opera and the role of animals, particularly dogs, which are linked through the thematic of lament. "My argument . . . is that one of the novel's striking achievements (which is also one of the reasons for its undeniable rebarbativeness) lies in its sharp insistence

that neither of these [opera and the care of animals] constitutes any kind of answer or way out, while at the same time it conveys or produces—in a way that only literature can do—an experience, beyond rationality and measured productivity, of their fundamental value" (177). One might think that Lurie's turn to opera and the care of animals indicates that literature, while of great importance, may not have the unique value or privileged position Attridge ascribes to it. Indeed Lurie also turns from his early affinity with Byron to a concern with the latter's scorned and aging lover and her daughter, who recalls his daughter Lucy. He even links opera and dogs via the fantasy of introducing a dog into his (virtual) opera: "Would he dare to do that: bring a dog into the piece, allow it to loose its own lament to the heavens between the strophes of lovelorn Teresa's? Why not? Surely, in a work that will never be performed, all things are permitted?" (215). Still, one might also ask to what extent Lurie's seeming turn, while not simply a "literary" gesture, remains entangled in forms of identification and projection more than compassion. See also Attridge's "Age of Bronze, State of Grace: Music and Dogs in Coetzee's *Disgrace*," *Novel* 34, no. 1 (2000): 98–121, where he contestably but inventively sees the "giving up" of the dog not as sacrifice or as expiation but as a pure, excessive, singular gift comparable to the "truly inventive" work of art.

57. On this issue see my *History and Its Limits*, chap. 3 on "traumatropisms."

58. Sounding a bit like Derrida in answering a question, Elizabeth Costello asserts that "to respond adequately . . . would take more time than I have, since I would first want to interrogate the whole question of rights and how we come to possess them" (107). For a history of the emergence of human rights, see Samuel Moyn, *The Last Utopia: Human Rights in History* (Cambridge: Harvard University Press, 2010). In Moyn's account, human rights came forth as a distinctively moral concept, opposed to state sovereignty and offering an unconventional revision of political action. Its salience is recent (the 1970s being crucial). Despite his stress on contingency, Moyn presents human rights as the "last utopia," which arose as the minimalist aftermath of communism, Marxism, and other more totalizing visions. One might argue that the centrality of at least an anthropocentric notion of human rights has been challenged by a concern for the animal as well as the environment, including but not limited to "animal rights." Perhaps one has here a presentiment of the "next utopia." I note that Coetzee has indicated significant interest in literary theory, including the work of Derrida. By contrast, Sebald is overly harsh about the role of theory. In rather traditional terms, he asserts that "of the many Kafka studies to have appeared in the 1950s, it is almost incredible to observe how much dust and mold have already accumulated on these secondary works, inspired as they are by the theories of existentialism, theology, psychoanalysis, structuralism, post-structuralism, reception aesthetics, or system criticism, and how unrewarding is the redundant verbiage on every page." He commends "the conscientious and patient work of editors and factual commentators" and of those who "have concentrated mainly on reconstructing a portrait of the author in his own time" ("Kafka Goes to the Movies," in *Campo Santo*, 154). Sebald's own work, including his scholarly work, would seem to fit neither category, although it does include real or fictive portraits and at times problematic speculation (for example, in *After Nature* concerning the putative homosexuality of Matthias Grünewald, put forward in a manner reminiscent of Freud on Leonardo da Vinci).

59. The TRC did not have the judicial power to impose or even recommend penalties and was criticized both for its seeming sacrifice of justice for the sake of reconciliation and for its amnesty provision concerning perpetrators, which none-theless took the severity and political motivation of the criminal offense into account, granted amnesty to only about 12% of over seven thousand petitioners, and included abuses by those affiliated both with the apartheid government and with the African National Congress. The report of the TRC fully satisfied few and was criticized particularly by former (or current) apartheid supporters and by ANC proponents who argued that human rights abuses could not be ascribed to those defending a just cause. On the controversy surrounding the TRC, see, for example, the now classic work of Antjie Krog, *Country of My Skull: Guilt, Sorrow, and the Limits of Forgiveness in the New South Africa*, intro. Charlayne Hunter-Gault (1998; New York: Three Rivers Press, 1999). Krog observes that "few women have testified about rape, and fewer, if any, have named the rapists." She also notes that "South African law defines rape as occurring only between a man and a woman and involving the penetration of the penis into the vagina. Acts of forced oral or anal sex and penetration by foreign objects are not considered rape. But the Truth and Reconciliation Commission has to establish whether one can rape with a political motive and whether the raping of nonpolitical women to keep the comrades busy is indeed a political act" (239). See also her discussion of the opposition of Afrikaner leaders and the unsuccessful attempt of the ANC, despite its internal divisions, to obtain a court order to block the publication of the TRC report (374–83).

60. In "Ethics and Politics in Tagore, Coetzee, and Certain Scenes of Teaching," *Diacritics* 32, no. 3–4 (2002): 17–31, Gayatri Chakravorty Spivak argues for a reading of the novel from Lucy's perspective: "When Lucy is resolutely denied focalization, the reader is provoked, for he or she does not want to share in Lurie-the-chief-focalizer's inability to 'read' Lucy as patient and agent" (22). Yet, as I intimate, any such reading has to be limited and self-questioning in view of the limitations in the development of Lucy as character and focalizer. In his recent *Diary of a Bad Year* (New York: Viking, 2008), Coetzee makes a statement about his "political thought" that leaves one in doubt about whether to take it as expressing a "position" or as a series of ironic modulations of opinion (perhaps more what his erotic/intellectual muse Anja would term a preferred "Soft" rather than a "Hard Opinion"):

> If I were pressed to give my brand of political thought a label, I would call it pessimistic anarchistic quietism, or anarchist quietistic pessimism, or pessimistic quietistic anarchism: anarchism because experience tells me that what is wrong with politics is power itself; quietism because I have my doubts about the will to set about changing the world, a will infected with the drive to power; and pessimism because I am skeptical that, in a fundamental way, things can be changed. (Pessimism of this kind is cousin and perhaps even sister to belief in original sin, that is, the conviction that humankind is imperfectible.)
>
> But do I really qualify as a thinker at all, someone who has what can prop-erly be called thoughts, about politics or about anything else? I have never been easy with abstractions or good at abstract thought. (203)

61. After having sex with Bev, Lurie reflects: "His thoughts go to Emma Bovary strutting before the mirror after her big afternoon. *I have a lover! I have a lover!* sings

Emma to herself. Well, let poor Bev Shaw go home and do some singing too. And let him stop calling her poor Bev Shaw. If she is poor, he is bankrupt" (150).

62. Lurie adamantly refuses to see the rape of Lucy as sacrificial, as she seems tempted to do at one point, although a sacrificial perspective does not inform her understanding of the relation between humans and other animals. In a series of doublings or displaced repetitions, sacrifice is also evoked in the initial sexual encounter of Lurie and Melanie ("the dark one") and the killing of the two "black-faced" Persian "slaughter-sheep" at Petrus's party celebrating the birth of his son (or, in Lurie's opinion, his new status on the farm). These scenes, along with the seeming sacrifice of the dog, resonate, perhaps parodically, with the account of Abraham and Isaac in *Genesis* 22, and Melanie's last name has an obvious relation to that of Abraham's beloved son. On the latter point, I benefited from a discussion with Adeline Rother.

63. In *Giving Offense: Essays in Censorship* (Chicago: University of Chicago Press, 1996), Coetzee makes a statement that may be compared to Lucy's in which he, perhaps too unproblematically, relies on a binary opposition in appealing to a "construct" or "foundational fiction" (in contrast to "essential being") that sets humans apart from animals but may someday bring an ascription to animals of their own "dignity" and protection against currently accepted forms of use and abuse:

> Affronts to the innocence of our children or to the dignity of our persons are attacks not upon our essential being but upon constructs—constructs by which we live, but constructs nevertheless. . . . The infringements are real; what is infringed, however, is not our essence but a foundational fiction to which we more or less wholeheartedly subscribe, a fiction that may well be indispensable for a just society, namely, that human beings have a dignity that sets them apart from animals. (It is even possible that we may look forward to a day when animals will have their own dignity ascribed to them, and the ban will be reformulated as a ban on treating a living creature like a thing.)
>
> The fiction of dignity helps to define humanity and the status of humanity helps to define human rights. There is thus a real sense in which an affront to our dignity strikes at our rights. Yet when outraged at such affront, we stand on our rights and demand redress, we would do well to remember how insubstantial the dignity is on which those rights are based. (14)

4. Historical and Literary Approaches to the "Final Solution"

1. Saul Friedländer, *Nazi Germany and the Jews*, vol. 1, *The Years of Persecution, 1933–1939* (New York: HarperCollins, 1997) and *Nazi Germany and the Jews,* vol. 2, *The Years of Extermination, 1939–1945* (New York: HarperCollins, 2007). The first volume is 436 pages, and the second, 870 pages. Friedländer received the Pulitzer Prize for the second volume, on which I concentrate, with references to it indicated by page number. Born in 1932, Saul Friedländer is from a German-speaking Prague Jewish family, was a hidden child in France, moved to Israel, and has taught in Switzerland (Graduate Institute of International Studies in Geneva), Israel (Hebrew University of Jerusalem and Tel Aviv) and the United States (UCLA).

2. Jonathan Littell, *Les Bienveillantes* (Paris: Gallimard, 2006). The novel is 906 pages. Translated as *The Kindly Ones*, trans. Charlotte Mandel (New York: Harper,

2009).I refer to the French text and provide my own translations. Born in 1967, Littell is from a New York Jewish family (the original family name was Lidsky) yet went to France at the age of three and spent much time in Paris where he attended lycée. He received his BA from Yale, one of the universities where French theory has had a particularly prominent place. After college and work in an international humanitarian organization (People Against Hunger), he returned to France, although he has been living recently in Barcelona. In a limited but important fashion, Littell's approach and self-understanding emulate or parallel those of other significant figures of the recent past, such as Giorgio Agamben, Maurice Blanchot, and Slavoj Žižek, in ways I shall try to elucidate, especially in notes. My analysis raises the question of the extent to which the notoriety of the novel may be due to the way it instantiates influential approaches to both literature and the Holocaust in terms of an aesthetic of the sublime, excess, radical ambiguity (resolvable at best into irony and paradox), and fatalistic entry into an incomprehensible "heart of darkness." Crucial here is the notion that something (paradigmatically, the Holocaust) both demands representation or explanation and ultimately is beyond comprehension, narrative, or even words.

3. In France, Littell was awarded the Prix Goncourt and the Grand Prix pour le Roman de l'Académie Française. Responses to the novel in the United States have been mixed. See, for example, the engaged, largely favorable review of Liran Razinsky, "History, Excess and Testimony in Jonathan Littell's Les Bienveillantes, French Forum 33, no. 3 (Fall 2008): 69–87; the very positive yet rather bland review of Daniel Mendelsohn, "Transgression," New York Review of Books 56 (March 26, 2009), available online at http://www.nybooks.com/articles/22452 (accessed November 8, 2010); the generally positive review of Susan Rubin Suleiman, "When the Perpetrator Becomes a Reliable Witness of the Holocaust : On Jonathan Littell's Les Bienveillantes," New German Critique 36, no. 1 (2009): 1–19; the very negative review of Ruth Franklin, "Night and Cog," New Republic (April 1, 2009): 38–43; and the measured, well-informed review of Samuel Moyn, "A Nazi Zelig: Jonathan Littell's The Kindly Ones," Nation December 3, 2009, available online at http://www.thenation.com/ doc/20090323/moyn/print (accessed November 8, 2010). Reviews in France were largely positive, at times hyperbolic, including the response of the noted writer and Holocaust survivor Jorge Semprún, one of the members of the jury awarding Littell the Prix Goncourt. A notable exception was that of mixed and at times very critical reviews by some historians. See the extensive, often supportive discussion in Le débat 144 (mars–avril 2007): 3–69, including "Conversations sur l'histoire et le roman" with Littell by Richard Millet and Pierre Nora and essays by Florence Mercier-Leca, Georges Nivat, and Daniel Bougnoux. Pierre Nora praised the novel and exclaimed: "I am among those whom your book shattered [sidérés]. It is for me an extraordinary literary and historical phenomenon" (25). For the largely positive response of a social scientist who criticizes historians for reading the book as a historical thesis rather than a literary work, see Jean Solchany, "Les Bienveillantes ou l'histoire à l'épreuve de la fiction," Revue d'histoire moderne & contemporaine 54, no. 3 (2007): 160–78. Yet Solchany's understanding of a literary reading as well as of the "linguistic turn" is such as to validate any interpretation in terms of reader response, however projective and unsupported by procedures cogently argued to be operative in the text. For a

scathing castigation of certain largely negative reviews of the book in Germany, see Klaus Theweleit, "On the German Reaction to Jonathan Littell's *Les Bienveillantes*," *New German Critique* 106 (Winter 2009): 21–34, where Theweleit offers a very favorable reading of Littell's book, seeing it in good part as a novelized version of his own *Male Fantasies*. For contrasting psychoanalytic readings of the novel taken more or less on the level of a case history, see the uncritically positive reaction of André Green, in the *Revue française de psychanalyse* (March 2007): 907–10, and the harsh critique of Henri Dudet, "Les Bienveillantes mises en question," *Psychanalyse* 11, no. 1 (2008): 105–17. Perhaps the most subtle and critical psychoanalytic reading, which is combined with a pointed literary critique, is Julia Kristeva's "A propos des *Bienveillantes* (De l'abjection à la banalité du mal)," *L'Infini* 99 (Summer 2007): 23–35. All translations, unless otherwise indicated, are my own. My thinking also benefited from reading Mary (Kate) Horning's unpublished paper, présented at the Cornell University European History colloquium, comparing Littell's novel and Bernhard Schlink's *Der Vorleser* (1995; Zurich: Diogenes Taschenbuch Verlag, 1997; *The Reader*, trans. Carol Brown Janeway [New York: Vintage, 1998]).

4. I have not seen a case made for the formally innovative nature of Littell's use of musical categories instead of chapter or section headings, and I do not see how the categories (Toccata, Allemandes I et II, Courante, Sarabande, Menuet [en rondeaux], Air, and Gigue) play an effective role in the discourse or movement of the text.

5. Saul Friedländer, *Memory, History, and the Extermination of the Jews of Europe* (Bloomington: University of Indiana Press, 1993): 110–11. Himmler's Posen speech (or speeches) had an important performative role in rallying the elite at a very difficult moment in the war for the Nazis, after the defeats at Stalingrad and in Africa. Among other notorious statements, Himmler at Posen says the following to his SS generals and other high-ranking personnel (insiders who, through their experience with mass murder, really understood it or were "in the know"): "Most of you know what it means to see a hundred corpses [or "dead bodies"—*Leichen*] lie side by side, or five hundred, or a thousand. To have endured this [*durchgehalten zu haben*] and, except for cases of human weakness, to have remained decent [or upright—*anständig geblieben zu sein*], that is what has made us hard." *A Holocaust Reader*, ed. Lucy Dawidowicz (West Orange, NJ: Behrman House, 1976), 133, translation modified. Nazi hardness was itself apparently a question of those "in the know" enduring, or bearing up, in the face of an aporia or antinomy: beholding scenes of mass slaughter (which one also perpetrated, although this remains unstated) and remaining upright or decent. It may not be irrelevant to note that standing upright is one criterion often invoked to differentiate humans from other animals. In his *Le sec et l'humide: Une brève excursion en territoire fasciste* (Paris: Gallimard, 2008), which is intended as a study of the fascist imaginary as seen through Léon Degrelle's *La campagne en Russie* (Paris: La Diffusion du Livre, 1949), Jonathan Littell points out that fighting in an upright or erect position was the ideal of the fascist soldier, which was undermined by the requirements of taking an abject, crouching position against partisans and tanks (39). Littell's approach in this book is essentially an application of the phenomenological-Deleuzian mode of analysis of Klaus Theweleit, who provides a very supportive "postface." The nature of the rather fluid, seemingly transhistorical analysis, which downplays ideology, might apply not only to fascists, indeed "male soldiers" in general,

but also to other groups, for example, certain bodybuilders or other athletes, even many of those resisting fascism. See also the discussion in Philippe Carrard, *The French Who Fought for Hitler* (New York: Cambridge University Press, 2010), esp. 105. Of course the conditions of trench warfare in the First World War were antithetical to the ideal of "uprightness," and the stereotypical cringing Jew was the antithesis of the upright soldier.

6. Jeffrey A. Trachtenberg, "Facing the Holocaust," *Wall Street Journal*, Feb. 28, 2009, W9, available online at http://online.wsj.com/article/SB123578783301898945. html (accessed November 8, 2010).

7. Peter Scowen, "Inside a 'Perverted Fairyland,'" *Globe Books*, May 1, 2009, available online at http://www.theglobeandmail.com/books/article1127739.ece (accessed November 8, 2010).

8. Littell, "The Executioner's Song," interview with Assaf Uni in *Haaretz*, May 30, 2008, available online at http://www.haaretz.com/hasen/spages/988410.html (accessed November 8, 2010).

9. Interview with Littell by Samuel Blumenfeld, *Le Monde*, November 17, 2006, available online at http://thekindlyones.wordpress.com/littell-interview-with-samuel-blumenfeld/ (accessed November 8, 2010).

10. "Conversations sur l'histoire et le roman," 20. Littell does not further explicate his relations to Bataille, Blanchot, and Beckett. On Bataille, especially with respect to sacrificial regenerative violence, see my *History and Its Limits: Human, Animal, Violence* (Ithaca: Cornell University Press, 2009), 102–8, as well as the more or less convergent analysis in Stefanos Geroulanos, *An Atheism That Is Not Humanist Emerges in French Thought* (Stanford: Stanford University Press, 2010), 184–94. Many of Blanchot's texts are extremely elusive. But in his virulent 1948 essay "Literature and the Right to Death," included in *The Work of Fire* (*La part du feu*), trans. Charlotte Mandel (1949; Stanford: Stanford University Press, 1995), Blanchot contends that "revolutionary action is in every respect analogous to action as embodied in literature: the passage from nothing to everything, the affirmation of the absolute as event and of every event as absolute." The Reign of Terror becomes a paradigmatic event indicating that "every citizen has a right to death" not as "a sentence passed on him" but as "his most essential right" (319). And Sade become "the writer par excellence . . . who cuts off people's heads the way you cut off a cabbage" and whose "oeuvre is nothing but the work of negation" (321). Blanchot concludes by defending a seemingly fatalistic, putatively unstoppable generalization of radical ambiguity whereby "nothing can prevent [the "amazing power of the negative, or freedom" bound up with the "right to death"] from continuing to assert itself as continually differing possibility, and nothing can stop it from perpetuating an irreducible *double meaning*, a choice whose terms are covered over with an ambiguity that makes them identical to one another even as it makes them opposite. This original double meaning . . . is the source of literature . . . and the question it asks is the question asked by literature" (343–44). Blanchot's line of thought would seem to imply that this "radical ambiguity," which leaves little room for critical judgment, would apply indiscriminately to the relation between perpetrator and victim (as well as collaborator and resister). In his *Writing of Disaster*, trans. Ann Smock (1980; Lincoln: University of Nebraska Press, 1986), I think one finds enacted a radically ambiguous slippage between the historical, the

transhistorical, and the quasi-transcendental with respect to the unstable figuration of the Shoah. As Ethan Kleinberg observes in *Generation Existential: Heidegger's Philosophy in France, 1927–1961* (Ithaca: Cornell University Press, 2005): "Blanchot saw the Shoah as a singular and fundamentally ahistorical event, but also as the moment by which all history and meaning will now be understood" (225). See also the analysis in Geroulanos, *Atheism That Is Not Humanist*, 251–67.

11. Littell, "Conversations sur l'histoire et le roman," 9.

12. Littell, "Conversations sur l'histoire et le roman," 10–11, 23.

13. "Conversations sur l'histoire et le roman," 33 (in dialogue with Pierre Nora). In this exchange Littell asserts that he finds Ian Kershaw's biography of Hitler to be "the most accomplished synthesis in relation to all preceding writing. Kershaw describes the Nazi system as a bureaucracy directed by a charismatic chief" (35). Hence Littell places major emphasis on Hitler's "obsession" with the Jews. This does little to elucidate the nature of that "obsession" and even construes it in aleatory or radically contingent terms with respect to the genocide. He hypothesizes that if Hitler had been "obsessed with the 'Gypsies,' they would have been the objects of a totalizing 'final solution.'" In the "conversation," the only way Littell can account for the excesses of others is to point to the desire to do Hitler's will, and the relation to Hitler also explains the conflicts between elements of the bureaucracy. Whatever one makes of this rather reductive account, it does not play a significant role in the novel, where there is much about the bureaucracy but too little about its relation to Hitler or even about Hitler's role, which was of crucial importance even if it does not explain all significant aspects of the genocide and its excesses, as certain passages in the novel itself would indicate, including the ones I quote from pages 95 and 137.

14. Such markers are active in a text that might superficially be seen as similar to Littell's in its procedures, notably in the role of the pseudodialogic, complicity-seeking narrator, the "judge-penitent" Jean-Baptiste Clamence—Albert Camus's *La chute* (*The Fall*) of 1956. On the latter, see my *History and Memory after Auschwitz* (Ithaca: Cornell University Press, 1996), chap. 3. One might argue that some perspective is provided on Aue by other characters who make episodic or evanescent appearances, such as his occasionally perceptive but largely apolitical sister Una or her aged, wealthy, paralytic husband von Üxküll (staunchly anti-Semitic yet an aficionado of Schönberg and largely enveloped in the world of abstract music [457–58]). One might also mention certain of Aue's acquaintances (notably the genteel, sylphide-like Hélène) or various fellow Nazis who serve as interlocutors (such as Voss, a linguist who finds "race" a concept "without theoretical value" [281] and against whom Aue defends the "idealistic" basis of the Nazi *Weltanschauung* [283] and finds "exaggerated" a rejection *en bloc* of racial anthropology, ultimately insisting on the need for an act of "faith" [284]). But the question is whether others ever become "focalizers" or offer viable critical alternatives, especially in light of Aue's central role as narrator.

15. Kristeva, "A propos des *Bienveillantes*," 31 (my trans.). There is some difficulty in translating "perpetrator" into French. "*Bourreau*" means executioner, hangman, or torturer. Dictionaries (such as Harper-Collins) offer "*auteur*" as in "*l'auteur d'un crime.*" "*Exécuteur*" has been used (and criticized), and recently there has been a revival

of the sixteenth-century term *"perpétreur"* since *"perpétrer"* and *"perpétration"* are still in current use. See the discussion in Kurt Jonassohn with Karin Solveig Björnson, *Genocide and Gross Human Rights Violations in Comparative Perspective* (New Brunswick, NJ: Transaction, 1998), 143–44.

16. Littell's figuration of Aue is curiously similar (in an inverted manner) to Giorgio Agamben's view of the *Muselmann* in *Remnants of Auschwitz: The Witness and the Archive*, trans. David Heller-Roazen (New York: Zone Books, 1999). In Agamben's extreme hyperbole, the *Muselmann*, as "life in its most extreme degradation," becomes "the touchstone by which to judge and measure all morality and degradation" (24). Agamben also has a pervasive idea of the "gray zone" approximating or mingling perpetrator and victim such that the problem of the perpetrator-victim (for example, in Jewish councils or the *Sonderkommando*) does not emerge as a specific problem whose incidence varies with historical circumstances in a manner allowing for distinctions between perpetrators and victims, including cases of perpetrators who are not in any pertinent sense victims, and victims who are not perpetrators. See my discussion in *History in Transit: Experience, Identity, Critical Theory* (Ithaca: Cornell University Press, 2004), 155–94.

17. See, for example, Bataille's *Madame Edwarda* of 1941 in *My Mother; Madame Edwarda; The Dead Man,* trans. Austryn Wainhouse, intro. Yukio Mishima (New York: Marion Boyars, 1995), 135–59. The carefully framed yet ribald and boisterous humor in Mel Brooks's *The Producers* is, I would suggest, a noteworthy instance of the Bakhtinian carnivalesque, which continually tests and may transform but does not simply obliterate limits. In general Bataille assumes an identification between sacrificer and sacrificed such that victimization and the perspective of the victim are not posed as explicit, variable, and important problems. The latter tend to remain obscure in a pervasive gray zone, as if sacrifice were always essentially a question of a god sacrificing itself.

18. Here one might recall Sartre's argument about the Flaubert-narrator's nihilistic, indeed genocidal relation to objects of narration. See *L'idiot de la famille*, 3 vols. (esp. vol. 3) (Paris: Gallimard, 1971–72) and my more qualified discussion in *"Madame Bovary" on Trial* (Ithaca: Cornell University Press, 1982), 81–99 and 121–25.

19. The sheer bulk of documentary material may be found excessive by some readers, threatening to overwhelm Littell's "literary" aspirations. See, for example, the response in Antoine Compagnon, "Nazisme, histoire et féerie: Retour sur *Les Bienveillantes*," *Critique* 726 (November 2007): 881–96.

20. Binjamin Wilkomirski's *Fragments: Memories of a Wartime Childhood*, trans. Carol Brown Janeway (1995; New York: Schocken, 1996). See also my discussion in *Writing History, Writing Trauma* (Baltimore: Johns Hopkins University Press, 2001), 32–34.

21. See Frederick Taylor, *Dresden: Tuesday, February 13, 1945* (New York: HarperCollins, 2004), 6. The notoriously vicious Clemens and Weser are also mentioned frequently in Victor Klemperer's *I Will Bear Witness: A Diary of the Nazi Years, 1942–1945*, trans. Martin Chalmers (1995; New York: Random House, 1999). For example: "Hirschel then waited in another room to be taken away; in this room he met Eger, who had been arrested the same day. After a while Inspector Weser came in— the animal, who also struck us and spat on us. At first he was only taunting: 'I hear

you said I was the worst—well, you won't see your Community again.' At that point a long hospital train went past. 'Weser suddenly went into a frenzy, raining blows on both of us. 'You people are to blame for that . . . . Normally, I can't harm a soul, but I want to murder every Jew. I want to kill your two boys as well. . . . You won't come back'" (176).

22. Littell's book is itself dedicated indiscriminately to "the dead." One may also note that the name of the shadowy, obese, flatulent, cat-loving, nubile-entouraged Doctor Mandelbrod, a Nazi whom many critics have seen as a stock figure displaced from a James Bond film, summons up "mandelbrot," the Jewish bread or biscotti.

23. Aue's sister Una herself asserts that "in killing the Jews . . . we have wanted to kill ourselves, to kill the Jew in us, to kill that which in us resembled the idea that we made for ourselves of the Jew" (801–2). In more ambiguous terms, Aue, in reading Hitler's speeches with reference to Jews, asks himself whether "the Führer, without knowing it, was not describing himself," indeed, in "concentrating the will of the *Volk* . . . if he were speaking of himself, he did not speak of us all?" (636).

24. Alluding to the excesses of France on the eve of the First World War and the pogroms in Russia, Aue asserts that "to impute all our faults to anti-Semitism alone" would be "a grotesque error . . . I hope you will not be too surprised that I devalue in this way anti-Semitism as the fundamental cause of the massacre of the Jews: this would be to forget that our politics of extermination would look much further. By the time of the defeat . . . we had already, besides the Jews, accomplished the destruction of all Germans who were physically handicapped and incurably mentally ill, the major part of Gypsies, and millions of Russians and Polish. And one knows that our projects were even more ambitious" (615). In this relativizing, zero-sum, oversimplifying combination of accuracy and misprision, Aue presupposes that not construing anti-Semitism as the "fundamental cause" of all Nazi violence, mass murder, and "exterminatory" projects, implies its devaluation, even with respect to Jews.

25. See, for example, Žižek's "Neighbors and Other Monsters: A Plea for Ethical Violence" in Slavoj Žižek, Eric L. Santner, and Kenneth Reinhard, *The Neighbor: Three Inquiries in Political Theology* (Chicago: University of Chicago Press, 2005). I would note that Žižek explicitly criticizes fascism. But, as I note in the epilog of this book, his own discourse on violence as nonstrategic, foundational, intrinsic to language, even "divine" is very problematic, for example, in *Violence* (New York: Picador, 2008), esp. 198–200.

26. Littell, "Conversations sur l'histoire et le roman," 40. Nora's question is on p. 39.

27. See Antoine Compagnon, "Nazisme, histoire et féerie." One should also note the mysterious, unnamed little twins who are cared for by Aue's mother and stepfather Moreau until the latter are killed. Then the twins are taken by his sister Una. In looking at a photo of the twins in the midst of his coprophagic phantasmagoria in the abandoned house of Una and von Üxküll, during the Russian advance, Aue thinks the twins may be Una's but blocks the recognition that he may be their father (816).

28. For an intensive study of the SS-Einsatzgruppen Trial, Case No. 9, at which Ohlendorf was the leading defendant, see Hilary Earl, *The Nuremberg SS-Einsatzgruppen Trial, 1945–1958: Atrocity, Law, and History* (New York: Cambridge University Press, 2009). Earl summarily concludes: "The truth is that Ohlendorf would not have

carried out his orders so willingly unless he believed they were right" (139). Peter Staudenmaier's 2010 Cornell University PhD dissertation, "Between Occultism and Fascism: Anthroposophy and the Politics of Race and Nation in Germany and Italy, 1900–1945," includes a discussion of the way the Gestapo and the SD, which saw itself as the guardian of Nazi ideology, succeeded in June 1941 in bringing about, despite significant points of resistance within the regime, an all-out assault against "esoteric" or "occult" associations along with "sects." (The assault occurred just before the invasion of Russia and after Rudolf Hess's embarrassing flight to Britain on May 10, 1941, attributed, in face-saving fashion, to "occult" influences on him.) These "esoteric" associations included Freemasons (often perceived as linked with Jews), theosophists, and anthroposophists (whose movement had been founded and inspired by Rudolf Steiner, at times mistakenly taken as a Jew, to the dismay of certain of his followers). Neither Friedländer nor Littell discusses this development. Interestingly, Otto Ohlendorf was among those inclined to support anthroposophy, apparently because of its "spiritual" orientation.

29. Littell interview by Samuel Blumenfeld, *Le Monde*, November 17, 2006.

30. Blumenfeld, *Le Monde*, November 17, 2006.

31. Littell discusses this episode on pp. 730–31.

32. Friedländer's attempt to devote sustained attention to these voices and their disruptive effects is the basis for claims concerning the novelty of his work both in historiographical and in literary terms (whether with respect to modernism, melodrama, or immediacy typically contrasted with theory).

33. In his introduction to the first volume on "the years of persecution, 1933–1939," Friedländer has a somewhat different formulation of his objective, which does not refer to disbelief. He affirms "the aim of creating a sense of estrangement counteracting our tendency to 'domesticate' that particular past and blunt its impact by means of seamless explanations and standardized renditions. That sense of estrangement seems to me to reflect the perception of the hapless victims of the regime, at least during the thirties, of a reality both absurd and ominous, of a world altogether grotesque and chilling under the veneer of an even more chilling normality" (5). Of course, given the seemingly incredible magnitude of events, "disbelief" was invoked by perpetrators to antagonize and disconcert victims ("no one will ever believe you") and feared by victims as the incredulous response of those not experiencing the events. As Primo Levi reports the words of an SS man (and his statement is echoed by others to the point of now being almost "uncannily" familiar): "However the war may end, we have won the war against you: none of you will be left to bear witness, but even if someone were to survive, the world will not believe him. . . . People will say that the events you describe are too monstrous to be believed." *The Drowned and the Saved*, trans. Raymond Rosenthal (New York: Random House, 1989), 11–12.

34. *Memory, History, and the Extermination of the Jews of Europe,* 115n13. I find Friedländer's formulation here to be problematic. For Himmler and those in accord with him, there may have been a "negative sublime" in genocidal action. But the commentator need not reaffirm it in his or her own "voice." In other words, one may suggest or contend that there may well have been a role for the "negative sublime" in the "elated" experience or view of certain perpetrators without repeating it

(through "use" in contrast to "mention") in one's own "voice" or account, however unintentionally. (A free indirect style, which Friedländer at times seems to employ, approximates "use" and "mention" and may sometimes not be sufficiently alert to the admittedly difficult problem of distinguishing them.)

35. Friedländer is often associated with the notion of the uniqueness of the Holocaust. See, for example, Gavriel D. Rosenfeld, "The Politics of Uniqueness: Reflections on the Recent Polemical Turn in Holocaust and Genocide Scholarship," *Holocaust and Genocide Studies* 3 (1999): 28–61. Yet Rosenfeld accords Friedländer a special status with respect to the inadequacy of general theories that attempt to encompass the Holocaust and mentions an essay in which Friedländer refers to "the absolute character of the anti-Jewish drive of the Nazis." "On the Possibility of the Holocaust: An Approach to a Historical Synthesis," in *The Holocaust as Historical Experience*, ed. Yehuda Bauer and Nathan Rotenstreich (New York: Holmes & Meier, 1981), 2. I noted in the introduction to this book Friedländer's tendency to avoid the terms "Holocaust" and "uniqueness," referring instead to the exceptionality (or centrality in German history) of Auschwitz, the Shoah, or the "Final Solution." He refers to "the exceptionality of this trespassing" in *Memory, History, and the Extermination of the Jews of Europe*, 50. He perhaps comes closest to a notion of uniqueness when he asserts that "the Nazi regime attained what is, in my view, some sort of theoretical outer limit. . . . Once a regime decides that groups, whatever the criteria may be, should be annihilated there and then and never be allowed to live on Earth, the ultimate has been achieved. This limit, from my perspective, was reached only once in modern history: by the Nazis" (82–83). In *Nazi Germany and the Jews*, he answers the call he puts forth at the end of the chapter in which the foregoing quotation appears: the call for "a historicization which would not lend itself to being easily used for the relativization of the Nazi past, its banalization, and ultimately for the elimination of its criminality from human memory" (83). This call and Friedländer's overall success in answering it may be accepted even by those who would question whether the "ultimate" has been reached only once in modern history or raise doubts about the significance of the claim to uniqueness (notably in light of its ideological abuses).

36. Standard works in this respect are Henry Friedlander, *The Origins of Nazi Genocide: From Euthanasia to the Final Solution* (Chapel Hill: University of North Carolina Press, 1995) and Guenter Lewy, *The Nazi Persecution of the Gypsies* (New York: Oxford University Press, 2000). Nazis closely associated or even conflated Bolsheviks and Jews, but Communist Party officials or members who were not Jews might be subjected to extremely harsh or even murderous treatment, notably in the ruthless movements of the *Einsatzgruppen*. As Friedländer notes in his second volume, on "the years of extermination, 1939–1945," Heydrich's initial charge to the latter on September 7, 1939, was that "the leading strata of the population should be rendered harmless," including Polish elites (14). Henry Friedlander sees much continuity between the euthanasia program and the Holocaust. While he finds various reasons for the killing, sterilization, and persecution of "Gypsies," including alleged "asocial conduct," Lewy (whose book carries an endorsement from Saul Friedländer on its dust jacket cover) notes that "party stalwarts and many 'race scientists' invoked the racial factor and the need to protect the 'purity' of 'German blood'" (219)

from "contamination" (221). He also observes: "Following the German invasion of the Soviet Union, Gypsies there were targeted as a blanket category (like Jews and Communist functionaries) of people who were to be destroyed" (220). He adds that "the losses in life experienced by the Gypsy community at the hands of the Nazis are clearly horrendous" (222). Still, Lewy insists that "Gypsies were not selected for extermination 'because they existed,'" and "no overall plan for the extermination of the Gypsy people was ever formulated and . . . the evidence shows that none was implemented" (225). Indeed, for him "what makes the murder of the Jews unique is not the number of victims but the intent of the murderers. Only in the case of the Jews did Nazis seek to annihilate physically every man, woman and child. This program of total extermination therefore deserves its own appellation—Holocaust or the Hebrew Shoah" (226). One may note that intention carries a great burden in this view and that there is no attempt at comparison with other genocides, which need not serve to diminish the significance of any given genocide.

37. On page 557 of vol. 2, Friedländer simply reasserts the opposition in a context in which he apparently believes it obviates the need for further explanation.

38. Friedländer, *Reflections of Nazism: An Essay on Kitsch and Death* (1982; Bloomington: University of Indiana Press, 1984).

39. See especially my *Writing History, Writing Trauma*. I would also propose that one function of historiography is to foster *Angstbereitschaft* (in Freud's term)—a readiness to feel anxiety that may counteract traumatization, come with empathic unsettlement (or a sense of estrangement), and help prepare for effective action.

40. The desire not to betray the dead is a strong motivation in certain survivors, for example, Charlotte Delbo, and may impede processes of mourning or render them impossible. Of course the question is what counts as betrayal or as keeping faith.

41. Lynne Sharon Schwartz, ed., *The Emergence of Memory: Conversations with W.G. Sebald* (New York: Seven Stories Press, 2007), 88.

42. Although he is from a Jewish family, Littell does not see himself as writing from a subject-position related to some form of Jewish "identity," however complex. In a manner that resonates with both universalistic and French republican values, he insists: "I approach [the Shoah] not as a Jew but as a human being." "Conversations sur l'histoire et le roman," 44. I would note that Littell has been critical of recent Israeli policy, notably in the occupied territories, seeing Israel as traumatized and even rendered "paranoid" by the Holocaust and asserting in his interview ("The Executioner's Song") with Assaf Uni in *Haaretz*: "There is nothing like genocide in the territories, but they are doing absolutely atrocious things."

43. See the forum in *History and Theory* 48:3 (2009), including Alon Confino, "Narrative Form and Historical Sensation: On Saul Friedländer's *The Years of Extermination*," 199–219; Amos Goldberg, "The Victim's Voice and Melodramatic Aesthetics in History," 220–37, and Christopher Browning, "Evocation, Analysis, and the 'Crisis of Liberalism,'" 238–47. See also Wulf Kannsteiner, "Success, Truth, and Modernism in Holocaust Historiography: Reading Saul Friedländer Thirty-Five Years after the Publication of *Metahistory*," *History and Theory* 48:2 (2009): 25–53. To the best of my knowledge, no commentator remarks on the fact that Friedländer follows common usage in referring repeatedly to Nazi "brutality" despite the anthropocentrism and

nonexplanatory nature of the term. The appeal to animal epithets or analogies seems entirely unexceptionable but is nonetheless deserving of critical analysis, both in the work of historians and in the discourse of perpetrators as well as victims. For Nazis, Jews were seen as pigs, dogs, rats, vermin, parasites, bloodsuckers, and so forth. For Jewish victims, Nazis were often seen as brutes, beasts, monsters, or even demons, and Jews at times (including Primo Levi) saw themselves as being treated like animals because of Nazi abuse. On the fraught question of human-animal relations, see my *History and Its Limits,* chap. 6.

44. On this issue, see my analysis of Dan Stone's analogous defense of a turn to cultural history in Holocaust historiography, "A Response to 'Holocaust Historiography and Cultural History' by Dan Stone," *Dapim* 23 (2009): 47–52. See also Stone's approach in "Biopower and Modern Genocide," in *Empire, Colony, Genocide: Conquest, Occupation, and Subaltern Resistance in World History*, ed. A. Dirk Moses (New York: Berghahn Books, 2008), 162–79, which refers to and in important ways converges with arguments I have made.

45. Friedländer (ed.), *Probing the Limits of Representation: Nazism and the "Final Solution"* (Cambridge: Harvard University Press, 1992), 1–21, esp. 6–7.

46. Friedländer, *Probing the Limits of Representation,* 7.

47. There are ironies in Friedländer's account, but I think they are situational rather than structural, for example, with respect to the unintentional effect of Jewish resistance. In "Narrative Form and Historical Sensation," Alon Confino notes the contradiction or at least tension between the desire to convey "disbelief" and "a compelling rendition of [an] interpretive framework [that] would work toward domesticating disbelief" (203). He nonetheless asserts that *The Years of Extermination* has been "received worldwide as an exemplary work of history" because "it has found the right balance of tone, narrative, and interpretation" (200). At the center of Confino's own reflections is the question: "How to write a historical narrative of the Holocaust that *both* offers explanations of the unfolding events *and* also suggests that the most powerful sensation about those events, at the time and since, is that they are beyond words?" (200–201). He argues that Friedländer has chosen a "literary form" that "embeds" explanation and interpretation in narrative. The seeming return to chronicle is itself a valid "literary" option that comes after—not before—theory in Friedländer's work. Confino's own key notion of "sensation"— related by him to intuition, a "feel" for experience, and even the sublime—evokes Friedländer's "quasivisceral reaction" and poses some of the same problems. His overall approach to Friedländer's work affirms a questionable sequential relation between theory and narrative; it also harmonizes the dissonance between some of the earlier theoretical essays and *Nazi Germany and the Jews*. And it does not raise the question of whether it is invariably desirable to have a balanced account of an unbalanced situation or whether it may be worthwhile to devote special attention to "unbalanced" dimensions of historical processes, especially when they are underemphasized in the literature.

48. See, for example, Ford Maddox Ford, "A Personal Remembrance" and Ian Watt "Impressionism and Symbolism in *Heart of Darkness*," in the Norton Critical Edition of *Heart of Darkness*, ed. Paul B. Armstrong, 4th ed. (New York: W. W. Norton, 2006), 316–22 and 349–64.

49. At the very beginning of the second volume, Friedländer makes use of a tell-tale anecdote. His opening sentences are: "David Moffie was awarded his degree in medicine at the University of Amsterdam on September 18, 1942. In a photograph taken at the event, Professor C. U. Ariens Kappers, Moffie's supervisor, and Professor H. T. Deelman stand on the right of the new MD, and assistant D. Granaat stands on the left" (xiii). No photo accompanies the description. A footnote tells the reader where the photo may be found, and, even without the reference, one may readily imagine the official photograph to which the text alludes. The final paragraph of the introduction resonates with the initial sentence, informing the reader that "the new MD, like all the carriers of this sign [the star sewn on his coat, with its "repulsive inscription"], was to be wiped off the face of the earth. Once its portent is understood this photograph triggers disbelief. Such disbelief is a quasivisceral reaction, one that occurs before knowledge rushes in to smother it" (xxvi). Then follows the passage on disbelief I quoted earlier. The "quasivisceral" reaction of disbelief is supposedly the immediate effect of a dissonance between a description of a photograph, recognized after the fact as portentous, and understanding that the person in it, surrounded by unknown figures, "was to be wiped off the face of the earth." But this effect may not be furthered by the possibly reassuring concordance of the beginning and the end of the introduction or by the imageless invocation of the photograph in which Moffie has already disappeared. The effect might be seen as melodramatic but in a manner that need not be dismissive or lead to the conflation of melodrama and "kitsch." Indeed, the effect is itself disrupted by the fact that Friedländer on the first page of the introduction tells the reader that Moffie was among the 20 % of the Jews of Holland who survived the war (xiii), hence making any concordance between beginning and end tenuously depend on an unrealized intention. Moreover, any arguably melodramatic elements are episodic and overshadowed by a primarily elegiac tone as Friedländer recounts what becomes, after a certain point, a narrative of the seemingly inexorable death and destruction of the Jews of Europe. I benefited from a discussion with Peter Staudenmaier about the role of the elegiac in Friedländer.

50. In "Evocation, Analysis, and the 'Crisis of Liberalism,'" Christopher Browning makes many valuable observations yet ultimately proposes the "crisis of liberalism" as an overall concept informing Friedländer's account, despite the latter's disclaimer about the possibility of any "single conceptual framework" and his manifest insistence on redemptive anti-Semitism. The frequently invoked concept of a crisis of liberalism, perhaps deployed most influentially some fifty years ago in Carl Schorske's *Fin-de-siècle Vienna* (New York: Random House, 1961), appears but is not given special prominence in Friedländer's account. On Schorske's appeal to the crisis of liberalism, see my *History & Criticism* (Ithaca: Cornell University Press, 1985), chap. 3.

51. The index lists fifty-one references to Hitler, twenty-six to Klemperer, sixteen to Czerniaków, and seven to Hillesum.

52. Friedländer affirms that, in part because of Hitler's "constant harangues against the Jews . . . as early as during the first months of 1942, even 'ordinary Germans' knew that the Jews were being pitilessly murdered" (334). But whether or to what extent they shared Hitler's animus raises another set of questions.

53. This comment brings up the question of protocols, if not taboos, in representing the Nazi genocide. Here one has the controversial issue of the use Holocaust

analogies, which attests to the "symbolic capital" accrued by the Holocaust as a transnational and even transhistorical point of reference yet forecloses the question of how analogies or comparisons are made as well the functions they serve. Boria Sax, without identifying or asserting a moral equivalence between them, compares factory farms and concentration camps, making the noteworthy point that "one of the results of the taboo against comparisons to the Holocaust is that it gives analogies an excessive rhetorical force." *Animals in the Third Reich: Pets, Scapegoats, and the Holocaust,*" foreword Klaus P. Fischer (New York: Continuum, 2000), 18. Although one might still question its necessity and political effectiveness, Sax's analogy would probably be more acceptable to the extent one took the treatment of animals seriously and judged certain conditions of factory farming to be atrocious. I would also mention the intricate issue of "Holocaust humor," which has not received the attention it merits. For one early, restricted treatment of the problem, see Terrence Des Pres, "Holocaust Laughter?," in *Writing and the Holocaust,* ed. Berel Lang (New York: Holmes & Meier, 1988), 216–33. See also Steve Lipman's fragmentary, uneven, but informative and at times illuminating *Laughter in Hell: The Use of Humor during the Holocaust* (Northvale, NJ: Jason Aronson, 1993). Lipman points out that Nazis were manifestly upset by humor and ridicule directed at them. For example, Goebbels, in one of his *Sprachregelungen* (language rules) banned Chaplin's name from the German press upon the appearance of *The Great Dictator* in 1940 (237). After the war Chaplin himself said that had he known of the "actual horrors" of German concentration camps he "could not have made The Great Dictator . . . could not have made fun of the homicidal insanity of the Nazis" (quoted 237). With respect to victims, Lipman's primary emphasis is on the way humor and laughter serve as strategies of survival and at times of resistance, indeed how "humor is one of the greatest gifts God gave mankind to pull itself out of despair" (x). The latter is obviously not its only role, notably in cynical perpetrators or even desperately ironic survivors (for example, the disconcerting perpetrator-victim Tadeusz Borowski).

54. For a moving collection of photos of shtetl life in the 1930s in places such as Warsaw, Lublin, Lodz, and Vilna, with some commentary, see Roman Vishniac, *A Vanished World,* foreword by Elie Wiesel (1947; New York: Farrar, Straus & Giroux 1983). Wiesel sees Vishniac as "a supreme witness" and remarks: "It is his love for the dead which touches us so deeply. He loves them all: the rabbis and their pupils, the peddlers and their customers, the beggars and the cantors, the sad old men and the smiling young ones. He loves them because the world they live in did not, and because death has already marked them for its own—death and oblivion as well" (unpaginated).

55. One notable example of such a nontraditional book is Art Spiegelman's *Maus,* which is supplemented by a CD-ROM including Spiegleman's interviews with his father Vladek, a survivor whose working through of the past, to the extent it exists, is very limited and poses problems for "Artie's" own attempt to come to terms with the past, its effects on his parents and in turn on himself. Spiegelman's two volumes are entitled *Maus: A Survivor's Tale; My Father Bleeds History (Mid-1930s to Winter 1944)* (New York: Pantheon Books, 1986) and *Maus II: A Survivor's Tale and Here My Troubles Began* (New York: Pantheon Books, 1991). See also *The Complete Maus* CD-ROM, produced by Elizabeth Scarborough (New York: Voyager, 1994)

56. See, for example, the different approaches in Isabel V. Hull, *Absolute Destruction: Military Culture and the Practices of War in Imperial Germany* (Ithaca: Cornell University Press, 2005), especially with respect to the well-documented 1904 German genocide against the Herero in Namibia, and Olivier Le Cour Grandmaison, *Coloniser, Exterminer: Sur la guerre et l'État colonial* (Paris: Fayard, 2005), especially on extremely violent if not genocidal action by other powers (notably the Belgians and the French) in Africa, as well as my discussion of these works in *History and Its Limits*, esp. 114–16. See also Benjamin Brower, *A Desert Named Peace: The Violence of France's Empire in the Algerian Sahara, 1844–1902* (New York: Columbia University Press, 2009) and the essays in Moses, *Empire, Colony, Genocide*. Many of the contributions in the latter book stress the "eliminationist" incentive of "settler colonialism" or "settler imperialism" (notably in Australia and the Americas), which might have flash points (or, in the phrase of A. Dirk Moses, "genocidal moments") of violence but was a more sustained, repetitive process of occupation, displacement, confinement, and at times assimilation that might at times obliterate the cultures or even the people of indigenous societies.

57. Christopher Browning, in his *Remembering Survival: Inside a Nazi Slave-Labor Camp* (New York: W. W. Norton, 2010), makes extensive use of survivor testimonies, including oral ones, in an attempt to provide a historically accurate reconstruction of events in a slave-labor camp. He does not explore the complex problem of experience and its relation to event as mediated by memory. See Samuel Moyn's insightful review in *The Jewish Review of Books* 1 (Spring 2010), available online at http://www.jewishreviewofbooks.com/publications/detail/ordinary-memory (accessed November 8, 2010).

58. A larger problem is the extent to which analogs of these factors or forces are or are not active in other historical contexts, notably contexts involving "ethnic cleansing," colonial domination, and extreme collective violence.

59. Not "stealing cigarettes, watches, and money from the victims" was a crucial indication of remaining decent or upright (*anständig*) for Himmler, a norm in fact riddled by prevalent "corruption" in the SS. Just before the earlier-quoted lines (beginning "most of you know what it means to see a hundred corpses"), Himmler at Posen intimates that not only future generations but even in his own time the large majority of Germans themselves might not be "in the know," even if they knew about the killing of Jews or at least (in accordance with the structure of the open secret) knew enough to realize they did not want to know more. He states: "I am referring to the evacuation of the Jews, the annihilation of the Jewish people. This is one of those things that are easily said. 'The Jewish people is going to be annihilated' says every party member. 'Sure, it's in our program, elimination of the Jews, annihilation—we'll take care of it.' And then they all come trudging, 80 million worthy Germans, and each of them has his one decent Jew [*seinen anständigen Jude*]. Sure, the others are swine, but this one is an A-1 Jew [*ein prima Jude*]. Of all those who talk this way, not one has seen it happen, not one has been through it [*keiner hat es durchgestanden*]." It is after this appeal to an experiential knowledge of those "in the know," in contrast to those who do not realize that there is no such thing as a good, decent, or upright Jew, that the recording seems to register brief laughter or chuckling in the audience. If that is the case, the reaction is, I think, directed not at

Himmler as a sign that one does not take him seriously but at those 80 million worthy Germans not "in the know," who are not part of the experiential, perhaps even sacrificial, band of comrades. The 80 million are among the uninitiated who do not get the point of the genocide or realize that it is "an unwritten, never-to-be-written [or unnamed or unmentioned—niemals genanntes und niemals zu nennendes] page of glory [Ruhmesblatt]." Himmler refers to the uninitiated in a rather clipped, mocking tone, and he may underestimate the extent to which a significant number of the 80 million were "in the know."

60. By "thoroughly different dynamics," I think Friedländer is referring to such "secular" factors as the "machinery of destruction," industrialized mass murder, bureaucracy, geopolitics, biopower, and so forth, which are important and have been constituents of the dominant line of historical analysis, even though their interaction or imbrication with more sacralizing or quasi-ritual and sacrificial dimensions is very underdeveloped or simply denied. When the latter are acknowledged, it may be in the mistaken form of reaction or a "regression" to barbarism or even to animality rather than as components of a complex, even riven "modernity" where they appear (however deceptively) to be "thoroughly different" or uncanny and may be repressed or disavowed.

61. In the introduction to the second volume, Friedländer asserts: "Hitler's personal hold on the vast majority of Germans stemmed from and expressed, as far as the content of his message went, three different and suprahistorical salvation creeds: the ultimate purity of the racial community, the ultimate crushing of Bolshevism and plutocracy, and the ultimate millennial redemption (borrowed from Christian themes known to all). In each of these traditions the Jew represented evil per se. In that sense, Hitler's struggle turned him into a providential leader as, on all three fronts, he was fighting against the same metahistorical enemy: the Jew" (xx).

62. This more encompassing dynamic was perhaps most evident during the waves of killing actions of the *Einsatzgruppen* and their support groups as well as at the end of the war with its sweeping forays, forced marches, and chaotic violence, at times in the disintegrating camps themselves. On the early actions of the *Einsatzgruppen* and their "helpers," see the elated scenes of killing documented in *"The Good Old Days": The Holocaust as Seen by Its Perpetrators and Bystanders*, ed. Ernst Klee, Willi Dressen, and Volker Riess, foreword Hugh Trevor-Roper, trans. Deborah Burnstone (1988; New York: The Free Press, 1991).

63. On the anti-Semitic Richard Wagner in this respect, including his praise of the Jewish political writer Ludwig Börne, "who in his eyes exemplified the redemption from Jewishness into 'genuine manhood' by 'ceasing to be a Jew,'" see Friedländer, *Years of Persecution*, 88. For Friedländer, however, "the intellectual foundations of redemptive anti-Semitism were mainly fostered and elaborated by the other Bayreuthians, especially after the composer's death, during the reign of his widow Cosima: Hans von Wolzogen, Ludwig Schemann and, first and foremost, the Englishman Houston Stewart Chamberlain" (89).

64. After the completion of this chapter, a book was published devoted to Friedländer: Christian Wiese and Paul Betts, eds., *Years of Persecution, Years of Extermination: Saul Friedländer and the Future of Holocaust Studies* (London: Continuum, 2010). Along with the essays in *History and Theory* 48, the book (which reprints only

Alon Confino's essay) presents a noteworthy set of thought-provoking assessments of Friedländer's masterwork. The contributions most pertinent to my argument are by Doris Bergen, Raphael Gross, A. Dirk Moses, Peter Pulzer, Nicholas Stargardt, and Dan Stone.

5. The Literary, the Historical, and the Sacred

1. The issue of motivations, even when they are ideologically shaped or even engendered, usually falls outside the range of concerns in formalist criticism as well as in much restrictedly empirical historiography.

2. Especially noteworthy is T. E. Hulme's definition of Romanticism as spilt religion—something quoted by M. H. Abrams in *Natural Supernaturalism: Tradition and Revolution in Romantic Literature* (New York: W. W. Norton, 1971), at page 68 in the course of tracing the complex relations of Romanticism to religion, its structures, and motifs—a problem discussed by many others, including Northrop Frye and Hans Blumenberg. In Abrams the focus is on English and to a lesser degree French writers with little on German literature but much on philosophy. See also the different, but in certain ways supplementary, approach of Philippe Lacoue-Labarthe and Jean-Luc Nancy, *L'absolu littéraire: Théorie de la littérature du romanticism allemand* (Paris: Editions du Seuil, 1978). The book intersperses translations of texts or fragments of texts by early German Romantics and philosophical Idealists, including Karl Wilhelm Friedrich and August Wilhelm Schlegel, Novalis (Friedrich Leopold von Hardenberg), Friedrich Wilhelm Joseph Schelling, and others, and sees a close linkage between the projects of the two interacting groups. Indeed, Lacoue-Labarthe and Nancy view early German Romanticism as a genre-subverting, deconstructive initiative that emphasized the quasi-divine self-creation (or autopoeisis) of the subject through "literary" production. For the authors, we are still within this frame of reference, which they think should be critically examined. The commentary in their book (unfortunately without the crucially important selections from the writers they discuss) is published in English as *The Literary Absolute: The Theory of Literature in German Romanticism*, trans. Philip Barnard and Cheryl Lester (New York: State University Press of New York, 1988). The religion of art or the role of art as a surrogate or competitor with respect to religion has played an important role in the wake of Romanticism, including Wagner's *Gesamtkunstwerk* and Freud's role-reversing reference in *Civilization and Its Discontents* to those who may need religion because they do not have art or *Kultur*. Of course, this is not the only thing of interest in Freud concerning the complex relations between religion and seemingly secular formations, including psychoanalysis, for example, with respect to attempts at therapeutic exorcism of hauntingly possessive forces, possibly requiring what could be construed as the analyst's (thaumaturgic?) touch to facilitate a movement toward a "cure" in an analysis.

3. Morris was part of the pre-Raphaelite brotherhood, some of whose figures, such as Dante Gabriel Rossetti, were closer to art for art's sake and sought inspiration in Romantic poetry and medieval art. In Morris as in Ruskin, these emphases were supplanted by a turn toward the arts-and-crafts movement, which envisioned art as serving life, notably through the mediation of architecture. They closely related art and craft, sought a craft-like component in all work, and took a markedly political

direction in Morris's democratic variant of guild socialism as well as in Ruskin's more authoritarian vision of social reform. Their approach was related to the broader and still active concern with the "quality of life," including a significant aesthetic dimension, which countered to some extent the narrowly economic, profit-maximizing forms of capitalism—a concern that was important for John Maynard Keynes and others in the Bloomsbury circle. Art for art's sake itself was not invariably a simplistic utopian or escapist notion but might explicitly be seen as problematic, and it could be put to work as a protest against commodification and commercialization, as it manifestly was in Flaubert and Baudelaire as well as in Virginia Woolf.

4. See, for example, Renato Poggioli, *Theory of the Avant-Garde*, trans. Gerald Fitzgerald (1962; New York: Harper & Row, 1968) and Peter Bürger, *Theory of the Avant-Garde*, trans. Michael Shaw, intro. Jochen Schulte-Sasse (1974; Minneapolis: University of Minnesota Press, 1984) as well as Friedrich Nietzsche, *The Birth of Tragedy from the Spirit of Music*, trans. and commentary Walter Kaufmann (1872; New York: Vintage Books, 1967).

5. For more differentiated analyses of Marx, see my *Rethinking Intellectual History: Text, Context, Language* (Ithaca: Cornell University Press, 1983) and *Soundings in Critical Theory* (Ithaca: Cornell University Press, 1989), esp. chap. 6.

6. See, for example, my *Emile Durkheim: Sociologist and Philosopher*, rev. ed. (1972; Aurora, CO: Davies Group, 2001). Pierre Bourdieu is close to Durkheim's quasi-theological or metaphysical understanding of sociology when he argues that it provides the key to all other problems, including those of literature and art. See, especially, his *Rules of Art: Genesis and Structure of the Literary Field*, trans. Susan Emanuel (1992; Stanford: Stanford University Press, 1996). In both practical and theoretical terms, the evaluative and emotional concern with (or "investment" in) the social might variably take particularistic, general, and universalizing turns, and different tensions arise with different combinations, emphases, and priorities. Durkheim tried to harmonize commitments to the family, the work group (or renewed *corporation*), the nation, and the international "community." In the past generation, the rise of "identity politics" (or what the French term *communautarisme*) has, especially with respect to immigration and ethnic diversity, brought newer challenges that have been sources of controversy, especially with respect to the issue of the compatibility of particular group commitments and social or religious practices, on the one hand, and universalistic "republican" values, on the other. See, for example, Joan Wallach Scott, *The Politics of the Veil* (Princeton: Princeton University Press, 2007) and, focusing on the American context, Linda Martin Alcoff, Michael Hames-Garcia, Satya P. Mohanty, and Paula M. Moya, eds., *Identity Politics Reconsidered* (New York: Palgrave, 2006).

7. Karl Löwith, *Meaning in History: The Theological Implications of the Philosophy of History* (Chicago: University of Chicago Press, 1949). Less critical than Löwith's, the work of Carl Schmitt is nonetheless important in this context. For a critical review of a recent delimited attempt to inquire into the problem of secularization by the noted philosopher Charles Taylor, see Martin Jay, "Faith-Based History," *History and Theory* 48 (2009): 76–84, which treats Taylor's *A Secular Age* (Cambridge: Harvard University Press, 2007). As Jay states, Taylor's objective (which is quite distant from the orientation of the present book) is "to explain the rise of something called secularism in the Latin Christian West and to defend religion—in particular the liberal Catholicism in which he frankly and proudly believes—against the threat posed to

it by that rise" (77). For Jay, Taylor arrives at on-the-one-hand-on-the-other-hand conclusions that are not surprising: "Religion can both embolden some believers to think that they share in divine wisdom and remind others that there are mysteries that they, as imperfect creatures, are unable to solve. It can therefore serve as stimulus to both arrogance and humility, both confidence and doubt, and the historical record abounds with examples of each" (84). See also Hent de Vries, ed., *Religion: Beyond a Concept* (New York: Fordham University Press, 2009), an imposing monument along the path of the postsecular turn, which resonates in limited ways with Derrida's approach, especially "Faith and Knowledge: The Two Sources of 'Religion' at the Limits of Reason Alone." For an informative work that problematizes the opposition between the religious and the secular, reconfiguring an understanding of flagellation and tracing the reactivation of "mystical" tropes in art and "aesthetic experience," see Niklaus Largier and Graham Harman, *In Praise of the Whip: A Cultural History of Arousal* (2001; New York: Zone Books, 2007).

8. For an informative survey of violence in the twentieth century, see Enzo Traverso, *L'histoire comme champs de bataille: Interpréter les violences du XXe siècle* (Paris: La Découverte, 2011).

9. For a study of terrorism that emphasizes the importance of historical temporality and the way terrorism was seen or experienced as accelerating the pace of history with impatience and at times with apocalyptic expectations, see Claudia Verhoeven, *The Odd Man Karakazov* (Ithaca: Cornell University Press, 2009).

10. See Jean-François Lyotard, *The Postmodern Condition: A Report on Knowledge*, trans. Geoff Bennington and Brian Massumi, foreword Fredric Jameson (1979; Minneapolis: University of Minnesota Press, 1984).

11. "Critique of Violence," in Walter Benjamin, *Reflections: Essays, Aphorisms, Autobiographical Writings*, ed. and intro. Peter Demetz, trans. Edmund Jephcott (New York: Harcourt Brace Jovanovich, 1978), 277–300.

12. Derrida, "The Force of Law: The 'Mystical' Foundation of Authority," *Cardozo Law Review* 11 (1990): 920–1045.

13. The Italian Futurist Filippo Tommaso Marinetti may no longer be a common reference point. But his thought embodies in an accentuated form many of the motifs that inform the cult of violence. For him poetry was a violent assault on the forces of the unknown. And art essentially involved ruinous and incendiary violence, cruelty, and injustice. Art did not simply produce aesthetic effects but was essentially at one with life and sought an outlet in politics. The Futurist Party he founded in 1918 was absorbed the following year into the Fascist Party of Mussolini, the political figure he idolized. Marinetti, however, did not support anti-Semitism and even publicly criticized it, thus marking the distance between his form of fascism and Nazism, as was the case for many other Italian fascists. See Umbro Apollonio, ed., *Futurist Manifestos*, trans. Robert Brain et al., intro. Umbro Apollonio, new afterword Richard Humphreys (Boston: MFA Publications, 2001). In his glorification of war and the experience of combat, his admiration for advanced technology, his devotion to speed, and his sense of regeneration through violence, Marinetti is in certain ways comparable to Ernst Jünger in Germany. Georges Sorel is another prominent yet currently eclipsed figure of the interwar period who influenced Mussolini (as well as Walter Benjamin among others) and whose apology for violence played a role in

both "leftist" anarcho-syndicalism and fascism. The lability in his ideological positions that nonetheless gravitated around the regenerative and redemptive power of violence makes him a symptomatic figure, even if one would hesitate to assign him the key role in fascist ideology for which Ze'ev Sternhell argues. See, for example, Sternhell's *Neither Right nor Left: Fascist Ideology in France*, trans. David Meisel (1983; Berkeley: University of California Press, 1986). T. E. Hulme translated Sorel's important *Reflections on Violence* (1915; New York: Peter Smith, 1941), which resoundingly concluded by attributing to violence the "high ethical values" that would bring "*salvation* to the modern world" (295).

14. See my discussion of Heidegger in *Representing the Holocaust: History, Theory, Trauma* (Ithaca: Cornell University Press, 1994), chap. 5 and in *History and Its Limits: Human, Animal, Violence* (Ithaca: Cornell University Press, 2009), chap. 5. Some of the points touched on in the next few paragraphs are discussed more extensively in *History and Its Limits*, chap. 4. For a critical study of the reception of Heidegger in France, which ranges broadly and casts light on many related problems, including the relation between philosophy and theology, see Ethan Kleinberg, *Generation Existential: Heidegger's Philosophy in France* (Ithaca: Cornell University Press, 2005). For a careful, illuminating inquiry into a famous 1929 debate bearing on the question of what it means to be "human," see Peter E. Gordon, *Existential Divide: Heidegger, Cassirer, Davos* (Cambridge: Harvard University Press, 2010). The profascist and anti-Semitic orientation of the "modernist" Ezra Pound and the anti-Semitism of T. S. Eliot have been much discussed, although there is still controversy about their precise nature and how they affect their literary works. On Pound, see *Ezra Pound and History*, ed. Marianne Korn (Orono, ME: National Poetry Foundation, University of Maine, 1985); Tim Redman, *Ezra Pound and Italian Fascism* (New York: Cambridge University Press, 1991); and Leon Surette, *Pound in Purgatory* (Bloomington: University of Illinois Press, 1999). On Eliot, see Anthony Julius, *T.S. Eliot, Anti-Semitism, and Literary Form* (New York: Thames and Hudson, 2003) as well as my discussion of this book in *History and Memory after Auschwitz* (Ithaca: Cornell University Press, 1998), 199–200. See also Paul Morrison, *The Poetics of Fascism: Ezra Pound, T.S. Eliot, Paul de Man* (New York: Oxford University Press, 1996), and on de Man, see my discussion in *Representing the Holocaust: History, Theory, Trauma* (Ithaca: Cornell University Press, 1994), chap. 4.

15. For insight into the legal system and an analysis of one of its important judges in the Third Reich and postwar Germany, see Raphael Gross, "'The Ethics of a Truth-Seeking Judge': Konrad Morgen, SS Judge and Corruption Expert," in *Years of Persecution, Years of Extermination: Saul Friedländer and the Future of Holocaust Studies*, ed. Christian Wiese and Paul Betts (London: Continuum, 2010), 193–209. In a regime that could be seen (with Carl Schmitt) in quasi-theological terms as instituting a permanent state of exception, whereby the sovereign will of the leader was tantamount to the law and the rule for individuals was not only a distorted Kantian imperative to do one's duty in obeying orders but to act in a difficult situation as one thought the *Führer* would act, there were also pockets of seemingly strict legality that overcompensated for the general abrogation of a rule of law. (The latter, however, could be seen as paradoxically authorized by the "Enabling Act" [*Ermächtigungsgesetz*] of 1933.) Konrad Morgen, as discussed by Gross, rejected

traditional religion, was not opposed to the persecution of Jews and other victims, and became Himmler's "corruption expert," fanatically scrupulous and, in the eyes of some, "murderous" in ferreting out "corruption" in the SS and initiating what might well have been over seven hundred criminal procedures, at times indicting high-ranking SS officers (193–95). Gross asserts that Morgen's case "plays a central role" in Jonathan Littell's *Les Bienveillantes* (Paris: Gallimard, 2006; translated as *The Kindly Ones,* trans. Charlotte Mandel [New York: Harper, 2009]), and he contrasts Morgen with SS officer Kurt Gerstein, subject of an early book by Saul Friedländer. Gerstein made a sincere attempt to bring to public attention what was happening to Jews under the Nazi regime and is recognized by Friedländer as a perhaps necessarily ambiguous resister. *Counterfeit Nazi—The Ambiguity of Good* (London: Weidenfeld & Nicolson, 1969), esp. 225–26. Gerstein was not fully rehabilitated but declared "tainted" (*belastet*) by the Spruchkammergericht (the civilian court responsible for the denazification process in postwar Germany), although he was in 1965 reassigned to the group of the exonerated by Ministerpräsident Kurt Georg Kiesinger. Morgen was exonerated by the court and kept a positive assessment of himself that was shared by the public, despite preliminary proceedings against him for alleged participation in the deportation and murder of Hungarian Jews (198). Gerstein does not have an analog in Littell's novel.

16. Breton, *Manifestoes of Surrealism,* trans. Richard Seaver and Helen R. Lane (Ann Arbor: University of Michigan Press, 1969), 125.

17. Blanchot, "Terrorisme comme méthode de salut publique," *Combat* 1, no. 7 (July 7, 1936); my translation.

18. Bataille, "Concerning the Accounts Given by the Residents of Hiroshima," in *Trauma: Explorations in Memory,* ed. and intro. Cathy Caruth (Baltimore: Johns Hopkins University Press, 1995), 221–35. Bataille's essay, first published in 1947, takes the form of an extremely participatory reading of John Hersey's *Hiroshima* (1946; New York; Bantam, 1985). For an insightful study of Bataille and Lacan that retains its pertinence for still-debated issues, see Carolyn J. Dean, *The Self and Its Pleasures: Bataille, Lacan, and the History of the Decentered Subject* (Ithaca: Cornell University Press, 1992).

19. See Nicolas Abraham and Maria Torok, *The Shell and the Kernel,* ed. and trans. Nicolas Rand, vol. 1 (1987; Chicago: University of Chicago Press, 1994), esp. part 5. Along with many less problematic assertions, A. Dirk Moses has put forward a surprisingly affirmative presentation of the role of redemptive violence, arguing, for example, that "while liberals advocate justice, they are understandably uncomfortable with the redemptive violence entailed in the terror of history. Yet it is this non-consoling history that gives oppressed people the motivation to escape their exile and disempowerment." "Genocide and the Terror of History," *Parallax* 17 (2011): 90–108, quote at 103–4. Of course, not only stereotypical "liberals" (or others seeking "consolation") may draw back from redemptive violence, and trust in it may motivate in ways that prove to be massively destructive, deceptive, and disillusioning. Nor need such a caveat exclude an appeal to more situationally inflected defenses of strategic uses of violence. "The terror of history" is itself a rather indiscriminate term approximating the equation of history and trauma.

20. Fear of degeneration, along with social Darwinism, was prevalent well before the Nazis. Degeneration was a prominent sign of the inability to struggle and

survive in a Darwinian conception of the world. It provoked attempts to combat it through various means from "mental hygiene" and increases in population to war and colonial conquest. Indeed, colonialism could be legitimated as both a way of empowering the colonizer and of helping the colonized either to ascend to "world history" or to plunge toward extinction. Social Darwinism and the role of extinction in relation to colonialism is a recurrent motif in Sven Lindqvist, *"Exterminate All the Brutes": One Man's Odyssey into the Heart of Darkness and the Origins of European Genocide*, trans. Joan Tate (1992; New York: The New Press, 1996). The Zionist Max Nordau's influential *Degeneration* (1892) bemoaned the putative feminization of Jewish men rendered powerless by two thousand years of exile. Nordau opposed anti-Semitism while calling for a "muscle Judaism." Nordau's views find echoes in certain later Zionists. See, for example, Menachem Begin, *The Revolt*, rev. ed. (London: W. H. Allen, 1979). See also the critical study by Idith Zertal, *Israel's Holocaust and the Politics of Nationhood* (Cambridge: Cambridge University Press, 2005). For an account of the concept of degeneration, especially in France, Italy, and England, from 1848–1918, see Daniel Pick, *Faces of Degeneration: A European Disorder* (New York: Cambridge University Press, 1989). See also J. Edward Chamberlin and Sander L. Gilman, eds., *Degeneration: The Dark Side of Progress* (New York: Columbia Press, 1985) and Charles Bernheimer, *Decadent Subjects: The Idea of Decadence in Art, Literature, Philosophy, and Culture of the Fin de Siècle in Europe* (Baltimore: Johns Hopkins University Press, 2002).

21. See Lutz Koepnick, *Dark Mirror: German Cinema between Hitler and Hollywood* (Berkeley: University of California Press, 2002) and Jean-Michel Palmier, *Weimar in Exile: The Antifascist Emigration in Europe and America*, trans. David Fernbach (New York: Verso, 2006). The films in question were not entirely unproblematic. W. G. Sebald sees Fritz Lang's *Dr. Mabuse: The Gambler* (1922) as in certain ways symptomatic of destructive forces in German history: "Fritz Lang's film is a paradigm of the xenophobia that spread among Germans from the end of the nineteenth century onwards." *On the Natural History of Destruction* [*Luftkrieg und Literatur*], trans. Anthea Bell (1999; New York: The Modern Library, 2003), 103. He also relates the work of Syberberg to "the most dubious aspects of Expressionist fantasy" (49).

22. For a survey of art, film, and literature in Nazi Germany, see the essays in Jonathan Huener and Francis R. Nicosia, eds., *The Arts in Nazi Germany: Continuity, Conformity, Change* (New York: Berghahn Books, 2006). In his contribution to the book, "A Command Performance? The Many Faces of Literature under Nazism" (chap. 5, 111–34), Frank Trommler questions the tendency of scholars to "prefer to remain content with the established wisdom on the poor literary quality of party-controlled publications" (111). Trommler does not provide a coherent and comprehensive alternative to this generalization but does indicate why one need not be content with it. Instead, he offers an informed account of dilemmas faced during the Nazi period by literary writers, especially in the effort to construct a national culture while promoting the Nazi movement. Perhaps most significant is his indication of the propensity of the German readership not to go along with the regime's preferred exponents but instead to focus on science fiction, humor, or foreign novels. Trommler finds similar trends in the consumption of film and music, which may not be that surprising in light of Hitler's own, sometimes "transgressive" taste in films or the attempt of German popular cinema to imitate or emulate Hollywood, including

its "screwball" comedies as well as its immensely popular "entertainment" films (for example, in German films with Hans Albers or Zarah Leander).

23. See, for example, Simonetta Falasca-Zamponi, *Fascist Spectacle: The Aesthetics of Power in Mussolini's Italy* (Berkeley: University of California Press, 1997); Jeffrey Schnapp, *Staging Fascism: 18 BL and the Theater of Masses for Masses* (Stanford: Stanford University Press, 1996); Eric Rentschler, *The Ministry of Illusion: Nazi Cinema and Its Afterlife* (Cambridge: Harvard University Press, 1996); and Neil Levi, "The 'Degenerate Art' Exhibition as Political Spectacle," *October* 85 (Spring 1998): 41–64. The former insightful analyses do not, however, extensively explore the relations between the aesthetic and the ritualistic or sacralizing. See also David Carroll, *French Literary Fascism: Nationalism, Anti-Semitism, and the Ideology of Culture* (Princeton: Princeton University Press, 1995) for a discussion of key figures such as Georges Sorel, Charles Péguy, Charles Maurras, Robert Brasillach, Pierre Drieu La Rochelle, Louis-Ferdinand Céline, Lucien Rebatet, and Thierry Maulnier, as well as of the "case" of Paul de Man. One problem in Carroll's lucid and useful analysis is his reliance on Philippe Lacoue-Labarthe's understanding of the political as an aesthetic fiction of totality. This understanding induces both an overly unified (or "totalized") conception of fascism (hence participating in certain self-understandings of fascism, particularly in Italy) and a downplaying of such factors as the sublime, the sacred, the phobic, and the quasi-ritual. For a discussion of the transnational self-understanding of fascists that was nonetheless subject to variations in practice and ideology adapted to specific contexts, see Federico Finchelstein, *Transatlantic Fascism: Ideology, Violence, and the Sacred in Argentina and Italy, 1919–1945* (Durham: Duke University Press, 2010). Especially noteworthy is his treatment of the clerically inflected form of fascism that emerged in Argentina. For a forceful study stressing the role of the phobic and even the quasi-ritualistic, see James M. Glass, *"Life Unworthy of Life": Racial Phobia and Mass Murder in Hitler's Germany* (New York: Basic Books, 1997). Despite the overly generalizing and "pathologizing" turns in his argument, Glass brings out the complexity of "racial hygiene" theories that confusingly mingled phantasmatic, ritual, and scientific (or scientistic) orientations.

24. See *The Goebbels Diaries*, ed., trans., and intro. Louis Lochner (Garden City, NY: Doubleday and Company,1948). On May 4, 1942, for example, Goebbels writes of Hitler: "Lieutenant Colonel Scherf of GHQ has sent me a compilation of quotations on the nature of genius by great Germans. . . . These quotations are very comforting in judging the present situation. Taken as a whole they almost give one the impression of an apotheosis of the Fuehrer. One cannot imagine a better justification of his nature, his personality, and his actions" (205). Goebbels had a low estimation of Italian fascism: "One might almost say that fascism has reacted upon the creative life of the Italian people somewhat like sterilization. It is, after all, nothing like National Socialism. While the latter goes deep down to the roots, fascism is only a superficial thing. That is regrettable, but one must recognize it clearly. National Socialism is really a way of life [*eine Weltanschauung*]. It always begins at the beginning and lays new foundations for life. That's why our task is so difficult, but also so beautiful, and the goal ahead is well worth our best effort" (71) [entry for February 6, 1942]. The goal centrally included the relentless, "purifying" extermination of the Jews: "The Fuehrer once more expressed his determination to clean up the Jews in Europe pitilessly. There must be no sentimentalism about it. The Jews have deserved the

catastrophe that has now overtaken them. Their destruction will go hand in hand with the destruction of our enemies. We must hasten this process with cold ruthlessness" (86) [entry for February 14, 1942]. Goebbels's insistence on belief (*Glaube*) and on a grail-like quest is pronounced.

25. While open to criticism for the way its presentation of the suffering of Germans tends to marginalize the treatment of Jews and other victims of the regime, Oliver Hirschbiegel's 2004 film *Der Untergang* (*Downfall*) is exceptional in its portrayal of Goebbels (played by Ulrich Matthes) both aesthetically and in its enactment of the historical Goebbels's dedication to Hitler. Quite remarkable as well is the portrayal of Hitler himself (played by Bruno Ganz). For a carefully illustrated, informative study of art under the Nazis, with its ideological and purifying or regenerative functions, including the attempt to serve the will of the *Führer*, see Peter Adam, *Art of the Third Reich* (New York: Harry N. Abrams, 1992). Concerning the Nazi aversion to modern art and architecture, Adam observes: "We must never forget that the people who went along with this kind of middle-of-the-road art at the same time went along with the *Weltanschauung* which—known or unknown to them—led to mass murder" (305).

26. Friedländer, *Nazi Germany and the Jews*, vol. 2, *The Years of Extermination, 1939–1945* (New York: HarperCollins, 2007), 394.

27. The German title is *Die Macht der Bilder: Leni Riefenstahl*, which I find more anodyne and less apt than the English.

28. W. G. Sebald, *Austerlitz*, trans. Anthea Bell (New York: Random House, 2001), 168.

29. In her famous essay, "Fascinating Fascism," in *Under the Sign of Saturn* (New York: Farrar, Straus & Giroux, 1972), 73–108, Susan Sontag argued that "fascist aesthetics" informed Riefenstahl's first book on the Nuba (*The Last of the Nuba*) because the photography of Nuba peoples stressed purity, the lack of pollution, the triumph of the strong over the weak, and the authentic, as did her earlier documentary films under the Nazi regime. It would, however, be dubious to take this constellation of traits as distinctive of a coherent fascist aesthetic, although each of them in a specific way played a role in the Third Reich as well as more or less different roles in other times and places.

30. After finishing what I thought was the final version of this chapter, I came across an important book of essays addressing questions bearing on my discussion: Roger Griffin, Robert Mallett, and John Tortorice, eds., *The Sacred in Twentieth-Century Politics: Essays in Honour of Professor Stanley G. Payne* (New York: Palgrave Macmillan, 2008). In my estimation, the essays addressing pertinent topics largely support the argument I make.

31. The essay by Derrida appears in *Religion*, ed. Jacques Derrida and Gianni Vattimo (1996; Stanford: Stanford University Press, 1998). Derrida was of Algerian Jewish (Sephardic) background and over time became increasingly interested in the issue of his (and others') complex, problematic "identities." See, for example, his "Abraham, the Other," in *Judeities, Questions for Jacques Derrida*, ed. Bettina Bergo, Joseph Cohen, and Raphael Zagury-Orly (New York: Fordham University Press, 2007). In part for comparative purposes, I note an excellent discussion of developments in theology and religious thought in postwar Germany, which find no echo in Derrida and deserve greater prominence in critical-theoretical discussions of

recent tendencies in and around religion: Dagmar Herzog's "The Death of God in West Germany: Between Secularization, Postfascism, and the Rise of Liberation Theology," in *Die Gegenwart Gottes in der modernen Gesellschaft: Transzendenz und religiöse Vergemeinschaftung in Deutschland*, ed. Michael Geyer and Lucian Hölscher (Göttingen: Wallstein, 2006), 425–60. Herzog offers a broad-ranging analysis, including the role of the Holocaust in prompting reconfigurations of religious thought, notably in the work of Dorothee Sölle who rejected the notion of an omnipotent God and stressed the participation of divinity in suffering and vulnerability, relating the Holocaust to problems raised by American military action in Vietnam as well as to the plight of "third world" poor (seen as an "enduring Auschwitz" [*ein Dauer-Auschwitz*, 459]). Moreover, Herzog offers an account of Christian liberation theology and its role in creating an alliance between rethought religion and the political left. She also offers the sobering observation that, "while before and during the Third Reich Christians frequently blamed popular gentile secularization on the purported cultural dominance of Jews in Weimar, after 1945 popular gentile secularization was frequently blamed on the National Socialists. This easy substitution is indicative of some wider resistance among Christians to self-confrontation" (453).

32. For example, I do not agree with the notion of an originary *coup de force* or performative decision that precedes and founds all normativity, law, institution, or constitution (17–18), a theme familiar from Derrida's "Force of Law: The 'Mystical' Foundation of Authority," *Cardozo Law Review* 11 (1990): 920–1045, esp. 941–43. See also my commentary on the latter essay as it was presented at a conference at Cardozo Law School where it did not as yet include the footnotes and "postscriptum" on Nazism and the "final solution" (973–74 and 1040–45). My response is entitled "Violence, Justice, and the Force of Law," *Cardozo Law Review* 11 (1990): 1065–78. See as well my discussion in *History and Its Limits*, 98–102. I also question what seems at times to be a biomechanistic fatalism that construes in absolute and quasi-transcendental, rather than explicitly speculative and analogical, terms a notion of the autoimmune that not only must be self-defeating but also goes to the extreme in the direction of excess, violence, and sacrifice—what Derrida at one point refers to as "the terrifying but fatal logic of the *auto-immunity of the unscathed*" ("The Two Sources of 'Religion' at the Limits of Reason Alone," 44)—what might perhaps be seen as a variant of the death drive. But I find more suggestive the idea that anything seemingly immune or unscathed runs "a risk of auto-immunity" that "haunts the community and its system of immunitary survival like the hyperbole of its own possibility" (47).

33. See, for example, Philippe Lejeune, *Le pacte autobiographique* (Paris: Seuil, 2005).

34. Derrida, *Gift of Death*, trans. David Wells (1992; Chicago: University of Chicago Press, 1995).

35. Rudolf Otto, *The Idea of the Holy*, trans. John W. Harvey (1917; Oxford: Oxford University Press, 1923). Otto links the holy, the numinous, the *mysterium tremendum*, and the totally other. Otto's discussion at times evokes Kant's treatments of the noumenal and the sublime, and it has unsettling echoes in certain views of the Holocaust itself. On the latter problem, see my *History and Its Limits*, chap 3.

36. In line with other dimensions of Derrida's argument, one may qualify the opposition he draws here by noting that the sacred and belief play a role in Heidegger, not only in the explicitly pro-Nazi writings of 1933–34 but in others as well, for example, *The Origin of the Work of Art* of 1935 or various commentaries on poets such as Hölderlin and Trakl. Heidegger's later prose in particular has an incantatory quality that might almost be read as a prayer-like attempt to lure the absent gods back into the temples they are seen as having deserted (in *The Origin of the Work of Art*). See my discussion of the latter in *History and Its Limits,* chap. 5. Levinas developed a theology of radical transcendence of the totally other somehow linked to an ethics of infinite responsibility to (or in the face of) the other human being (not other animals). It was accompanied by an affirmation of Jewish exceptionalism (or chosenness) and a martyrological notion of the victim whereby persecution revealed the presence of the divine. On the latter issues, see his "Being-Jewish," trans. Mary Beth Mader, *Continental Philosophy Review* 40 (2007): 205–10, esp. 209, and his *Carnets de captivité,* ed. Rodolphe Calin and Catherine Chalier (Paris: Grasset/MEC, 2009), esp. 179–80. See also the unpublished essay of Ethan Kleinberg, "Not Yet Marrano: Levinas, Derrida, and the Ontology of 'Being-Jewish,'" presented December 7, 2008, for the conference *The Jewish Question in French Philosophy after the Holocaust* at UCLA.

37. One may ask whether this logic and perhaps a scapegoat mechanism at least "haunt" methodologies based on the ideal type or analytic model, even in such a careful thinker as Max Weber, where the ideal type is linked to a quest to discover the difference or even uniqueness of the "West."

38. I would reiterate the point that the mutual marking (or "*différance*") of seeming binary opposites, rendering dubious any notion of an "as such," does not imply conceptual meltdown, utter confusion, or the indiscriminate generalization of a "gray zone." One may argue that in empirical reality and in normative judgment there may be strong and even decisive contrasts, for example, between perpetrators who are not in any pertinent sense victims and victims who are not in any pertinent sense perpetrators, as well as a variable "gray zone" of perpetrator-victims whose understanding poses intricate problems in analysis and judgment. One might speculate that a goal of critical thought and practice is to overcome, insofar as possible, a situation wherein decisive binary opposites are applicable, including the entire grid of victimization in which perpetrator, victim, and perpetrator-victim play a prominent role. This would involve the overcoming of any sacrificial frame of reference that involved victimization and a notion of regeneration through violence (which I take to be a sacrificial motif).

39. In Derrida, *Writing and Difference*, trans., intro., and notes Alan Bass (1967; Chicago: University of Chicago Press, 1978), chap. 10.

40. See, for example, the analysis in Werner Ustorf, "The Missiological Roots of the Concept of 'Political Religion,'" in *The Sacred in Twentieth-Century Politics,* ed. Griffin, Mallett, and Tortorice, 36–50, and, in the same book, Klaus Vondung, "What Insights Do We Gain from Interpreting National Socialism as a Political Religion?," 107–18, esp. 110. As a striking instance of an apparently unself-conscious quest for purity, involving incredible instances of avoidance, dissociation, and denial, one may cite the case of Franz Stangl, commandant of Sobibor and then of Treblinka. In his

conversations with the journalist Gita Sereny conducted while he was in prison, he gives no sign of feelings of elation during his time in the death camps. But he wore a white riding habit, complete with a crop, as he oversaw the abuse and killing of hundreds of thousands of Jews in conditions of extreme filth, including the putrefaction of dead bodies. See Gita Sereny, *Into That Darkness: An Examination of Conscience* (New York: Random House, 1983). Interviewing Stangl, Sereny asks incredulously: "But, even so, how could you go into the camp in this get-up?" Stangl could give only inconsequential rationales such as the availability of linen, the heat, and the fact that riding on horseback was "the best mode of transport" given the bad state of the roads (118). On the relation of everyday needs and an aesthetic of purity for the SS, Sereny writes: "There were, of course, no sanitary napkins, or even newspapers, and the girls used large leaves—burdock leaves if they could find them—to protect themselves. But any blood showing on a dress meant death; it was unaesthetic, and the SS were very keen on aesthetics" (237–38). (But here I doubt whether aesthetics formed a discrete, autonomous sphere.) On the novelistic embellishment of abuse, such as the fiction of a harem of young boys for a putatively homosexual SS man, Max Biala (earlier common spelling [163] but given, with reference to the following quotation, as "Biele or Bielas"), she asserts: "It does seem extraordinary that novelists find it necessary to invent such tales when the appalling truth is surely far more 'dramatic'" (259).

41. See, for example, Hans Ulrich Gumbrecht's *Production of Presence* (Stanford: Stanford University Press, 2004) and Eelco Runia, "Spots of Time" (in the "Forum on Presence"), *History and Theory* 45:3 (2006): 305–16. For a critical analysis of the turn to presence, see Ethan Kleinberg, "Presence *in Absentia*," *Storia della Storiografia* 55 (2009): 43–59. Especially significant in historiography are the contributions to an important recent book, *Practicing History: New Directions in the Writing of History after the Linguistic Turn*, ed. Gabrielle Spiegel (New York: Routledge, 2005). See my discussion in *History and Its Limits*, 45–52. A form of presence or immediacy seems to be the object of Frank Ankersmit's recent quest for sublime experience as the crux of an authentically historical relation to the past. *Sublime Historical Experience* (Stanford: Stanford University Press, 2005). A curious parallel may be found in Michael Fried's exploration over the years of the contrast between absorption, which is presumably the genuine inspiration of modernist art, and theatricality with its diversionary concern for the viewer, which is its degraded, almost sacrilegious antithesis—a contrast that has recently modulated into an impossible dialectic in which the recurrent temptation of theatricality calls for resistance in any truly absorbing aesthetic endeavor. *Why Photography Matters as Art as Never Before* (New Haven: Yale University Press, 2008). Also significant in this respect is the more general animus against representation (pronounced in Lyotard) as a kind of fall from abstraction and sublime unrepresentability. With respect to the Holocaust, this view brings with it a *Bilderverbot* in which any image must be an unacceptable desecration or reprehensible "consolation" that infringes the sublime or even sacral immensity of extreme, unsymbolizable trauma allowing only for indirection and allusion. A paradigmatic figure with respect to this view is Claude Lanzmann whose intransigence goes beyond the caveats of Theodor Adorno to become almost doctrinal. Hence even Georges Didi-Huberman's subtle, self-questioning analysis of photographs of victims at Auschwitz

(two of which are apparently of recently gassed bodies being cremated), smuggled out by *Sonderkommando* and intended to document and bear witness to atrocity, is condemned as simply inadmissible. See Didi-Huberman, *Images in Spite of All: Four Photographs from Auschwitz*, trans. Shane B. Lillis (2003; Chicago: University of Chicago Press, 2008); Claude Lanzmann, interview in *Le Monde,* January 19, 2001; and the critiques, inspired by Lanzmann, by Gerard Wajcman in "De la croyance photographique," *Les temps modernes* 56 (2001): 47–83; and Elizabeth Pagnoux, "Reporter photographique à Auschwitz," *Les temps modernes* 56 (2001): 84–108. The initial part of Didi-Huberman's study was published before his book as part of an exhibition catalogue. For a thought-provoking discussion of the above problems, see Michael S. Roth, *Living with the Past: Essays on History, Critical Theory, and Photography* (New York: Columbia University Press, 2011), esp. chap. 14.

42. See, for example, Michael Burleigh and Wolfgang Wippermann, *The Racial State: Germany, 1933–1945* (New York: Cambridge University Press, 1991).

43. See Eric L. Santner, *On Creaturely Life: Rilke, Benjamin, Sebald* (Chicago: University of Chicago Press, 2006) and Jane Bennett, *The Enchantment of Modern Life: Attachments, Crossings, and Ethics* (Princeton: Princeton University Press, 2001). See also Vincent Lloyd, *The Problem with Grace: Reconfiguring Political Theology* (Stanford: Stanford University Press, 2011).

44. For a discussion of these problems as well as those evoked in the preceding paragraph, see *History and Its Limits*, esp. chap. 3. As W. G. Sebald writes of Jünger and Alfred Andersch, considering the latter as the former's disciple: "When a morally compromised author claims the field of aesthetics as a value-free area it should make his readers stop and think. The burning of Paris was, for Ernst Jünger, a wonderful sight! Frankfurt burning, as seen from the Main, is for Andersch 'a terrifyingly beautiful image.'" *On the Natural History of Destruction,* 131. The sense of the glamour and sublimity of war was of course not confined to figures such as Jünger and Andersch. Winston Churchill wrote of the battle of Omdurman (1898), where superior weapons enabled Lord Kitchener to slaughter thousands of dervishes in the Sudan: "It was the last link in the long chain of those spectacular conflicts whose vivid and majestic splendour has done so much to invest war with glamour" (quoted in Lindqvist, *"Exterminate All the Brutes,"* 53). Even more lyrical is Lord Garnet Wolseley, commander of the British troops in the first Ashanti war (1874–76): "It is only through experience of the sensation that we learn how intense, even in anticipation, is the rapture-giving delight which the attack upon an enemy affords. . . . All other sensations are but as the tinkling of a doorbell in comparison with the throbbing of Big Ben" (quoted Sebald, *On the Natural History of Destruction,* 54). One of Lindqvist's major themes is the prevalence of support for violence and even genocide with respect to European colonialism, which he sees (at times in too direct a manner) as preparing the way for the Nazi genocide against the Jews. With respect to the latter, he overestimates the role of the quest for *Lebensraum* in Hitler and the Nazis (158–60).

45. *Mein Kampf,* trans. Ralph Manheim (1925; Boston: Houghton Mifflin, 1971), 50. On the founding trauma, see especially my *History and Its Limits*, chap. 3.

46. These confused relations are both critically explored and at times uncritically enacted in the work of certain important postwar artists, notably the painter Anselm

Kiefer and the filmmaker Hans-Jürgen Syberberg. The work of the Slovenian group Leibach is also significant in this respect. Syberberg's epically grandiose, brilliantly montage-laden, mesmerizing 1978 film *Our Hitler* (*Hitler, Ein Film aus Deutschland*) highlights crucial problems, with what may sometimes be a participatory fascination as well as decidedly dubious amalgamations (Hollywood, Hitler, Jews, money). The film is pervaded by a "steely romanticism" (in Goebbels's phrase) that may turn maudlin (for example, in the recurrent refrains of *"Deutschland, Deutschland Über Alles"* or in the appeals to *Heimat* [homeland], *Heimweh* [homesickness], and *Sehnsucht* [nostalgia], as in the apostrophe to Caspar David Friedrich, famous for his "sublime" landscapes, whom Hitler is accused of forever ruining for Germans). Perhaps the primary stress in the film is on the morbidly melancholic, kitsch-Wagnerian, charismatic, grail-seeking, believing, apocalyptic, and redemptive dimensions of the Nazi movement, culminating in a bloody sacrificial incentive. The open question is whether the latter's forceful performativity and imperative sweep are effectively counteracted by the film's many ironic and deflationary alienation effects. One especially problematic scene has a dreamy, melancholic, passive, Jewish yet Syberberg-like narrator (played by Harry Baer) as a puppeteer manipulating and possibly ventriloquating a Hitler puppet, stripping layers of uniforms from the monomaniacally declaiming *Führer* to reveal ultimately the figure of the Devil. This disturbing scene, manifestly inspired by the more complex exchange between Adrian Leverkühn and the Devil who is his own shape-shifting, diabolic projection, differs from Mann's *Doctor Faustus* in that in Syberberg Hitler seems to become an unproblematized projection of a Jewish narrator who tries to convince the *Führer* that one of his greatest mistakes was to exclude the Jews, who wanted nothing better than to be good Germans and to follow the leader. In any case, whether on the level of supporting argument or on that of symptomatic evidence, Syberberg can be invoked as reinforcing certain arguments I make or even as excessively stylizing and taking them too far. On these problems, see, for example, Eric L. Santner, *Stranded Objects: Mourning, Melancholia, and Film in Postwar Germany* (Ithaca: Cornell University Press, 1990); Andreas Huyssen, *Twilight Memories: Marking Time in a Culture of Amnesia* (New York: Routledge, 1995); and Ernst van Alphen, *Caught by History: Holocaust Effects in Contemporary Art, Literature, and Theory* (Stanford: Stanford University Press, 1997).

47. On the question of clerico-fascism in Argentina and Italy, see Finchelstein, *Transatlantic Fascism,* esp. chap. 4.

48. With respect to Nazism, see the comprehensive assessment by Christian Wiese, "An 'Indelible Stigma': The Churches between Silence, Ideological Involvement, and Political Complicity," in *Years of Persecution, Years of Extermination,* ed. Wiese and Betts, 157–92. Wiese argues that "Christian theology and the policy of the Churches, as well as a widespread social mentality determined by demonizing stereotypes of the 'alien,' dangerous Jew, actively and often consciously prepared the ground for the National Socialist policy of disenfranchisement and—a few exceptions apart—contributed to the fate of the Jewish minority through consistent desolidarization and quiet surrender" (166).

49. Stanley Payne, *A History of Fascism, 1914–1945* (Madison: University of Wisconsin Press, 1995). See also his essay in Griffin, Mallett, and Tortorice, *The Sacred in Twentieth-Century Politics.* For approaches to defining fascism, see George L. Mosse,

The Fascist Revolution: Toward a General Theory of Fascism (New York: Howard Fertig, 1998); Ze'ev Sternhell, *The Birth of Fascist Ideology* (Princeton: Princeton University Press, 1994); and *Neither Right nor Left: Fascist Ideology in France,* trans. David Meisel (1983; Berkeley: University of California Press, 1986); Robert O. Paxton, *The Anatomy of Fascism* (New York: Knopf, 2004); Michael Mann, *Fascists* (Cambridge: Cambridge University Press, 2004); Emilio Gentile, *The Origins of Fascist Ideology, 1918–1925* (New York: Enigma, 2005); Roger Griffin, *The Nature of Fascism* (London: Routledge, 1993) and *A Fascist Century* (London: Palgrave, 2008); Enzo Traverso, "Interpreting Fascism: Mosse, Sternhell, and Gentile in Comparative Perspective," *Constellations* 15 (2008): 303–19; and Federico Finchelstein, "On Fascist Ideology," *Constellations* 15 (2008): 320–31.

50. See Michman's "Introducing More 'Cultural History' into the Study of the Holocaust: A Response to Dan Stone," *Dapim: Studies on the Shoah* 23 (2009): 69–75, esp. 75n, as well as his *The Emergence of Jewish Ghettos during the Holocaust,* trans. Lenn J. Schramm (New York: Cambridge University Press, 2011).

51. See Saul Friedländer, *Memory, History, and the Extermination of the Jews of Europe* (Bloomington: Indiana University Press, 1993); *Nazi Germany and the Jews,* vol. 1, *The Years of Persecution, 1933–1939* (New York: HarperCollins, 1997); and *Nazi Germany and the Jews,* vol. 2, *The Years of Extermination, 1939–1945* (New York: HarperCollins, 2007), as well as my discussion in the preceding chapter.

52. As Hannah Arendt (who relied heavily on the work of Raul Hilberg and Gerald Reitlinger) ironically observes: "The German 'radical' variety was fully appreciated only by those peoples in the East—the Ukrainians, the Estonians, the Latvians, the Lithuanians, and, to some extent, the Rumanians—whom the Nazis had decided to regard as 'subhuman' barbarian hordes." *Eichmann in Jerusalem: A Report on the Banality of Evil* (New York: Viking, 1963), 154. For a much more qualified account of the Holocaust in Latvia, see Andrew Ezergailis, *The Holocaust in Latvia, 1941–1944: The Missing Center* (Washington, DC: Historical Institute of Latvia, 1996).

53. See Robert O. Paxton, *Vichy France: Old Guard and New Order, 1940–1944* (New York: Knopf, 1972) and Robert O. Paxton and Michael Marrus, *Vichy France and the Jews* (New York: Schocken, 1981).

54. Jan T. Gross, *Neighbors: The Destruction of the Jewish Community in Jedwabne, Poland,* with a new afterword (2001; New York: Penguin Books, 2002). The book, touching on sensitive issues, provoked a heated controversy. See Anthony Polonsky and Joanna B. Michlic, eds., *The Neighbors Respond: The Controversy over the Jedwabne Massacre in Poland* (Princeton: Princeton University Press, 2004). See also the forum in the *Slavic Review* 61, no. 3 (Autumn 2002): 453–89, which includes a response by Gross (483–89) and an especially interesting article by Janine P. Holc, "Working Through Jan Gross's *The Neighbors,*" 453–59.

55. Jan T. Gross, *Fear: Anti-Semitism in Poland after Auschwitz: An Essay in Historical Interpretation* (2006; New York: Random House, 2007). For other commentators, the motivations for the pogrom were at least more complex, for example, involving the issue of Soviet control of Poland and even the role of Soviet-supported security personnel in the unfolding of the pogrom—complexities that need not be taken as incompatible with the points Gross may overemphasize.

56. One disconcerting occasion is filmed in Claude Lanzmann's *Shoah* (1985).

57. See, for example, Gross, *Neighbors*, 82–84.

58. I have earlier referred to the controversial but important book of Olivier Le Cour Grandmaison, *Coloniser, Exterminer: Sur la guerre et l'État colonial* (Paris: Fayard, 2005). On the German genocide directed against the Herero in 1904 (as well as military action against the Nama and Maji-Maji), see Isabel V. Hull, *Absolute Destruction: Military Culture and the Practices of War in Imperial Germany* (Ithaca: Cornell University Press, 2005). See also A. Dirk Moses, ed., *Empire, Colony, Genocide: Conquest, Occupation, and Subaltern Resistance in World History* (New York: Berghahn Books, 2008). In his contribution, on the 1905–7 Maji-Maji war in German East Africa, which he asserts "has been neglected in historiography and public memory" (307), Dominik J. Schaller argues that there was "genocidal responsibility" in so far as the German military in Tanzania "had exactly known what the consequences of their scorched-earth policy would be" in bringing about the death of hundreds of thousands of Africans (310). For a sustained attempt to relate Holocaust studies and postcolonial studies, see Michael Rothberg, *Multidirectional Memory: Remembering the Holocaust in the Age of Decolonization* (Stanford: Stanford University Press, 2009).

59. Along with contributions to Moses, *Empire, Colony, Genocide*, see Neil Levi, "No Sensible Comparison?: The Place of the Holocaust in Australia's History Wars," *History & Memory* 19 (2007): 124–56, which defends the Holocaust analogy.

60. See Charles Patterson, *Eternal Treblinka: Our Treatment of Animals and the Holocaust* (New York: Lantern Books, 2002) and Boria Sax, *Animals in the Third Reich: Pets, Scapegoats, and the Holocaust*, foreword Klaus P. Fischer (New York: Continuum, 2000). See also Arendt, *Eichmann in Jerusalem*, esp. 107–11. When Arendt famously refers to Eichmann's inability to "think," she places special emphasis not only on his tendency to speak only in endlessly repeated clichés, indicating a deficit of critical thought, but also on his lack of empathy, "namely, to think from the standpoint of somebody else" (49). To some extent Arendt may have shared this "lack" in so far as she put forward an objectified, "othering" portrayal of Eichmann himself and, in a different register, an unmodulated condemnation of the role of Jewish councils, which showed little sensitivity to the plight and double-bind situation of at least certain members. It is nonetheless noteworthy that judgment was at times rendered with respect to members of Jewish councils by those who survived and were formerly under their jurisdiction, including not only famous cases such as that of Abba Kovner and other resisters in the Vilna ghetto but, as Arendt notes (124), in an outburst during the Eichmann trial itself, in both Hungarian and Yiddish, against Pinchas Freudiger of Budapest. I would note that a limited attempt at "empathic" understanding of Eichmann does not mean that one would experience the glee (or what Arendt renders as the laughter) or the "extraordinary sense of elation" that Eichmann presumably (and repeatedly) asserted he would feel "jumping into his grave" while having on his conscience "the death of five million Jews" (45–46).

61. Joachim Remak, ed., *The Nazi Years: A Documentary History* (Englewood Cliffs, NJ: Prentice-Hall, 1969), 41. The affirmation from Göring's *Aufbau einer Nation* ["Building of a nation"] is quoted in Remak, 69.

62. Klaus Vondung, "The Sacralization of Politics," in *The Sacred in Twentieth-Century Politics*, ed. Griffin, Mallett, and Tortorice, 114. Jeffrey Herf, in his *The Jewish Enemy: Nazi Propaganda during World War Two and the Holocaust* (Cambridge: Harvard

University Press, 2006), investigates neglected sources (notably directives of the Reich Press Office and certain newspapers) and stresses the way Nazi leadership was both motivated by apocalyptic anxieties about a worldwide Jewish conspiracy and able to disseminate such a view to many others.

63. In *Bloodlands: Europe between Hitler and Stalin* (New York: Basic Books, 2010), Timothy Snyder provides a massively documented, admirably researched, often gripping account of the slaughter by Hitler and Stalin of some fourteen million people (noncombatants, including but not restricted to Jews) in the area between Germany and Russia, extending "from central Poland to western Russia, through Ukraine, Belarus, and the Baltic States" (viii). Stalin's reign of terror lasted longer than Hitler's assault and included the draconian 1929–33 collectivization of Ukrainian peasants, the "artificial" famine of the early 1930s, and the Great Terror of 1937–8. One of Snyder's principal points is that one should not single out Auschwitz in so far as such a gesture obscures the extent of the killings under both Hitler and Stalin that arguably included genocidal dimensions under the Soviet leader as well as Hitler. Indeed, Snyder wants to present the atrocities within a single spatial and temporal frame in a manner that shifts the focus in studying atrocities during the war and links the two dictators and their regimes, at least in terms of the immensity and ruthlessness of their killing operations. Despite sections on (sometimes lethal) ethnic cleansing and postwar Stalinist anti-Semitism, Snyder makes some pertinent comments in passing but does not have, as a key concern, inquiry into the motivations of Stalin's (or Hitler's) killings, terrorism, and incarcerations, providing for the most part a narrative punctuated by descriptions that allow the reader to encounter individual victims and not only (possibly mind-numbing) statistics. (Yet on page 336, for example, he notes that "once the war was over, the task was to insulate the Russian nation, and of course all of the other nations, from cultural infection." He goes on to refer to "dangerous intellectual plagues," "Russian purity," and "pollution . . . from western Europe or America, but also from cultures that crossed boundaries, such as the Jewish or the Ukrainian or the Polish" [336–37].) One question left in abeyance is whether there were, in the Soviet Union, quasi-religious currents that made the cult of personality with respect to Stalin more than a catchphrase and whether there was also a sense of pollution or contamination by certain "traitorous" and "dangerous" groups, including kulaks who might have been victims of class genocide in so far as their class position was essentialized into an inescapable, indelible status comparable to "race." See also the more interpretive effort of Mark Lipovetsky and Sven Spieker, "The Imprints of Terror: The Rhetoric of Violence and the Violence of Rhetoric in Modern Russian Culture," *Wiener Slawistischer Almanach, Sonderband* 64 (2006): 5–35, where they develop the argument that "the sacralization of modernity through the rituals of Soviet culture required constant terror" (7). Like Snyder, they bring out the inadequacy of appeals to the incomprehensibility or unrepresentability of events, which open the door to turns to the sacred or the sublime in the voices of commentators themselves. In one's own voice, one may well see atrocities as senseless or devoid of redeeming meaning and *not* transfigure them into occasions for sacred or sublime experiences, but a distinguishable question is what constellation of different meanings perpetration may have had for at least some of those undertaking it.

64. See Derrida, *The Post Card: From Socrates to Freud and Beyond,* trans. Alan Bass (1980; Chicago: University of Chicago Press, 1987).

65. For a relatively early yet still pertinent analysis of the Posen speech, see Peter Haidu, "The Dialectics of Unspeakability: Language, Silence, and the Narratives of Desubjectification," in *Probing the Limits of Representation: Nazism and the "Final Solution,"* ed. Saul Friedländer (Cambridge: Harvard University Press, 1992), 277–99.

66. Scott Spector has been working on the problem of ritual murder charges against Jews in fin-de-siècle Vienna and Berlin.

67. At one point in the recording of the speech, some members of the audience chuckle, but it is sarcastic laughter evoked by Himmler's ironic reference to those "80 million Germans," each of whom has "his one decent Jew," that is, those who do not fully "get" the incentive of the "final solution" where a decent Jew is a contradiction in terms and no Jew is in principle to be spared. For my earlier discussions of Himmler's words at Posen, see *Representing the Holocaust: History, Theory, Trauma;, History and Memory after Auschwitz;* and *Writing History, Writing Trauma,* esp. pp. 136–40. For one translation of the most infamous section of the speech, see *A Holocaust Reader,* ed. and trans. Lucy Dawidowicz (West Orange, NJ: Behrman House, 1976), 132–33.

68. In *Eichmann in Jerusalem,* Arendt notes Eichmann's "elation" with respect to things he said (for Arendt, "elating clichés" [53]), including his repeated assertion that he would jump with laughter (or glee) into his grave because of his role in the death millions of Jews (56). Yet (in banalizing fashion) she puts this down to Eichmann's propensity to brag (46–47), just as she sees Eichmann's primary if not sole motivation in terms of his careerism (50). She also sees Eichmann as having no hatred for Jews and as not being a fanatic, not recognizing that there may well be ideological fanaticism that is not reducible to general psychological traits. Arendt is justifiably wary of glorifying or demonizing Nazi excesses, although she does not notice how her own stress on the unprecedented nature of their crimes may do just that. Nor does she find alternatives to banality such as the recognition of sacralizing or "sublimating" incentives in certain dimensions of perpetrator behavior and motivation that one insistently does not take up in one's own voice. One might detect a curious form of "modernism," which could be related to unqualified claims for uniqueness and even to a certain Eurocentrism in Arendt's repeated insistence on the altogether unprecedented nature of the crimes of which Eichmann was accused—indeed her hyperbolic assertion that the failure to recognize this essentially new criminality on the part of "Israel, like the Jewish people in general," along with the attempt to relate the genocide to earlier catastrophes in Jewish history, "is actually at the root of all the failures and shortcomings of the Jerusalem trial" (267). Arendt convincingly criticizes Martin Buber's opposition to Eichmann's execution because it "might 'serve to expiate the guilt felt by many young persons in Germany'" (251), but she also criticizes the response of Karl Jaspers, who argued for an international tribunal, concluding that "it was disappointing to find him dodging, on the highest possible level, the very problem Eichmann and his deeds had posed," by which she seems to mean what she sees as the unprecedented nature of Nazi crimes and the problem of an appropriate penalty for them (252). (Arendt agreed with Jaspers on the need for an international tribunal on the grounds of her principled if essentialistic belief

that murder and genocide differed "in essence" and that "modern, state-employed mass murderers must be prosecuted because they violated the order of mankind, and not because they killed millions of people" [272].) She maintains that "administrative massacre" is a more appropriate terms than genocide, ignoring both dimensions of the "final solution" that were not simply administrative (such as the hands-on killing of the *Einsatzgruppen*) and the way it is problematic to present administrative massacre as unprecedented. (The genocide against the Herero in 1904 was arguably also an administrative massacre.) Among the philosophers who did not make public statements concerning the trial, she does not mention Martin Heidegger, whose response (or lack thereof) to the "final solution" was disappointing on virtually every level. Still, among the "lessons" Arendt derives from the trial, which, despite its anthropocentrism, is arguably preferable to "the lesson of the fearsome, word-and-thought-defying *banality of evil*" (252), is the following: "Politically speaking, it is that under conditions of terror most people will comply but *some people will not*, just as the lesson of the countries to which the Final Solution was proposed is that 'it could happen' in most places but *it did not happen everywhere*. Humanly speaking, no more is required, and no more can reasonably be asked, for this planet to remain a place fit for human habitation" (233).

69. Summarizing some of the scenes depicted in the documents collected in Ernst Klee, Willi Dressen, and Volker Riess, eds., *"The Good Old Days": The Holocaust as Seen by Its Perpetrators and Bystanders*, foreword Hugh Trevor-Roper (1988; New York: The Free Press, 1991), Trevor-Roper writes: "The most horrible photographs, and some of the most horrible narratives, in this book record the earlier stages in this [genocidal] process, for the first massacres, especially those in the Baltic states, were carried out in public. In Kaunas, Lithuania, where Einsatzkommando 3 operated, the Jews were clubbed to death with crowbars, before cheering crowds, mothers holding up their children to see the fun, and German soldiers clustered round like spectators at a football match. At the end, while the streets ran with blood, the chief murderer stood on the pile of corpses as a triumphant hero and played the Lithuanian national anthem on an accordion" (xii). Scenes recorded in this book accord with Timothy Snyder's account in *Bloodlands*. Snyder glosses Himmler's Posen speech in this manner: "Heinrich Himmler said that it was good to see a hundred, or five hundred, or a thousand corpses lying side by side. What he meant was that to kill another person is a sacrifice of the purity of one's own soul, and that making this sacrifice elevated the killer to a higher moral level" (400). I think the scenes indicated by Himmler may for him have been beyond good and evil, caused no damage to one's soul if undertaken with purity of intention (rather than personal self-interest), yet may have involved "elevating" sacrificial elements for those beholding (and perpetrating) them. Snyder goes on to comment: "Hermann Göring said that his conscience was named Adolf Hitler. For Germans who accepted their Leader, faith was very important. The object of their faith could hardly have been more poorly chosen, but their capacity for faith is undeniable" (400).

70. See, for example, Eric Kligerman, *Sites of the Uncanny: Paul Celan, Specularity, and the Visual Arts* (New York: Walter de Gruyter, 2007).

71. See, for example, Julia Kristeva, *The Powers of Horror*, trans. Leon S. Roudiez (1980; New York: Columbia University Press, 1982). Kristeva begins her important

book with a compelling discussion of the sacred, ritual purity, and the danger of contamination, but she does not bring her analysis (inspired in part by Mary Douglas) to
bear on her extensive discussion of Céline and fascism (or, more precisely, Nazism).
She certainly recognizes Céline's anti-Semitism but tends to analyze his novels in
restricted aesthetic or literary terms, not drawing out the relations between their
"visceral" style and his explicitly anti-Semitic pamphlets. There is an apologetic element in her view of Céline as revolutionary writer, even at one point a designation
of his fascism as a biographical need in terms that appear to separate it sharply from
his literary writing practice. More generally, Kristeva tended at the time to stress the
role of unarticulated, affective, presymbolic drives (*pulsions*), centrally including the
"death drive" or the Lacanian real, in accounting for revolutionary change in poetry
and art. Her orientation changes to a significant degree in later works, including
her "Forgiveness: An Interview" (with Alison Rice) in *PMLA* 117 (2002): 278–95,
and her critical comments on Jonathan Littell's *Les Bienveillantes*, which she does not
analyze or celebrate for its expression or acting out of phantasms. Instead, Kristeva
is critical of a practice in so far as it undercuts or eschews the role of critical judgment and framing devices in the writing and the understanding of literature. See her
"A propos des *Bienveillantes* (De l'abjection à la banalité du mal)," *L'Infini* 99 (Summer
2007): 23–35. See also David Carroll's critical analysis of Kristeva on Céline in
French Literary Fascism, 183–86, even though Céline, whose work Carroll himself
sees in terms of radically disruptive, unbounded, primal, even poetically "sublime"
initiatives (184), would seem to be a writer who goes against the grain of Carroll's
understanding of fascism in terms of an aesthetic-political totality.

72. Yet the camps could also include a more or less institutionalized "theater of
cruelty," including playing vicious "games" with beatings (at times on the buttocks
of naked women), fomenting hysteria or frenzy on the arrival of victims, shouting
and stampeding them on the way to gas chambers (with victims running in panic
along the so-called *Schlauch* [tube or tunnel] or *Himmelfahrt* [path to heaven]), using
dogs trained to be vicious (such as Kurt Franz's notorious Bari at Treblinka, trained
to attack victims' genitals), as well as Franz's "boxing matches" that went on until the
death of a combatant. Franz Stangl attributed the initiation of such procedures at
Treblinka to Christian Wirth, and Stangl fatalistically came to see them as irrevers-
ible. See the account in Gita Sereny, *Into That Darkness*, esp. 165 and 202. At least in
retrospect, Stangl showed little sign of elation but instead claimed that he hardened
or deadened himself to events through dissociation and numbing, coming to consider
prisoners little more than "cargo."

73. Friedländer, *Nazi Germany and the Jews* (2 vols.). The term is most discussed
in chapter 3 of volume 1. In the second volume, as I noted in the previous chapter,
Friedländer even refers at one point to "some kind of 'sacralized modernism'" (657).

74. These forces may have been in part active recently with respect to the "empire of evil," the enemy other, the haters of freedom, the elusive, omnipresent specter
of terror, and the often ill-defined terrorist. These seemingly "spiritual," mystified
categories have been used to justify extreme measures, including the denial of civil
liberties and the justification of torture and violence. They may even cover over and
legitimate the conversion of "collateral damage" into an explicit strategy in destroying property and doing violence to noncombatants. One such strategy, developed
by the Israeli Defense Force in Nablus in 2002 and later taken up by the American

military, is "walking through walls," whereby the streets are circumvented and small military units take control of a city by smashing holes in walls, causing havoc in those sheltered by them. See Eyal Weizman, *Hollow Land: Israel's Architecture of Occupation* (New York: Verso: 2007), 185–218. Violent scapegoating and victimizing sacrificialism, along with a distorted hazing mentality, may even be active in the bizarre carnivalesque forms of torture and punishment witnessed at Abu Graib. Moreover, without implying a simple identity with the Nazi genocide, I would make the nonetheless controversial point that the not uncommon attempt to purify the nation by getting rid of sources of contamination, which typically invites scapegoating, had an eerie enactment in the at times prejudicial, runaway "logic" informing the postwar *épuration* of collaborators in France, which included the sometimes carnivalesque shaving of the heads of some twenty thousand women reputed to be "horizontal collaborators" with the enemy. *Epuration* is usually translated poorly as "purge"— a word that exists in French—but would be better rendered by "cleansing" or "purification."

75. I make special mention of (1) oblation or gift giving insofar as it may be disentangled from victimization and (2) rituals for transitional points in social and personal life, including noninvidious carnivalesque practices.

76. One may list a series of seeming similarities. Formally, the statements are in certain ways close ("to see" and "most of you know"), appealing to tacit experiential knowledge bound up with affect and emotion. They constitute an appeal or a call ("come see or know with me") addressed to actual and possible communities. They could be interpreted as bases of a micrological approach to problems in which the seemingly small incident (a speech at Posen, a grain of sand) is the displaced locus of enormously momentous significance—a micrological approach found also in the novels of Virginia Woolf where the little, sometimes miraculous things in life are its saving graces (if only when artistically refashioned in retrospect) or in the histories of, say, Christopher Browning where the focus is on "ordinary," generally conformist "men" carrying out atrocious enormities on the basis of unexceptional, banal motivations such as peer pressure. (In Browning the more elated or sublime aspects tend to recede into the background if not fall out of the picture.) See Browning's *Ordinary Men: Reserve Police Battalion 101 and the Final Solution in Poland* (New York: HarperCollins, 1992). But only the most indiscriminate notion of the sublime or formalistic validation of juxtaposition and montage would make more of the limited similarities.

77. On Himmler and animals, see Felix Kersten, *The Kersten Memoirs, 1940–1945,* intro. H. R. Trevor-Roper, trans. Constantine Fitzgibbon and James Oliver (London: Hutchinson, 1956), esp. 116–18.

Epilogue

1. I discuss some of them in *History and Its Limits: Human, Animal, Violence* (Ithaca: Cornell University Press, 2009). For some impressive works taking one or more of these approaches, see Ulrich Baer, *Remnants of Song: Trauma and the Experience of Modernity in Charles Baudelaire and Paul Celan* (Stanford: Stanford University Press, 2000) and *Spectral Evidence: The Photography of Trauma* (Cambridge: MIT Press, 2002); Sam Durrant, *Postcolonial Narrative and the Work of Mourning: J.M. Coetzee, Wilson*

Harris, and Toni Morrison (Albany: State University of New York Press, 2004); David L. Eng and David Kazanjian, eds., *Loss*, afterword Judith Butler (Berkeley: University of California Press, 2003); and Ranjana Khanna, *Dark Continents: Psychoanalysis and Colonialism* (Durham: Duke University Press, 2003). Perhaps the paradigm-setting work for the prevalent de Manian-deconstructive form of trauma theory is Shoshana Felman and Dori Laub, *Testimony: Crises of Witnessing in Literature, Psychoanalysis, and History* (New York: Routledge, 1992).

2. *On the Natural History of Destruction*, trans. Anthea Bell (1999; New York: Modern Library, 2004). Sebald refers to what he terms the "horrified fixity of Walter Benjamin's 'angel of history'" (67) and, as I intimate in chapter 3, even sees it as the ultimate stance of Alexander Kluge, despite Kluge's "intellectual steadfastness" and even what Sebald earlier presents as "the prospect suggested here [by Kluge] of an alternative historical outcome, possible in specific circumstances" in "a serious call to work for the future in defiance of all calculations of probability" (64)—what might be seen as a call to a limited and however improbable but determined attempt to work through historical traumas and catastrophes.

3. Slavoj Žižek, Eric L. Santner, and Kenneth Reinhard, *The Neighbor: Three Inquiries in Political Theology* (Chicago: University of Chicago Press, 2005).

4. See Žižek, "Neighbors and Other Monsters: A Plea for Ethical Violence," in *Neighbor*, 134–90.

5. Žižek, *Violence* (New York: Picador, 2008), 1.

6. Žižek, *Violence*, 13.

7. See Žižek, *The Sublime Object of Ideology* (London: Verso, 1989), in which concentration camps are derived from "the fact that we are dealing here with the 'real' of our civilization which returns as the same traumatic kernel in all social systems" (50).

8. Žižek, *Violence*, 209–10. One may note that Hitler had a low estimation of businessmen, a manipulative attitude toward workers, and an opportunistic orientation to capitalism insofar as the latter served the interests of his regime (similar to his orientation toward churches).

9. See Saul Friedländer, *Nazi Germany and the Jews*, vol. 1 (New York: Haper-Collins, 1997), chap. 3. See also Michael Burleigh and Wolfgang Wippermann, *The Racial State: Germany, 1933–1945* (New York: Cambridge University Press, 1991).

10. Žižek, *Violence*, 198–200.

11. Žižek, *Violence*, 7.

12. See, for example, Žižek, *Tarrying with the Negative: Kant, Hegel, and the Critique of Ideology* (Durham: Duke University Press, 1993), chap. 5.

13. Žižek, *Tarrying with the Negative*, 170.

14. Žižek, *Tarrying with the Negative*, 3.

15. Žižek, *Violence,* 61.

16. J. M. Coetzee, *Disgrace* (New York: Penguin Books, 1999). One may also refer to the 1962 film *Les Dimanches de Ville D'Avray* (*Sundays and Cybèle*), directed by Serge Bourgignon. The film offers the story of the enchanted yet tragic relationship between two "outsiders"—a twelve-year-old orphan girl (played by Patricia Gozzi), abandoned by her mother and then by her father, and Pierre (played in a German-accented French by Hardy Krüger), a simple, yet perhaps dangerously disturbed, thirty-year-old Indochina war veteran who becomes her surrogate father/

sublimated lover. He thinks the girl may help him, for he is haunted by the sight of a woman and child killed in the crash of his plane on a bombing mission. The orphan girl is called Françoise yet has a secret name—that of the goddess Cybèle. She comes to reveal the name to Pierre (who notes its homophony with "*si belle*") with whom she shares a special world into which they enter when a stone thrown into a pond enables them to be within their magic circle. Pierre has a magical knife, taken from a fortune-teller, that enables the two to hear the spirits embodied in trees. An artist friend understands and respects their enchanted relationship, which for him is innocent and beautiful, but at first Pierre's girlfriend and her male friend (recently married but apparently still interested in her) are unsettled by, and suspicious of, the "abnormal" relationship. To the dismay of the girlfriend, who has begun to appreciate the enchanted relationship, the male friend calls the police when Pierre and Françoise/Cybèle cannot be found on Christmas Day. As gifts to Cybèle, Pierre has taken a fully decorated Christmas tree from the artist-friend's home and, with the knife, removes a rooster from the steeple of a church, a rooster for which the girl had jokingly asked. The final scenes show Pierre, lying with the sacrificial knife and rooster next to him, shot by police who interpreted the scene as one of (sacrificial?) murder. Then one sees the girl, annihilated and (re)traumatized by the killing, who answers the policeman's question by stating that she no longer has a name. Apparently, once one has experienced violence against a loved one, all names are gone, although the secret name itself may have had ambivalent powers. Pierre here may function as a scapegoat for those who kill him or want him out of the way, a status that may well apply to unwanted veterans returning from unpopular wars (both the Indochina war [1946–54] to which the film alludes and the Algerian war [1954–62] that came to a destabilizing, contested end at the time the film was made and released). Casting as Pierre an actor with a noticeable German accent gives an added twist to the status and resonance of the character that also invokes the aftermath of the Second World War.

17. Žižek, *Violence*, 64–65.

18. See Žižek, *The Ticklish Subject: The Absent Centre of Political Ontology* (London: Verso, 1999), 381–88. Could one read Coetzee's rendition in *Disgrace* of David Lurie's intransigence before the university board inquiring into his affair with a student as a parody of this scenario as well as of the Truth and Reconciliation Commission?

19. See Žižek, *The Indivisible Remainder: Essays on Schelling and Related Matters* (London York: Verso, 1996), and *Violence*.

20. Žižek, *Violence*, 52–53.

21. See Theodor W. Adorno, "The Meaning of Working Through the Past," in *Critical Models*, trans. Henry W. Pickford (New York: Columbia University Press, 1998), 89–103. A version of the essay, based on a lecture, was first published in 1959, and the term translated as "working through" is "*Ausarbeitung*" (and not Freud's "*Durcharbeitung*," although the process, initially discussed in terms of "*Verarbeitung*" [or "*verarbeiten*"], that Adorno affirms is very close to that analyzed by Freud but with more pronounced sociopolitical dimensions). The essay has also been translated by Timothy Bahti and Geoffrey Hartman as "What Does Coming to Terms with the Past Mean?," in *Bitburg in Moral and Political Perspective,* ed. and intro. Geoffrey Hartman (Bloomington: Indiana University Press, 1986), 114–29.

22. Žižek *Violence*, 201.

23. Žižek, introduction to *Virtue and Terror* (selected texts of Robespierre) (London: Verso, 2007), x–xi

24. For perspectives on this problem, see Mark Antliff, *Avant-Garde Fascism: The Mobilization of Myth, Art, and Culture in France, 1909–1939* (Durham: Duke University Press, 2007); Ze'ev Sternhell, *Neither Right nor Left: Fascist Ideology in France*, trans. Davis Maisel (Princeton: Princeton University Press, 1995); and Georges Bataille, *Visions of Excess: Selected Writings, 1927–1939*, ed. and intro. Allan Stoekl, trans. Allan Stoekl with Carl R. Lovitt and Donald M. Leslie, Jr. (Minneapolis: University of Minnesota Press, 1985).

25. Žižek, *Ticklish Subject*, 157.

26. Žižek, *Ticklish Subject*, 162–63.

27. Žižek, *Ticklish Subject*, 144.

INDEX